# HOTEL MANAGEMENT AND ADMINISTRATION

M. C. METTI

ANMOL PUBLICATIONS PVT. LTD.
NEW DELHI - 110 002 (INDIA)

**ANMOL PUBLICATIONS PVT. LTD.**

*H.O.*: 4374/4B, Ansari Road, Darya Ganj,
New Delhi-110 002 (India)
Ph.: 23278000, 23261597

*B.O.*: No. 1015, Ist Main Road, BSK IIIrd Stage
IIIrd Phase, IIIrd Block
Bangalore - 560 085 (India)
Visit us at: www.anmolpublications.com

*Hotel Management and Administration*

ISBN 978-81-261-3250-8

PRINTED IN INDIA

Printed at Mehra Offset Press, Delhi.

# Contents


*Preface* *vii*

1. An Introduction to Hotel 1
2. Entrepreneurship 16
3. Basics of Hotel Management 88
4. Management Theories 169
5. Distribution and Business 202
6. Action Research in Hotel Management 212
7. Organizational Learning 261
8. Administration in Hotel Management 273

*Index* 290

# Preface

The term management characterizes the process of and/or the personnel leading and directing all or part of an organization (often a business) through the deployment and manipulation of resources (human, financial, material, intellectual or intangible).

According to the Oxford English Dictionary, the word "manage" comes from the Italian *maneggiare* (to handle — especially a horse), which in turn derives from the Latin *manus* (hand).

Management has to do with power by position, whereas leadership involves power by influence. Mary Parker Follett, who wrote on the topic in the early twentieth-century, defined management as "the art of getting things done through people". One can also think of management functionally, as the action of measuring a quantity on a regular basis and of adjusting some initial plan; or as the actions taken to reach one's intended goal. This applies even in situations where planning does not take place. From this perspective, Frenchman Henri Fayol considers management consists of five functions: planning,organizing, leading ,co-ordinating and controlling.

Some people, however, find this definition, while useful, far too narrow. The phrase "management is what managers do" occurs widely, suggesting the difficulty of defining management, the shifting nature of definitions, and the connection of managerial practices with the existence of a managerial cadre or class.

One habit of thought regards management as equivalent to "business administration", although this then excludes management in places outside commerce, as for example in charities and in the public sector. Nonetheless, university departments which teach management usually get called "business schools".

Speakers of English may also use the term "management" or "the management" as a collective word describing the managers of an organization, for example of a corporation.

First-of-its-kind this book presents a balanced overview of the theory and practice of hotel strategies. With real-world examples in every chapter, it explains how and why the hotel management has gained international status and shows how to forecast future developments. Subjects covered include, Hotel Types, Entrepreneurship, Planning in management, Planning in Organasations and Market planning process, Leadership and Humanresorces Management etc.

Hope this book will serve as a first hand guide to the students and teachers alike.

Author

## Chapter 1

# An Introduction to Hotel

A hotel is an establishment that provides paid lodging, usually on a short-term basis. Hotels often provide a number of additional guest services such as a restaurant, a swimming pool or childcare. Some hotels have conference services and meeting rooms and encourage groups to hold conventions and meetings at their location.

Hotels differ from motels in that most motels have drive-up, exterior entrances to the rooms, while hotels tend to have interior entrances to the rooms, which may increase guests' safety and present a more upmarket image.

In Australia, a hotel may also be an establishment that serves alcoholic drinks, and usually meals in a casual setting but which does not necessarily provide accommodation. This type of establishment would more usually be called a pub or bar in other countries. In general use in Australia the terms '"hotel" and pub are usually taken to be synonymous.

In India, the word may also refer to a restaurant since the best restaurants were always situated next to a good hotel.

The word hotel derives from the French hotel, which referred to a French version of a townhouse, not a place offering accommodation (in contemporary usage, hôtel has the meaning of "hotel", and hotel particulier is used for the old meaning). The French spelling (with the circumflex) was once also used in English, but is now rare. The circumflex replaces the 's' once preceding the 't' in the earlier hostel spelling, which over time received a new, but closely related meaning.

## SERVICES AND FACILITIES

Basic accommodation of a room with only a bed, a cupboard, a small table and a washstand has largely been replaced by rooms with en-suite bathrooms and climate control. Other features found may be a telephone, an alarm clock, a TV, and broadband Internet connectivity. Food and drink may be supplied by a mini-bar (which often includes a small refrigerator) containing snacks and drinks (to be paid for on departure), and tea and coffee making facilities (cups, spoons, an electric kettle and sachets containing instant coffee, tea bags, sugar, and creamer or milk).

In the United Kingdom a hotel is required by law to serve food and drinks to all comers within certain stated hours; to avoid this requirement it is not uncommon to come across "private hotels" which are not subject to this requirement. However, in Japan the capsule hotel supplies minimal facilities and room space.

The cost and quality of hotels are usually indicative of the range and type of services available. Due to the enormous increase in tourism worldwide during the last decades of the 20th century, standards, especially those of smaller establishments, have improved considerably. For the sake of greater comparability, rating systems have been introduced, with the one to five stars classification being most common.

## TYPES OF HOTELS

### Boutique Hotels

Boutique hotel is a term originating in North America to describe intimate, usually luxurious or quirky hotel environments. Boutique hotels differentiate themselves from larger chain/branded hotels and motels by providing personalized level accommodation and services / facilities.

Sometimes known as "design hotels" or "lifestyle hotels," boutique hotels began in the 1980s in major cities like New York, London, and San Francisco. Very often it is the Morgans Hotel in Murray Hill of New York, that is awarded with the title of first boutique hotel in the world. It was opened by Ian Schrager in 1984 according to a design by Andrée Putman.

Typically boutique hotels are furnished in a themed, stylish and/or aspirational manner. Although usually considerably smaller than a mainstream hotel (often ranging from 3 to 100 guest rooms), boutique hotels can often have hundreds of rooms in major cities. Guest rooms and suites are fitted with telephony and Wi-Fi Internet, air-conditioning, honesty bars and often cable/pay TV. Guest services are attended to by 24 hour hotel staff. Many boutique hotels have on-site dining facilities, and the majority offer bars and lounges which may also be open to the general public.

Despite this definition, the popularity of the boutique term and concept has lead to some confusion about the term. Boutique hotels have typically been unique properties operated by individials or companies with a small collection. However, their successes have prompted established multinational hotel companies to establish their own brands. The most notable is Starwood Hotels and Resorts' W Hotels.

Currently, there is one publication dedicated to the boutique hotel, boutique DESIGN magazine, which is published quarterly. Boutique hotel resources are more commonly available online. One such site dedicated to boutique hotels is Tablet Hotels. There are also a number of sytlized design and coffee table books highlighting various properties throughout the world.

**Apartment Hotel**

An Apartment Hotel is a type of accommodation, described as "a serviced apartment complex that uses a hotel style booking system". It is similar to renting an apartment, but with no fixed contracts and occupants can 'check-out' whenever they wish.

Apartment hotels are flexible types of accommodation; instead of the rigid format of a hotel room an apartment hotel complex usually offers a complete fully fitted apartment. These complexes are usually custom built, and similar to a hotel complex contain a varied amount of apartments. The length of stay in these apartment hotels are very varied with anywhere from a few days to months or even years. Prices tend to be cheaper than hotels. The people that stay in apartment hotels use them as a home from home therefore they are usually fitted with everything the average home would require.

Apartment hotels were first created in holiday destinations as accommodation for families that needed to 'live' in an apartment rather than 'stay' as they would in a hotel. The apartments would provide a 'holiday home' but generally be serviced. Later on these apartments evolved to be complete homes, allowing occupants to do everything they would at home, such as cleaning, washing and cooking.

Essentially the apartment hotel combines the flexibility of apartment living with the service of a hotel. Many of the apartments take advantage of prime locations with panoramic views of cities seen through wall to ceiling windows. Suites usually include high quality finishes, broadband connection & interactive TV, servicing and integrated kitchen and bathroom. High quality leather sofas in the living area and king size beds bring the hotel experience to a whole new level. Those are the luxuries, they also come with the basics: satellite or cable TV, washer, dryer, dishwasher, cooker, oven, fridge, freezer, sink, shower, bath, wardrobes, all the furnishings to be expected in a luxury home.

**Bed and Breakfast**

A Bed and Breakfast often referred to as a B&B is a type of boarding house typically operating out of a large single family residence.

Guests are accommodated at night in private bedrooms and breakfast is served in the morning - either in the bedroom or, more commonly, in a dining room or the host's kitchen. Bathrooms can be private or shared (with other guests or with the family in smaller establishments) or en-suite (where the ablutions are directly accessed from the guest's bedroom).

B&Bs may be operated either as a primary occupation or as a secondary source of income. Staff often consists of the house's owners and members of their family who live there. Guests are usually expected to pay for their stay upon arrival and leave before noon (or earlier) on the day of departure. A big advantage of this type of hosted accommodation is the local knowledge of the host.

When guests stay more than one night, in some smaller B&Bs they will be expected to be away from the B&B during the main part of the day. This arrangement, however, may not be inconvenient since many popular B&Bs are located in beach and mountain areas, such as Hawaii, New England, and Colorado where daytime recreation and tourism activities are popular. One advantage of staying at a B&B is readier access to popular locations "off the beaten path" which may not be convenient to the city center.

Because most B&Bs are small, rarely with room for more than about 2-12 guests, it is advisable for anyone wanting to stay at a bed and breakfast to make reservations well in advance of their travel date. Consultation with a qualified travel agent knowledgeable in this type of accommodation may be helpful; However, many B&Bs belong to associations and have a web presence. Be aware that prices and tariffs described in various books and travel guides are often obsolete by the time they are published.

The B&B arrangement is actually a very old one; before the 20th century, it was quite normal for country travellers to spend the night at a private house rather than an inn, and the custom persists in many parts of the world. However, prior to the 19th century, this was strictly an informal arrangement constrained by acquaintance and social rank; a doctor might stay with a doctor or pharmacist, while a nobleman would only stay with the local gentry. The abbreviation of 'B&B' on roadside signs first became popular in the British Isles.

In the British Isles, breakfast is usually cooked on demand for the guest and usually features bacon, eggs, sausages, tomatoes, mushrooms, baked beans, etc but increasingly, because of either a desire of owners to economise or guests to minimise their calorie intake, a 'continental breakfast' is becoming more common.

In the British Isles where hotel prices are often outrageous, B&B's are a budget option and this tradition continues in many parts of the world.

However, many B&Bs in North America and New Zealand often consciously seek to recall earlier days; they are frequently established in attractive older houses that have been renovated and filled with antique furniture. In some cases in North America an existing inn will relabel itself as a "B&B" to improve business and move itself `up-market'.

In Ireland, most B&Bs serve a traditional Irish breakfast as a point of pride. In Cuba, which opened up to tourism in the 1990s after the financial support of the Soviet Union ended, a form of B&B called casa particular ("private home") became the main form of accommodation outside the tourist resorts.

The term "bed and breakfast" is also used to refer to a meal plan where breakfast is the only meal provided, commonly in package holidays, in a major hotel that may provide other meals to only some customers.

As they are often run by amateurs, with little lodge management experience, strict laws should govern the operation of B&Bs. However, regulations vary in each jurisdiction both in content and extent and in enforcement.

The most common regulations B&Bs must follow pertain to safety. They are required to have fire resistance, a sufficient fire escape plan in place, and smoke detectors in each guest room.

## Capsule Hotel

A capsule hotel, is a hotel system of extremely dense occupancy. Guest space is reduced in size to a modular plastic or fibreglass block roughly 2 m by 1 m by 1.25 m, providing room to sleep and little more, although facilities usually include a television and other electronic entertainment. These capsules are then grouped and stacked, two units high. Luggage is usually stored in a locker away from the capsule. Privacy is maintained by a curtain at the open end of the capsule but noise pollution can be high. Washing facilities are communal and there are often restaurants, or at least vending machines, and other entertainment facilities.

This style of hotel accommodation was developed in Japan and has not gained acceptance outside of the country. The Japanese capsule hotels vary widely in size, some having only fifty or so capsules and others over 700. They are often male-only. There are also capsule hotels with separate male and female sleeping quarters. Clothes and shoes are sometimes exchanged for a yukata and slippers on entry. A towel may also be provided. The benefit of these hotels is convenience and price, usually around ¥2000-4000 a night 21-29, $25–34, £15–20). Such hotels are not necessarily regarded as only an option for those with lower incomes—a typical customer would be the business salaryman after a night of drinking who has missed the last train home. Some capsule hotels offer low daytime discounts for those needing an afternoon nap.

The first capsule hotel was the Capsule Inn Osaka, designed by Kisho Kurokawa and located in the Umeda district of Osaka. It opened on February 1, 1979 and the initial room rate was ¥1,600.

These rooms can be seen in the movie The Fast and the Furious: Tokyo Drift. They were also used as a basis for sets in the film The Fifth Element. They also appear in the cyberpunk novel Neuromancer under the name of "coffin hotel."

**Casa Particular**

Casa particular is a phrase meaning private accommodation or private homestays in Cuba, very similar to bed and breakfast although it can also take the form of vacation rental. When the meaning is clear the term is often shortened to simply casa.

A casa particular is basically a private family establishment that provides paid lodging, usually on a short-term basis. In general under this term you can find full apartment and houses, rooms inside people homes, mini-apartments or rooms with separate entrance (studio or efficiency type rooms).

It is also considered a type of boarding house typically operated out of a single family residence where guests can be accommodated at night in private bedrooms (which may or may not be equipped with private baths) and where breakfast, sometimes continental and sometimes the full English variety, is served in the morning. The business may be operated either as a primary occupation or as a secondary source of income, and the staff often consists of the house's owner(s) and members of their family who live there.

Because they are usually small, rarely with room for more than about 5-6 guests, it is advisable for anyone wanting to stay at a particular casa particular during high season to make advance reservations. However, outside the season there is no need because there are often many such casas, causing competition and opening opportunities to strike a deal. Prices can then drop to 15 euro or even less for longer stays. During high season they can rise to over 30 euro. Many belong to associations, have a web presence, and are described in various books and travel guides:

Casas particulares can be recognised by a small sign on the door, with two blue triangles ('roofs') against a white background, which the owners obtain after paying a fixed per-room annual tax.

In some Cuban cities and tourist resorts, like Varadero, Playa Santa Lucia and Guardalavaca, local authorities determined that casas particulares would represent a threat to the hotel industry, and passed some legislation placing regulations and limits on the industry forbidding the operation of these establishments.

"Casa particular" literally means "private house" but it started to be used to mean "private accommodation" in 1997, when the Cuban government finally allowed Cubans to rent out rooms in their houses or apartments to tourists, providing Cuban families with new sources of incomc. As any other type of accommodation in Cuba such as hotels, camping and motels were owned by the government, the term "casa particular" stated that this kind of paid lodging was privately operated.

***Services and Facilities***

All rooms are clean, safe and upgraded to tourist standards. It ranges from basic accommodation of a room with a bed, a closet, a small table to full furnished independent apartments upgraded to western standards. Other features found may be a telephone, an alarm clock, and a TV. Food and drink may be supplied by a mini-bar (which often includes a small refrigerator) containing snacks and drinks (to be paid for on departure).

It is possible to have breakfast/dinner in the casa for price. Often breakfasts/dinners sold will decide if case owner will break even or not. So if it becomes clear that one plans to generally eat out, the price may go up because this is an important source of income.

Casas particulares have several advantages over other types of lodgings:

- The guest can quickly develop genuine Cuban relationships and become deeply involved in the culture of the country. Before he/she knows it, the guest will be part of the family. In a big resort one may only meet hotel workers and other tourists.
- The guest will enjoy the free and easy atmosphere, feel completely at home in the casa particular and will be able to invite friends over. The current regulations for state-run hotels don't allow to have Cuban guests invited to hotel rooms.
- It is almost always cheaper to stay in a private room than in a hotel.
- "Guests" are not usually allowed into the hotels. Usually one can take one local "guest" into his rented casa-particular.

- By renting a casa particular, the guest will be directly contributing to a person or family's standard of living. This is often obvious through the fact that casas particulares are freshly painted.

The cost and quality of casas particulares are usually indicative of the accommodation type and type of services available. Most of the casas particulares are rented for short term to travellers. Long term accommodation is also provided by some casas, especially for foreign students. In Havana, the casas particulares are usually family apartments and a smaller number of them are houses. In other cities, private accommodation is provided mainly in family houses.

Types of Casas Particulares rentals:

- Private Room: a room is rented out most of the times with private bathroom and a key to the apartment/ house is usually given to the guest.
- Private Room with independent entrance. Sometimes the house/apartment is split in order to allow this.
- Apartment: the guest can enjoy the privacy and independency of a full furnished apartment for his/ her vacations. Sometimes this apartment is part of house being split by a wall usually with a connecting door.
- Studio-type or mini-apartment: it is not an apartment with several rooms but just the bedroom, a kitchen-living-dining room and a bathroom.

**Condo-hotel**

A condo-hotel or a hotel-condo is a building used as both a condominium and a hotel. This type of residential building meets several needs that make it attractive. As development costs increase, the cost of hotel development can make developing new hotels difficult, especially in major cities. By selling the units as condos, the developer moves much of the development cost to the condo owners. By owning units that can be rented as hotel rooms, the owners are able to get a return on their investment allowing them the ability to own a residence in a resort or major city.

It should be noted that the U.S. Government is very strict about the type of advertising that can be done vis a vis Condo Hotel projects. Some condo projects have advertised themselves as "Real Estate Investments" - since the value of these condos as a real estate investment is not entirely clear - the U.S. Government currently disallows use of this reference when advertising condo hotels.

Condo hotels have been criticized in California for allowing developers to skirt laws designed to protect public access to beaches. Because such a facility has hotel rooms, it can be classified as a public accommodation, even though the majority of the units are privately held, and the facility does little to accommodate the public.

**Destination Hotel**

A destination hotel is a place of lodging whose inherent location and amenities attract visitors regardless of the route needed to arrive or the areawide features of interest. The destination hotel concept has existed at least since the 19th century and occupies a significant market share of all lodging in the world as of 2006. From the late 1980s to the present the extent of amenities and conference facilities has greatly expanded for many destination hotels. Destination hotels are also called destination lodgings and destination resorts. Considerable academic and business analysis has been conducted in the field of destination hotels. In the Arnold Encyclopedia of Real Estate a destination hotel is characterized as a place of lodging not chosen for convenience and not chosen for people in transit to other areas.

The following typically are characteristics of a destination hotel:

- Amenities which are quite complete and self-contained
- Upscale nature of the lodging operation
- Distinctive characteristics of the building, gardens or adjacent natural feature
- Activity set which makes leaving the property unnecessary

Since the 1800s, the traditional concept of a destination hotel has been based upon a venue which is typically remote and has a natural feature as its attraction. For example, the Kviknes Hotel in Norway is a difficult to reach remote location which provides visitors access to the scenic fjord at Balestrand. Historically there were certain built-in amenities such as gourmet cuisine, music recitals and shoreline trails; however, the amenities of modern (post 1980) destination hotels dwarf the scale of these earlier models. Many of the Las Vegas and Carribbean resort hotels have complete shopping malls, conference centers and large entertainment halls on site; thus, the contemporary version of a destination often features large on-site capital investment in activities, although the access to a local natural feature is still retained by many newer destination hotels.

**Luxury Resorts**

A luxury resort, sometimes referred to as an exclusive resort, is a very expensive vacation facility which is fully staffed and has been rated with five stars. Luxury resorts often boast many visitor activities and attractions such as golf, watersports, spa and beauty facilities, skiing, natural ecology and tranquility. Because of the extent of amenities offered, a luxury resort is also considered a destination resort.

A luxury resort is an elite luxury property which exhibits an exceptionally high degree of customer service and hospitality. A flawless execution of guest services will be the resort staff's and managements main concern. A luxury resort will commonly also feature a superb architectural interior and exterior design as well as an interesting physical location.

The interior design will normally be elegant with stylish bedroom decor, exceptional dining facilities, and manicured landscaping and meticulous grounds. Luxury resorts will often also be in based in exceptionally desirable and strategic worldwide locations, from beautiful tropical islands, to snow caked mountains, to scenic lakes and rivers, to exhilarating cities. The locations will often be famous for featured activities from skiing to golf, water spots, diving, fishing, sailing and nature walks to glamorous shopping and nightlife entertainment.

A luxury resort may vary greatly in character, style and theme from resort to resort. A luxury resort will, however, normally be characterized by a high level of luxury, sophistication and off course price. Accommodations are first class, whether they follow a classic and traditional nature or a more minimalist and modern styling. An unmatched level of comfort will be available at a luxury resort, as well as many personalized services and amenities.

**Extended Stay Hotel**

Extended stay hotels are a type of lodging with features unavailable at standard hotels. These features are intended to provide more home-like amenities. There are currently 27 extended stay chains in North America with at least 7 hotels, representing over 2,000 properties. There is substantial variation among extended stay hotels with respect to quality and the amenities that are available. Some of the economy chains attract clientele who use the hotels as semi-permanent lodging. Occasionally, these budget establishments can be the scene of criminal activity.

Extended-stay hotels typically have self-serve laundry facilities and offer discounts for extended stays, beginning at 5 or 7 days. They also have guestrooms (or "suites") with kitchens. The kitchens include at a minimum usually: a sink, a refrigerator (usually full size), a microwave oven, and a stovetop. Some kitchens also have dishwashers and conventional ovens.

Extended stay hotels are popular with business travelers on extended assignments, families in the midst of a relocation, and anyone else in need of temporary housing. Extended stay hotels are also used by travelers who appreciate the larger space a typical suite provides.

Residence Inn is credited with popularizing the "extended stay" concept. The chain was launched in 1975 in Wichita,

Kansas by Jack DeBoer, and acquired by Marriott Corporation in 1987. As of April 2005, there were over 450 Residence Inn hotels in the United States, Canada and Mexico. Some extended stay hotels are coming up in United Kingdom and Ireland as well.

One of today's most popular long term lodging brands came from the merger of Extended Stay America and Homestead Hotels. Both these chains were already well established when they combined in 2004 to become Extended Stay Hotels with over 670 owned and operated properties nationwide.

Another worldwide hotel chain, Choice Hotels International, franchisor for name brands such as Comfort Inn, Comfort Suites, Sleep Inn and Quality Inn, entered the extended stay market with their MainStay Suites brand. They proceeded to acquire the Suburban Extended Stay hotel chain in 2005, making them a sizeable extended stay system with over 150 hotels open and under development.

**Flophouse**

A flophouse or dosshouse is a place that offers very cheap lodging, generally by providing only minimal services. Occupants of flophouses generally share bathroom facilities and reside in very cramped quarters. The people who make use of these places are often transients, although some people will stay in flophouses for long periods of time—years or decades. Some people who live in flophouses may be just a step above homelessness. In the late 20th century, typical cost might be about US$6 per night. A typical flophouse might advertise its services with a sign such as "Hotel for Men; Transients Welcome".

Quarters in flophouses are very small, and may resemble office cubicles more than a regular room in a hotel or apartment building. A cubicle might only have wire mesh for a ceiling.

In the past, flophouses were sometimes called "workingmen's hotels" and catered to hobos and transient workers such as seasonal railroad and agriculture workers, or migrant lumberjacks who would travel west during the summer to work and then return to an eastern or midwestern city such as Chicago to stay in a flophouse during the winter. This is described in the 1930 novel The Rambling Kid by Charles Ashleigh and the 1976 book The Human Cougar by Lloyd Morain. Another theme in Morain's book is the gentrification which was then beginning and which has led cities to pressure flophouses to close.

George Orwell also discussed flophouses in the UK in his book Down and Out in Paris and London. He described them as having rather poor cleanliness standards, often issuing unwashed and badly stained blankets, and sometimes renting beds in a large common room resembling barracks more than private rooms. He noted that at the time he wrote the book (1933) the term "dosshouse" was already falling out of use.

Some city districts that currently have or once had flophouses in abundance became well-known in their own right, such as the Bowery in New York, New York.

The movies The Blues Brothers (1980) and Staying Alive (1983) both feature their lead characters living in flophouses. Another slang term for flophouses was mentioned in the movie Kids. This variation of the definition is a house or apartment (usually apartment) where substance abusers stay to party and abuse drugs and/or alcohol. Such people, whether employed or unemployed, lead a hedonist self-destructive lifestyle. If they are employed, their money usually goes to drugs and/or alcohol. Other bums and partygoers can also temporarily stay for parties.

Some low-end flophouses have graffiti sprayed on the walls and lack beds, instead just have matresses on the floor. Some of the characters in the film Trainspotting lived in these conditions. Michael Dominic's documentary film Sunshine Hotel (2001) follows the lives of the denizens of one of the few remaining Bowery flophouses.

# Chapter 2

# Entrepreneurship

Hospitality management is the name given to the collegiate academic major in which students are taught the business of running hotels, restaurants, and travel and tourism-related business.

The most famous hospitality school in management is located in Ithaca, NY: The Hotel School at Cornell University.

Another notable hospitality school is in Switzerland: the École hôtelière de Lausanne (EHL).The school currently offers three types of degrees. The primary programme, where students are educated in international hospitality management, leads to a Bachelor of Science (BOS) degree. Additionally, a prestigious MBA, the MHA (Master in Hospitality Administration) is offered. EHL has educated more than 25,000 hospitality industry executives who now make up a prestigious network for every member of the EHL community.

## ENTREPRENEURSHIP

Entrepreneurship is the practice of starting new organizations, particularly new businesses generally in response to identified opportunities. Entrepreneurship is often a difficult undertaking, as a majority of new businesses fail. Entrepreneurial activities are substantially different depending on the type of organization that is being started. Entrepreneurship ranges in scale from solo projects (even involving the entrepreneur only part-time) to major undertakings creating many job opportunities.

Many "high-profile" entrepreneurial ventures seek venture capital or angel funding in order to raise capital to build the business. Many kinds of organizations now exist to support would-be entrepreneurs, including specialized government agencies, business incubators, science parks, and some NGOs.

The understanding of entrepreneurship owes a lot to the work of economist Joseph Schumpeter and the Austrian School of economics. In Schumpeter (1950), an entrepreneur is a person who is willing and able to convert a new idea or invention into a successful innovation. Entrepreneurship forces "creative destruction" across markets and industries, simultaneously creating new products and business models others. In this way, creative destruction is largely responsible for the dynamism of industries and long-run economic growth. Despite Schumpeter's early 20th-century contributions, the traditional microeconomic theory of economics has had little room for entrepreneurs in their theoretical frameworks (instead assuming that resources would find each other through a price system).

Entrepreneurship received a boost in the formalized creation of so-called incubators and science parks where businesses can start at a small scale, share services and space while they grow, and eventually move into space of their own when they have achieved a large enough scale to be viable stand-alone businesses. Also, entrepreneurship is being employed to revitalize fading downtowns and inner cities, which may have excellent resources but suffer from a lack of spirited development.

For Frank H. Knight and Peter Drucker entrepreneurship is about taking risk. The behaviour of the entrepreneur reflects a kind of person willing to put his or her career and financial security on the line and take risks in the name of an idea, spending much time as well as capital on an uncertain venture.

Still another view of entrepreneurship is that it is the process of discovering, evaluating, and exploiting opportunities, which go on to reify themselves in the form of new business ventures. In this model an entrepreneur could be defined as "someone who acts with ambition beyond that supportable by the resources currently under his control, in relentless pursuit of opportunity" (a definition common to entrepreneurship professors Howard Stevenson and Jeffry Timmons). Pinchot coined the term Intrapreneurship to describe entrepreneurial-like activities inside organizations and government. The concept is commonly referred to as Corporate Entrepreneurship.

The place of the disharmony-creating and idiosyncratic entrepreneur in traditional economic theory (which describes many efficiency-based ratios assuming uniform outputs) presents theoretic quandaries. William Baumol has added greatly to this area of economic theory and was recently honored for it at the 2006 annual meeting of the American Economic Association.

## THE ENTREPRENEUR

Entrepreneurs have many of the same character traits as leaders. Similarly to the early great man theories of leadership, however, trait-based theories of entrepreneurship are increasingly being called into question. Entrepreneurs are often contrasted with managers and administrators who are said to be more methodical and less prone to risk-taking. Although such person-centric models of entrepreneurship have shown to be of questionable validity, a vast but clearly dated literature studying the entrepreneurial personality found that certain traits seem to be associated with entrepreneurs:

- For example, in 1961, David McClelland described the entrepreneur as primarily motivated by an overwhelming need for achievement and strong urge to build.
- Collins and Moore (1970) studied 150 entrepreneurs and concluded that they are tough, pragmatic people

driven by needs of independence and achievement. They seldom are willing to submit to authority.

- Bird sees entrepreneurs as mercurial, that is, prone to insights, brainstorms, deceptions, ingeniousness and resourcefulness. They are cunning, opportunistic, creative, and unsentimental.
- Busenitz and Barney claim entrepreneurs are prone to overconfidence and over generalisations.
- According to Cole, there are four types of entrepreneur: the innovator, the calculating inventor, the over-optimistic promoter, and the organisation builder. These types are not related to the personality but to the type of opportunity the entrepreneur faces.
- Burton W. Folsom, Jr. distinguishes between what he calls a political entrepreneur and a market entrepreneur. The political entrepreneur uses political influences to gain income through subsidies, protectionism, government-granted monopoly, government contracts, or other such favorable arrangements with governments. The market entrepreneur operates without special favors from government.

## CHARACTERISTICS OF ENTREPRENEURSHIP

- The entrepreneur has an enthusiastic vision, the driving force of an enterprise.
- The entrepreneur's vision is usually supported by an interlocked collection of specific ideas not available to the marketplace.
- The overall blueprint to realize the vision is clear, however details may be incomplete, flexible, and evolving.
- The entrepreneur promotes the vision with enthusiastic passion.
- With persistence and determination, the entrepreneur develops strategies to change the vision into reality.

- The entrepreneur takes the initial responsibility to cause a vision to become a success.
- Entrepreneurs take prudent risks. They assess costs, market/customer needs and persuade others to join and help.
- An entrepreneur is usually a positive thinker and a decision maker.

## Entrepreneur

An entrepreneur (a loanword from French) is a person who undertakes and operates a new enterprise or venture and assumes some accountability for the inherent risks. In the context of the creation of for-profit enterprises, entrepreneur is often synonymous with founder.

Most commonly, the term entrepreneur applies to someone who establishes a new entity to offer a new or existing product or service into a new or existing market, whether for a profit or not-for-profit outcome.

Business entrepreneurs often have strong beliefs about a market opportunity and are willing to accept a high level of personal, professional or financial risk to pursue that opportunity. Business entrepreneurs are often highly regarded in U.S. culture as critical components of its capitalistic society.

- An entrepreneur is a person who organizes and manages any enterprise, esp. a business, usually with considerable initiative and risk.
- An employer of productive labour; contractor.
- Is the one to deal with or initiate as an entrepreneur.

## Role of Entrepreneur in an Organization

An entrepreneur is someone who organizes a system. He is the person who creates and/or sells a product or service in order to gain profit. However, there is a general sense that entrepreneurship involves the establishment of a new venture while adopting some of the risk and being ready for failure. There is no general definition for the word, as it has been used in a large variety of ways. Some scholars of entrepreneurship, such as Prof. W. Long have tried to develop a specific definition by studying the evolution of the word's usage.

### Entrepreneur as a Risk Bearer

An entrepreneur is an agent who buys factors of production at certain prices in order to combine them into a product with a view to selling it at uncertain prices in future. Uncertainty is defined as a risk, which cannot be insured against and is incalculable. There is a distinction between ordinary risk and uncertainty. A risk can be reduced through the insurance principle, where the distribution of the outcome in a group of instances is known. On the contrary, uncertainty is a risk, which cannot be calculated. The entrepreneur, according to Knight, is the economic functionary who undertakes such responsibility of uncertainty, which by its very nature cannot be insured, or capitalized or salaried to. Mark Casson has extended this notion to characterize entrepreneurs as decision makers who improvise solutions to problems which cannot be solved by routine alone.

### Entrepreneur as an Organizer

An entrepreneur is one who combines the land of one, labour of another and the capital of yet another, and, thus, produces a product.

By selling the product in the market, he pays interest on capital, rent on land and wages to laborers and what remains is his or her profit.

### Entrepreneur as a Leader

Scholar R. B. Reich considers leadership, management ability, and team-building as essential qualities of an entrepreneur.

Entrepreneur is sometimes mistakenly equated with "opportunist". An entrepreneur may be considered one who creates an opportunity rather than merely exploits it, though that distinction is difficult to make precise.

### Supply vs Demand Theories

Business academics have two classes of theories of how people become entrepreneurs, called supply and demand theories, after Economics. In the supply theory, entrepreneurs arise as they are born, with personality traits which drive them to become entrepreneurs. In the demand theory, anyone could be recruited by circumstance or opportunity to become an entrepreneur.

Several research studies have shown that entrepreneurs are convinced that they can command their own destinies. Behaviourial scientists express this by saying that entrepreneurs perceive the "locus of control" to be within themselves. It is this self-belief which stimulates the entrepreneur, according to supply-side theorists.

A more generally held theory is that entrepreneurs emerge from the population on demand, from the combination of opportunities and people well-positioned to take advantage of them. The entrepreneur may perceive that they are among the few to recognize or be able to solve a problem. In this view, one studies on one side the distribution of information available to would-be entrepreneurs and on the other, how environmental factors (access to capital, competition, etc.) change the rate of a society's production of entrepreneurs.

**Personality Characteristics**

John G. Burch lists the following traits typical of entrepreneurs:

- A desire to achieve: The push to conquer problems, and give birth to a successful venture.
- Hard work: It is often suggested that many entrepreneurs are workaholics.
- Desire to work for themselves: Entrepreneurs like to work for themselves rather than working for an organization or any other individual. They may work for someone to gain the knowledge of product or service that they may want to produce.
- Nurturing quality: Willing to take charge of, and watch over a venture until it can stand alone.
- Acceptance of responsibility: Are morally, legally, and mentally accountable for their ventures. Some entrepreneurs may be driven more by altruism than by self-interest.

- Reward orientation: Desire to achieve, work hard, and take responsibility, but also with a commensurate desire to be rewarded handsomely for their efforts; rewards can be in forms other than money, such as recognition and respect.
- Optimism: Live by the philosophy that this is the best of times, and that anything is possible.
- Orientation to excellence: Often desire to achieve something outstanding that they can be proud of.
- Organization: Are good at bringing together the components (including people) of a venture.
- Profit orientation: Want to make a profit; but the profit serves primarily as a meter to gauge their success and achievement.

## FUNCTIONS OF MANAGEMENT

### PLANNING

Planning is the (psychological) process of creating and refining a plan, or integrating it with other plans. The term is also used to describe the formal procedures used in such an endeavour, such as the creation of documents, diagrams, or meetings to discuss the important issues to be addressed, the objectives to be met, and the strategy to be followed. Beyond this, planning has a different meaning depending on the political or economic context in which it is used.

Planning refers to the practice and profession associated with land use planning, urban planning or spatial planning. In many countries, the operation of town and country planning system is often referred to as 'planning' and the professionals which operate the system are known as 'planners'.It is a process which is decided in advance what is to be done in the coming future.

#### Objectives for Non-profit-making Organizations

In the case of non-profit organizations the objectives may be less than clear. Keith Blois suggested five main reasons for the differences from 'commercial' organizations:

1. Ambiguous Goals [more actors and groups of actors are involved
2. Lack of Agreement in Means-End Relationships [even where there is consensus on the goal there may be disagreement on how to get there]
3. Environmental Turbulence [non-profit organizations seem to be exposed more to turbulence than commercial ones
4. Unmeasurable Outputs [unfortunately, by definition, non-profit organizations do not have the classically convenient simplicity of 'bottom-line profit'
5. The Effects of Management Intervention are Unknown [the lack of precision caused by factors 1-4 is problem enough, but the 'culture' seems to add further barriers to managing these organizations

Even so, Kotler and Andreasen suggested some possible objectives for such organizations:

1. Surplus Maximization [equivalent to profit maximization]
2. Revenue Maximization [as for profit-making organizations]
3. Usage Maximization [maximizing the numbers of users and their usage]
4. Usage Targeting [matching the capacity available]
5. Full Cost Recovery [breaking even]
6. Partial Cost Recovery [minimizing the subsidy]
7. Budget Maximization [maximizing what is offered]
8. Producer Satisfaction Maximization [satisfying the wants of staff]

**Planning in Organizations**

Planning is also a management function, concerned with defining goals for future organizational performance and deciding on the tasks and resources to be used in order to attain those goals. To meet the goals, managers will invest significant resources for training and incentives to motivate employees. Planning is the process of setting objectives and determining how to accomplish them

Simply it is the act of thinking before doing. It access us in predecting the about the future. So,it serve as the standard for the function of controlling if there is any devation.

**The Marketing Planning Process**

In most organizations 'strategic planning' is an annual process, typically covering just the year ahead. Occasionally, a few organizations may look at a practical plan which stretches three or more years ahead.

To be most effective, the plan has to be formalized, usually in written form, as a formal 'marketing plan'. The essence of the process is that it moves from the general to the specific; from the overall objectives of the organization down to the individual action plan for a part of one marketing programme. It is also an iterative process, so that the draft output of each stage is checked to see what impact it has on the earlier stages - and is amended accordingly.

**The Corporate Plan**

The starting point for the marketing plan, and the context within which it is set, is the corporate plan. In most marketing-oriented organizations the contents of the corporate plan will closely match those of the marketing plan itself; but it will also include the plans for the disposition of the other internal resources of the organization. Thus, the corporate plan is likely to contain three main components:

The first category is intimately involved with the customers. In marketing terms, although there are many other factors to take into account, the most important definition of where the company is revolves around where it is in the market (and hence where it is with its consumers). The same is largely true of the second stage as well; since, no matter how much its managers may wish otherwise, where the company can realistically expect to go is totally in the hands of its customers. It is only at the third stage that the 4 Ps come into play as vehicles for moving the company to reach its objectives.

## Corporate Objectives

The overall objectives of commercial organizations are conventionally supposed to be financial. However, other aims are also possible. Many companies choose long-term growth (which may be quite different to revenue maximization in the short term). Almost all have an implicit, and very powerful, aim of survival.

One of the best known 'alternatives', that of 'satisficing' (rather than profit maximization), came from Herbert Simon: "In one way or another, they [alternative theories] incorporate the notions of bounded rationality: the need to search for decision alternatives, the replacement of optimization [profit-based objectives] by targets and satisficing [minimal] goals, and mechanisms of learning and adaptation."

Pfeffer and Salancik said that: "We prefer to view organizations as coalitions altering their purposes and domains to accommodate new interests, sloughing off parts of themselves to avoid some interests, and when necessary, becoming involved in activities far afield from their stated central purposes. Organizations are social instruments of tremendous power and energy, and the critical issue becomes who will control this energy and for what purpose."

If we accept the traditional assumption, as to the financial basis of the objectives behind the corporate plan, these objectives are ideally meant to be quantified in numerical and, in particular, financial terms.

In the most general terms, though, the 'objectives' behind a strategy address two questions: ''Where' do we want to be?' and ''When' do we expect to be there?'

### *Forecasting*

This can be a very complex topic but can, in general, be roughly divided into two parts;

### *Short-Term Forecasting*

This is the type of forecasting you will recognise. It is normally based upon a projection of historical trends, usually focused on sales volumes. There are many sophisticated techniques, increasingly using large amounts of computing power, but in essence all of these try to separate out the four main components:

1. Long term trends probably represent the most important information you are trying to extract from the mass of data before you.
2. Medium term cycles are supposed to result from regular economic ups and downs (from boom to bust) which used to be encapsulated in a 5 year 'business cycle' which, unfortunately, became unpredictable in the 1980s. The much quoted 'Kondratieff Cycles' are much longer, if they exist at all, being of the order of 25 - 50 years; and hence do not normally enter into shorter term forecasts.
3. Seasonal is the pattern within a single year, a pattern which most suppliers who are affected by it know well.
4. Random fluctuations, which do not fit regular patterns, afflict all products and services, and make computer analysis a very difficult proposition.

The end result of all these patterns superimposed may appear very confusing indeed. Despite all the sophistication on offer, therefore, by far the best advice is to keep it as simple as possible. The human eye is much better at resolving the complications shown above than the most powerful computer. Thus, the best approach to forecasting (and certainly the best check on any more sophisticated technique) is 'eyeballing' the sales charts! With some practise you should be able to sort out the main features of what is happening - and that is better than most computer models achieve.

The evidence is that the sophistication adds little or nothing to the accuracy (though it does to the image of the forecasters, and the prices they charge). Worst of all, such unnecessary complexity hinders your understanding of what is going on under the covers of the computer (and hides the fact that most forecasts are really based on human judgement). In any case, even if historical trends are accurately analysed, there is no guarantee that the future will be the same as the past. It is much better that you surface all the assumptions, and make your own judgements in full knowledge of what is involved.

Two very simple techniques to use (if nothing else but as a check on the forecasts others are trying to sell to you);

- Eyeballing - the technique I mentioned above is the first, and best, method. It merely requires you to plot historical results graphically; and then look for the patterns. Trust your own judgement - until you are proved wrong.
- Exponential Smoothing - this is the mathematical technique which reportedly gives the best results; probably because it is so simple, and consequently easily understood. Indeed, it is a very impressive title for a simple, but useful, mathematical technique; which can quite easily be handled manually. It just allows greater weight to be given to recent periods. Instead of, for example, the average trend over the whole of the last year being calculated, the sales data for each of the months is given a weighting, depending on how recent that month was. It simply takes the previous forecast, and adds on the latest 'actual' sales figure; except that it does this in a fixed proportion, which is chosen to reflect the weighting to be given to the latest period. The general form is; $Ft+1 = Ft + aEt$ where $Ft+1$ is the new forecast you are calculating, $Ft$ is the previous one and $Et$ is the deviation (or 'error') of the actual performance recorded against that previous period forecast; and 'a' is the weighting to be given to the most recent events. Exponential smoothing will not, in this simple form, allow for seasonality; though more sophisticated (but less easily understood) versions can do this.

## Long-Term Forecasting

This tends to be qualitative (as compared with the quantitative, numeric, focus of short term forecasts). It is even more dependent on judgement; and most of the more complicated approaches to it (such as Delphi, or Jury methods) aim to reduce the risks implicit in the judgement by spreading the process over panels of experts. It does not, in the final analysis, absolve the manager from backing his or her own judgement (which is probably better informed, in terms of the specific situation, than that of the 'experts').

Of all the techniques the most useful involves developing complementary scenarios, which allow for the uncertainties involved; as well as expanding the viewpoint of all the managers involved in the process. Unfortunately, in the form most often described it can also be the most complex and sophisticated of these techniques - and in this form perhaps only the very large corporate planning team at Shell have used it really effectively. A much simplified approach, based on the version which Shell recommend for their line managers who are not part of their corporate planning group, is more practical for most organisations. In this simplified version of the form originally described by Shell[1] the four steps to this process are:

1. Identify the important variables
2. Brainstorm to find the possible outcomes
3. Link these together in a series of alternative scenarios
4. Refine these scenarios

    1. Identify the important variables - what (in the whole of the external environment, not just the marketing environment) are the most important factors which will determine the future of the organisation.
    2. Brainstorm to find the possible outcomes - work through the different outcomes which different alternatives for these variables may lead to.

3. Link these together in a series of alternative scenarios - start to build six or seven scenarios ('stories' about the future of the organisation, or more importantly its market) which are able to contain these different alternatives.
4. Refine these scenarios - then work on the scenarios until they are condensed to two or three meaningful alternative (but complementary) descriptions of the future.

## CORPORATE MISSION

Behind the corporate objectives, which in themselves offer the main context for the marketing plan, will lie the ''corporate mission; which in turn provides the context for these corporate objectives. This 'corporate mission' can be thought of as a definition of what the organization is; of what it does: 'Our business is...'.

This definition should not be too narrow, or it will constrict the development of the organization; a too rigorous concentration on the view that 'We are in the business of making meat-scales', as IBM was during the early 1900s, might have limited its subsequent development into other areas. On the other hand, it should not be too wide or it will become meaningless; 'We want to make a profit' is not too helpful in developing specific plans.

Abell suggested that the definition should cover three dimensions: 'customer groups' to be served, 'customer needs' to be served, and 'technologies' to be utilized.

Thus, the definition of IBM's 'corporate mission' in the 1940s might well have been: 'We are in the business of handling accounting information [customer need] for the larger US organizations [customer group] by means of punched cards [technology].' Fortunately, as the name itself (International Business Machines) indicates, IBM already had a wider perspective (and its corporate mission was virtually defined by its name).

## CORPORATE VISION

Perhaps the most important factor in successful marketing is the 'corporate vision'. Surprisingly, it is largely neglected by marketing textbooks; although not by the popular exponents of corporate strategy - indeed, it was perhaps the main theme of the book by Peters and Waterman, in the form of their 'Superordinate Goals'. Theodore Levitt said: "Nothing drives progress like the imagination. The idea precedes the deed."

If the organization in general, and its chief executive in particular, has a strong vision of where its future lies, then there is a good chance that the organization will achieve a strong position in its markets (and attain that future). This will be not least because its strategies will be consistent; and will be supported by its staff at all levels. In this context, all of IBM's marketing activities were underpinned by its philosophy of 'customer service'; a vision originally promoted by the charismatic Watson dynasty.

Henry Mintzberg explained: "... in some cases, in addition to the mission there is the 'sense of mission', that is, a feeling that the group has banded together to create something new and exciting. This is common in new organizations".

What a worthwhile vision consists of is, however, usually open to debate; hence the reason why such visions tend to be associated with strong, charismatic leaders. But the vision must be relevant. The message for the marketer is that, to be most effective, the marketing strategies must be converted into a powerful long-term vision; if such a vision does not already exist.

## MARKETING AUDIT

The first formal step in the marketing planning process is that of conducting the marketing audit. Ideally, at the time of producing the marketing plan, this should only involve bringing together the source material which has already been collected throughout the year - as part of the normal work of the marketing department.

The emphasis at this stage is on obtaining a complete and accurate picture. In a single organization, however, it is likely that only a few aspects will be sufficiently important to have any significant impact on the marketing plan; but all may need to be reviewed to determine just which 'are' the few.

In this context some factors related to the customer, which should be included in the material collected for the audit, may be:

- Who are the customers?
- What are their key characteristics?
- What differentiates them from other members of the population?
- What are their needs and wants?
- What do they expect the 'product' to do?
- What are their special requirements and perceptions?
- What do they think of the organization and its products or services?
- What are their attitudes?

A 'traditional' - albeit product-based - format for a 'brand reference book' (or, indeed, a 'marketing facts book') was suggested by Godley more than three decades ago:

1. Financial data —Facts for this section will come from management accounting, costing and finance sections.
2. Product data —From production, research and development.
3. Sales and distribution data - Sales, packaging, distribution sections.
4. Advertising, sales promotion, merchandising data - Information from these departments.
5. Market data and miscellany - From market research, who would in most cases act as a source for this information.

His sources of data, however, assume the resources of a very large organization. In most organizations they would be obtained from a much smaller set of people (and not a few of them would be generated by the marketing manager alone). It is apparent that a marketing audit can be a complex process, but the aim is simple: 'it is only to identify those existing (external and internal) factors which will have a significant impact on the future plans of the company'.

It is clear that the basic material to be input to the marketing audit should be comprehensive. Accordingly, the best approach is to accumulate this material continuously, as and when it becomes available; since this avoids the otherwise heavy workload involved in collecting it as part of the regular, typically annual, planning process itself - when time is usually at a premium. Even so, the first task of this 'annual' process should be to check that the material held in the current 'facts book' or 'facts files' actually 'is' comprehensive and accurate, and can form a sound basis for the marketing audit itself.

The structure of the facts book will be designed to match the specific needs of the organization, but one simple format - suggested by Malcolm McDonald - may be applicable in many cases. This splits the material into three groups:

1. 'Review of the marketing environment'. A study of the organization's markets, customers, competitors and the overall economic, political, cultural and technical environment; covering developing trends, as well as the current situation.
2. 'Review of the detailed marketing activity'. A study of the company's marketing mix; in terms of the 4 Ps - product, price, promotion and place.
3. 'Review of the marketing system'. A study of the marketing organization, marketing research systems and the current marketing objectives and strategies.

The last of these is too frequently ignored. The marketing system itself needs to be regularly questioned, because the validity of the whole marketing plan is reliant upon the accuracy of the input from this system, and 'garbage in, garbage out' applies with a vengeance.

The analysis of this material will, no doubt, require significant effort. In the first instance it is a matter of selection, of sorting the wheat from the chaff. What is important, and will need to be taken into account in the marketing plan that will eventually emerge from the overall process, will be different for each product or service in each situation. One of the most important skills to be learned in marketing is that of being able to concentrate on just what is important.

It is important to say not just what happened but why. The process of marketing planning encompasses all of the marketing skills. However, a number of these may be particularly relevant at this stage:

- 'Positioning'. The starting point of the marketing plan must be the consumer. It is a matter of definition that his or her needs should drive the whole marketing process. The techniques of positioning and segmentation therefore usually offer the best starting point for what has to be achieved by the whole planning process.
- 'Portfolio planning'. In addition, the coordinated planning of the individual products and services can contribute towards the balanced portfolio.
- '80:20 rule'. To achieve the maximum impact, the marketing plan must be clear, concise and simple. It needs to concentrate on the 20 per cent of products or services, and on the 20 per cent of customers, which will account for 80 per cent of the volume and 80 per cent of the 'profit'.
- '4 Ps'. The 4 Ps can sometimes divert attention from the customer, but the framework they offer can be very useful in building the action plans.

## MARKETING OBJECTIVES

It is only at this stage (of deciding the marketing objectives) that the active part of the marketing planning process begins'.

This next stage in marketing planning is indeed the key to the whole marketing process. The marketing objectives state just where the company intends to be; at some specific time in the future. James Quinn succinctly defined objectives in general as: "Goals (or objectives) state 'what' is to be achieved and 'when' results are to be accomplished, but they do not state 'how' the results are to be achieved".

They typically relate to what products (or services) will be where in what markets (and must be realistically based on customer behaviour in those markets). They are essentially about the match between those 'products' and 'markets'. Objectives for pricing, distribution, advertising and so on are at a lower level, and should not be confused with marketing objectives. They are part of the marketing strategy needed to achieve marketing objectives.

To be most effective, objectives should be capable of measurement and therefore 'quantifiable'. This measurement may be in terms of sales volume, money value, market share, percentage penetration of distribution outlets and so on. An example of such a measurable marketing objective might be `to enter the market with product Y and capture 10 per cent of the market by value within one year'. As it is quantified it can, within limits, be unequivocally monitored; and corrective action taken as necessary.

The marketing objectives must usually be based, above all, on the organization's financial objectives; converting these financial measurements into the related marketing measurements.

It is conventionally assumed that marketing objectives will be designed to maximize volume or profit (or to optimize the utilization of resources in the non-profit sector), by creating demand or rejuvenating existing demand, say; although the various sub-objectives may indicate many different routes to achieving such optimization. However, as Kotler suggested (in the earlier edition of his book), there may be a number of other objectives:

- Synchromarketing
- Demarketing
- Counter-marketing

1. Synchromarketing - The aim may be to 'redistribute' existing sales (which are already at optimum levels) so that they occur at times, or in places, which the supplier prefers. Thus, for example, organizations which have highly seasonal sales (which make inefficient use of resources) may want to increase non-seasonal sales. Walls achieved this by balancing its summer sales of ice-cream with pies and sausages, demand for which peaks in winter. The suppliers of central-heating oil offer special deals for those customers willing to restock their tanks in summer.
2. Demarketing' - Demand may sometimes exceed supply. In these circumstances the emphasis will be on rationing scarce supplies. Occasionally the supplier, rather than bring on-stream expensive new plant, may seek to persuade customers to buy less (or be less dissatisfied with the scarcity). Some suppliers of electrical energy (electricity generators in Europe and the USA) have heavily advertised energy conservation measures to achieve this end (otherwise, the cost of meeting the peak winter loads would be very high - and unprofitable).
3. Counter-marketing - In what is usually a public-sector activity (but is occasionally undertaken by the private sector, where some uses of a product are damaging the corporate image), there may be an objective of stopping consumption completely. The anti-tobacco and anti-drug campaigns are the most obvious examples; but McDonald's campaigns to stop its customers dropping litter, or the brewers' campaigns to stop drinking and driving, fall into this category.

**Emergent Strategy**

In this case, the intended strategy, decided upon traditionally or incrementally, is overtaken by events in two main ways. One, which will probably be recognised by the organisation, is that of unrealised strategy; where it proves impossible to implement the chosen strategy in practice.

Less obvious is the emergent strategy which is decided by events in the external environment; and, thus, forced upon the organisation. This may not necessarily be recognised, in its totality, by the organisation - since many of its implications may be hidden. As markets become more complex, however, such emergent strategies are becoming more common.

Many organizations see both these processes in terms of failure - they have been forced, usually by unpredictable events, to abandon their own strategy. There is, accordingly, a tendency for these unwelcome facts to be ignored until they are so obvious that they cannot be avoided. This is a major error. Such deviations must be recognised (probably through one or other form of environmental analysis coupled with networking) as soon as possible- so that the organisation can react in good time.

A much more powerful approach is, though, to be proactive; so seize upon these deviations as the basis for future developments. What needs to be recognised is that emergent strategies are the most powerful of all. They must, by definition, be dierctly derived from the needs of the market - where even successful deliberate strategies may not ideally match market needs but may achieve their targets by sheer force (especially where conviction marketing lies behind them). Emergent strategies are, thus, likely to be vigorous ones.

There are two main approaches to capitalising on such emergent strategies. The first of these, favoured in the West, is the umbrella strategy. This is a form of very positive delegation, in that the overall strategies, the umbrella, are very general in nature - and allow the lower level managers, who are closest to the external environment, the freedom to react to these changes.

A much more direct, and hence even more powerful, approach is that favoured by the Japanese corporations. They integrate emergent strategies with their own. Indeed it is arguable that, in terms of marketing, to a large extent they use emergent strategies instead of their own deliberate strategies. This is evidenced as much by an attitude of mind as by any other feature. They deliberately go out to look for symptoms of such emergent trends which can be detected in the performance of their own products. More than that, though, they often deliberately launch a range of products rather than a single one to see which is most successful. It is almost as if they deliberately seek out the emergent strategies by offering the best environment for them to develop - the very reverse of the Western approach which seeks to avoid them! The Japanese then go on to build on these emergent strategies with a number of very effective tools - most of which are designed to overcome the major problem which accompanies emergent strategies, that they emerge on the scene much later than deliberate ones (and are likely to be visible to all the competitors at the same time) so that time is the essence. Thus, time management techniques (including parallel development along with flexible manufacturing and JIT) which have been developed by the Japanese offer them a significant competitive advantage in handling such emergent strategies.

## MARKETING STRATEGIES

There are numerous definitions of what strategy is, but again James Quinn again gave a succinct general definition: "A strategy is a 'pattern' or 'plan' that 'integrates' an organization's 'major' goals, policies and action sequences into a 'cohesive' whole"

He went on to explain his view of the role of 'policies', with which strategy is most often confused: "Policies are rules or guidelines that express the 'limits' within which action should occur.

Simplifying somewhat, marketing strategies can be seen as the means, or 'game plan', by which marketing objectives will be achieved and, in the framework that we have chosen to use, are generally concerned with the 4 Ps. Examples are:

**Product**

- Developing new products, repositioning or relaunching existing ones and scrapping old ones
- Adding new features and benefits
- Balancing product portfolios
- Changing the design or packaging

**Price**

- Setting the price to skim or to penetrate
- Pricing for different market segments
- Deciding how to meet competitive pricing

**Promotiom**

- Specifying the advertising platform and media
- Deciding the public relations brief
- Organizing the salesforce to cover new products and services or markets

**Place**

- Choosing the channels
- Deciding levels of customer service

In principle, these strategies describe how the objectives will be achieved. The 4 Ps are a useful framework for deciding how the company's resources will be manipulated (strategically) to achieve the objectives. It should be noted, however, that they are not the only framework, and may divert attention from the real issues. The focus of the strategies must be the objectives to be achieved - not the process of planning itself. Only if it fits the needs of these objectives should you choose, as we have done, to use the framework of the 4 Ps.

The strategy statement can take the form of a purely verbal description of the strategic options which have been chosen. Alternatively, and perhaps more positively, it might include a structured list of the major options chosen.

One aspect of strategy which is often overlooked is that of 'timing'. Exactly when it is the best time for each element of the strategy to be implemented is often critical. Taking the right action at the wrong time can sometimes be almost as bad as taking the wrong action at the right time. Timing is, therefore, an essential part of any plan; and should normally appear as a schedule of planned activities.

Having completed this crucial stage of the planning process, you will need to re-check the feasibility of your objectives and strategies in terms of the market share, sales, costs, profits and so on which these demand in practice. As in the rest of the marketing discipline, you will need to employ judgement, experience, market research or anything else which helps you to look at your conclusions from all possible angles.

At this stage, you will need to develop your overall marketing strategies into detailed plans and programmes. Although these detailed plans may cover each of the 4 Ps, the focus will vary, depending upon your organization's specific strategies. A product-oriented company will focus its plans for the 4 Ps around each of its products. A market or geographically oriented company will concentrate on each market or geographical area. Each will base its plans upon the detailed needs of its customers, and on the strategies chosen to satisfy these needs.

Again, the most important element is, indeed, that of the detailed plans; which spell out exactly what programmes and individual activities will take place over the period of the plan (usually over the next year). Without these specified - and preferably quantified - activities the plan cannot be monitored, even in terms of success in meeting its objectives.

It is these programmes and activities which will then constitute the 'marketing' of the organization over the period. As a result, these detailed marketing programmes are the most important, practical outcome of the whole planning process. These plans should therefore be:

- Clear - They should be an unambiguous statement of 'exactly' what is to be done.
- Quantified - The predicted outcome of each activity should be, as far as possible, quantified; so that its performance can be monitored.

- Focused - The temptation to proliferate activities beyond the numbers which can be realistically controlled should be avoided. The 80:20 Rule applies in this context too.
- Realistic - They should be achievable.
- Agreed - Those who are to implement them should be committed to them, and agree that they are achievable.

The resulting plans should become a working document which will guide the campaigns taking place throughout the organization over the period of the plan. If the marketing plan is to work, every exception to it (throughout the year) must be questioned; and the lessons learned, to be incorporated in the next year's plan.

## ORGANIZING

Organizing is the act of rearranging elements following one or more rules. It can also be seeing as the opposite of messing up.

One organized opposite could be disordered, since ordered is almost synonymous. The difference between ordered and organized is that something is only ordered as long as it is both organized and standardized.

Anything is commonly considered organized when it looks like everything has a correct order of placement. But it's only ultimately organized if any element has no difference on time taken to find it. In that sense, organizing can also be defined as the act to place different objects in sequential arrangement for better searching.

Organizations are groups of people frequently trying to organize some specific subject, such as political issues. So, even while organizing can be viewed as a simple definition, it can get as complex as organizing the world's information.

Historically, humans have always tried to organize ourselves. Be it on religion, through books and spoken word, or in science, through journals and studies, or in many other ways. Writing ideas in a book, not to talk to someone, but to specific catalog is also an attempt to organize information.

Science books are notable by their organization attempt of a specific subject. Encyclopedias, instead, usually try to organize any subject into one place, for faster indexing and seeking of meanings.

Recently there was the advent of computers and in the last decade, a huge Internet usage world wide. Notably, the Internet growth is directly related to the advent of websites to search the internet, which also means organizing the internet, since nobody would know how to get anywhere without either guessing, hints or those websites.

Organizing, in companies point of view, is the management function that usually follows after planning. And it involves the assignment of tasks, the grouping of tasks into departments and the assignment of authority and allocation of resources across the organization.

## LEADING

Management skills are a subset of leadership skills. I've often heard people try to separate them by saying that they are leaders, but not managers. In my experience the people who say this are generally failures when it comes to attracting followers which makes it difficult to consider them successful leaders.

A leader is someone who knows where to go. Management skills are how they actually get there. A college student who gets a bunch of friends together to take a weekend trip skiing is acting not only as a leader, but also as a manager. The student must take into account how much gas they have in their car, how much lift tickets are going to cost, invite people who have a reasonable chance of getting along with each other, etc.

Someone who is trying to act as a leader, but wants nothing to do with management is like a 7 year old who has found the keys to the family car and is overcome with the desire to drive to Disney World. Vision, a goal, and a sense of purpose are all present, but the ability to plan and execute is lacking.

That is a pretty good description of someone who wants to lead, but not manage. They may have wonderful ideas, but without the ability to plan and oversee the necessary work their ideas are not going to be realized—at least not by them. If their ideas do get implemented it will be done by another leader who embraces the management function.

While management is an important part of leadership, the reverse is not necessarily true. There are many people who are very skilled at implementing someone else's vision who are not leaders. The fact that these people exist can make some leaders feel justified in abdicating their responsibility to manage.

In its simplest form, management is the process of defining and measuring success. The leader who attempts to pass these responsibilities off to a different individual is unlikely to achieve 100% alignment between their vision and the actual work done by the organization. This doesn't mean that the organization will necessarily be ineffective, but if only 80% of the work being done is actually aligned with the vision, there is going to be a decrease in productivity overall.

A leader who sets the vision, defines success, and determines the measurements of success will be more effective than the same leader who wants to set the vision but refuses to undertake any work in the management area.

The word leadership can refer to:

1. The process of leading
2. The concept of leading
3. Those entities that perform one or more acts of leading.

The various meanings can lead to some confusion.

House defines "leadership" organizationally and narrowly as "the ability of an individual to influence, motivate, and enable others to share contribute toward the effectiveness and success of the organizations of which they are members". One can also characterize leadership by the period of the authority, as in "During the 1940s Russia was under Stalinist leadership". In formal hierarchies the term can also serve to describe the position or relationships which allow and legitimize the exercising of what one might term "leadership behaviour".

In some languages the term for a leader and the term for the principle of leadership have very different meanings. Furthermore, note the different connotations of a synonym of the word "leader" adopted from the German: the word Führer, and its accompanying ideas on the Führerprinzip.

In would-be controlling groups such as the military, political parties, ruling élites, and other belief-based enterprises like religions or businesses, the idea of leadership can become a Holy Grail and people can come to expect transformational change stemming from the leader; such entities may encourage their followers and believers to worship leadership, to respect it, and to strive (whether realistically or not) to become proficient in it. Ideally, one cannot buy or sell leadership in the military (or elsewhere); instead, leaders must ratify their position of command in the hearts and minds of their soldiers in order to obtain the best from them. Followers in such a situation may become uncritically obedient. Personal strategies that one can use to guard against the unrealistic expectations associated with belief in leaders include:

- Maintaining a questioning and skeptical attitude
- Bolstering confidence in one's own decision-making abilities

## Categories and types of Leadership

One can categorize the exercise of leadership as either actual or potential:

- Actual - giving guidance or direction, as in the phrase "the emperor has provided satisfactory leadership".

- Potential - the capacity or ability to lead, as in the phrase "she could have exercised effective leadership"; or in the concept "born to lead".

In both cases, as a result of the constancy of change some people detect within the late 20th and early 21st centuries, the act of learning appears fundamental to certain types of leading and leadership. When learning and leadership coalescee, one could characterize this as "learnership".

Leadership can have a formal aspect (as in most political or business leadership) or an informal one (as in most friendships). Speaking of "leadership" (the abstract term) rather than of "leading" (the action) usually implies that the entities doing the leading have some "leadership skills" or competencies. Several types of entities may provide or exhibit leadership, actual or potential, including:

- A person in a position or office of authority, such as a President or a chairperson
- A person in a position or office associated with expertise, skill, or experience, such as a team leader, a ship's captain, a chief engineer, a chief, or a parent
- A group or person in the vanguard of some trend or movement, as in fashion trend-setters
- A group of respected people, (called a "reference group" by sociologists) such as business commentators or union spokespersons
- A product that influences other product offerings in a competitive marketplace

Leadership can come from an individual, a collective group of leaders, or even from the disincarnate — if not mystical — characteristics of a celebrity figurehead (compare hero). Yet other usages have a "leadership" which does little active leading, but to which followers show great (often traditional) respect (compare the courtesy title reverend). Followers often endow the leader with status or prestige. Aside from the prestige-role sometimes granted to inspirational leaders, a more mundane usage of the word "leadership" can designate current front-runners that exercise influence over competitors, for example, a corporation or a product can hold a position of "market leadership" without any implication of permanence or of merited respect. Note that the ability to influence others does form an integral part of the "leadership" of some but not all front-runners. A front-runner in a sprint may "lead" the race, but does not have a position of "leadership" if he does not have the potential to influence others in some way. Thus one can make an important distinction between "being in the lead" and the process of leadership. Leadership implies a relationship of power — the power to guide others.

Analyzing the inspirational leader (one who can instill passion and direction into a group of individuals) requires an understanding of how the psychology of a group can affect the members of the group.

Different approaches to group dynamics (for example: Arthur F Carmazzi's ideas on "directive communication"; and Sigal Barsade's theory of "the ripple effect", see leadership as a product of awareness and command of the reactions and influences of a group on the emotions of the individual.

According to Arthur F Carmazzi, leadership does not involve changing the mindset of the group, but the cultivation of an environment that brings out the best (inspires) the individuals in that group... Each individual has various environments that bring out different facets from their own identity, and emotionally charged perceptions drive each facet within each environment. To lead, Carmazzi says, one must build a platform through education and awareness where individuals fill each others needs. Leaders accomplish this by knowing why people may react favorably to a situation in environment A, but get frustrated or disillusioned in environment B.

When leaders change their actions in accordance with their awareness of what those actions really mean, they affect the emotional and perceptive affects on a group. By taking control of the "standard" reactions to the actions of the group, a leader can in effect change the psychology of the group and change the culture of an organization.

**Leadership Associated with Positions of Authority**

In On Heroes, Hero-Worship, and the Heroic in History, Thomas Carlyle demonstrated the concept of leadership associated with a position of authority (auctoritas in Latin). In praising Oliver Cromwell's use of power to bring King Charles I to trial and eventual beheading, he wrote the following: "Let us remark, meanwhile, how indispensable everywhere a King is, in all movements of men. It is strikingly shown, in this very War, what becomes of men when they cannot find a Chief Man, and their enemies can."

From this viewpoint, leadership emerges when an entity as "leader" contrives to receive deference from other entities who become "followers". And as the passage from Carlyle demonstrates, the process of getting deference can become competitive in that the emerging "leader" draws "followers" from the factions of the prior or alternative "leaders".

In representative democracies the people retain sovereignty (popular sovereignty) but delegate day-to-day administration and leadership to elected officials. In the United States, for example, the Constitution provides an example of recycling authority. In the Constitutional Convention of 1787, the American Founders rejected the idea of a monarch. But they still proposed leadership by people in positions of authority, with the authority split into three powers: in this case the legislative, the executive, and the judiciary. Under the American theory, the authority of the leadership derives from the power of the voters as conveyed through the electoral college. Many individuals share authority, including the many legislators in the Senate and the House of Representatives.

If a group or an organization wants or expects identifiable leadership, it will require processes for appointing/acquiring and replacing leaders.

Traditional closed groups rely on bloodlines or seniority to select leaders and/or leadership candidates: monarchies, tribal chiefdoms, oligarchies and aristocratic societies rely on (and often define their institutions by) such methods.

Competence or perceived competence provides a possible basis for selecting leadership elites from a broader pool of potential talent. Political lobbying may prove necessary in electoral systems, but immediately demonstrated skill and character may secure leadership in smaller groups such as gangs.

Many organizations and groups aim to identify, foster and promote what they see as leadership potential or ability - especially among younger members of society.

The issues of succession planning or of legitimation become important at times when leadership (particularly individual leadership) might or must change due to term-expiry, accident or senescence.

Some cultures, especially those with a reverence for age and wisdom, see leadership as a standard part of the life-cycle of a person. Just as a youth becomes initiated into adulthood, so an adult may gain initiation as a leader. Such societies may require special reinforcement of the respect and kudos due to such senior members in order to maintain their position. If aged adults can no longer hunt or fight or play a full part in physical labour, for example, those adults' positions in society must rest on respect and implied wisdom and teaching roles, whether or not they show identified "leadership traits".

At certain stages in their development, the hierarchies of social ranks implied different degrees or ranks of leadership in society. Thus a knight led fewer men in general than did a duke; a baronet might in theory control less land than an earl. See peerage for a systematization of this hierarchy, and order of precedence for links to various systems.

In the course of the 19th and 20th centuries, several political operators took non-traditional paths to become dominant in their societies. They or their systems often expressed a belief in strong individual leadership, but existing titles and labels ("King", "Emperor", "President" and so on) often seemed inappropriate, insufficient or downright inaccurate in some circumstances. The formal or informal titles or descriptions they or their flunkeys employed express and foster a general veneration for leadership of the inspired and autocratic variety.

The whole structure of military hierarchies and the idea and the titles of an officer corps tend to reinforce the importance attached to leadership and to the chain of command in the military. Thus (for example) other ranks defer to Lieutenants who defer to Majors who defer to Colonels who defer to Generals who defer to Marshals. Similar elaborate structures of hierarchical leadership titles can occur in Christian churches (Deacon - Priest - Bishop - Archbishop - Cardinal) or in commercial enterprises (team leader - supervisor - line manager/middle manager - staff manager/ senior manager - vice president etc).

Informal, often spontaneously-generated titles or descriptions can provide informative insights. The use of "boss" in work-places and crime-syndicates may suggest a relatively loose hierarchy, while dubbing someone "chief" can express either instantaneous readiness to follow of an acknowledgment of collegiality.

Some titles can outstay their use. "Divine Augustus" fell prey to religious changes in the later Roman Empire. "Master" (or "Massa") has fallen out of general use in the American South, and "Baas" has new connotations in the new South Africa since the late 20th century.

Other honorifics can also change in accordance with social circumstances. Britons whose remote ancestors paid due deference to the local "lord" will now find that title more concentrated in the areas of politics and the law. Their American cousins have virtually confined the word "lord" to religious usage.

Richard Wrangham and Dale Peterson, in Demonic Males: Apes and the Origins of Human Violence present empirical evidence that only humans and chimpanzees, among all the animals living on earth, share a similar tendency for a cluster of behaviours: violence, territoriality, and competition for uniting behind the one chief male of the land.

By comparison, bonobos, the second-closest species-relatives of man, do not unite behind the chief male of the land. The bonobos show deference to an alpha or top-ranking female that, with the support of her coalition of other females, can prove as strong as the strongest male in the land. Thus, if leadership amounts to getting the greatest number of followers, then among the bonobos, a female almost always exerts the strongest and most effective leadership.

Some have argued that, since the bonobo pattern inverts the dominant pattern among chimpanzees and men with regard to whether a female can get more followers than a male, humans and chimpanzees both likely inherited gender-bias against women from the ancestors of the chimpanzees; gender-bias features as a genetic condition of men. And the bias against women having leadership as a position of authority occurs in most cultures in the world. As of 2002, Sweden had the highest percentage of women in the legislature: but only 43%. And the United States, Andorra, Israel, Sierra Leone, and Ireland tied for 57th place with less than 15% of the legislature women. Admittedly, those percentages significantly outclass the occurrence of female chimpanzees becoming alpha of the community by getting the most followers, but similar trends exist in manifesting a general gender-bias across cultures against females gaining leadership as a position of authority over followers.

An alternative explanation suggests that those individuals best suited to lead the a group will somehow rise to the occasion and that followers (for some reason) will accept them as leaders or as proto-leaders. In this scenario, the traits of the leaders (such as gender, aggressiveness, etc.) will depend on the requirements of a given situation, and ongoing leadership may become extrapolated from a series of such situations.

In cultural anthropology, much speculation on the origins of human leadership relates to the perceived increasing need for dispute resolution in increasingly densely-populated and increasingly complex societies.

Sometimes followership can occur without intentional leadership. Despite (or because of) its mythical origin, the image of swarms of lemmings which follow the first lemming off a cliff appears frequently in characterizing followers. The animal kingdom also provides the actual model of the bellwether function in a mob of sheep. And human society also offers many examples of emulation. The fashion industry, for example, depends on it. Fashion marketers design clothing for celebrities, then offer less expensive variations/imitations for those who emulate the celebrities.

Unintentional leadership can also occur from more pro-active forms followership. For example, in organizations which punish both leadership inaction and mistakes, and in which a predicament has no good solution, a common tendency involves declaring oneself a follower of someone else — metaphorically passing the buck.

Another example of followership without intentional leadership comes with the market leadership of a pioneering company, or the price leadership of a monopolist. Other companies will emulate a successful strategy, product, or price, but originators may certainly not desire this — in fact they often do all they can legally do to prevent such direct competition.

The term "leadership" sometimes applies (confusingly) to a winning position in a race. One can speak of a front-runner in a sprint or of the "leader" in an election or poll as in a position of leadership. But such "leadership" does not involve any influence processes, and the "leader" will have followers who may not willingly choose to function as followers. Once again: one can make an important distinction between "in the lead" and the process of leadership. Once again, leadership implies a relationship of power - the power to guide others.

Leading from the front, in a military sense, may imply foolhardiness and unnecessary self-exposure to danger: these do not necessarily make for successful long-term leadership strategies.

**Scope of Leadership**

One can govern oneself, or one can govern the whole earth. In between, we may find leaders who operate primarily within:

- Families
- Bands
- Tribes
- States and nations
- Empires

Intertwined with such categories, and overlapping them, we find (for example) religious leaders (potentially with their own internal hierarchies), work-place leaders (executives, officers, senior/upper managers, middle managers, staff-managers, line-managers, team-leaders, supervisors...) and leaders of voluntary associations.

Some anthropological ideas envisage a widespread (but by no means universal) pattern of progression in the organisation of society in ever-larger groups, with the needs and practices of leadership changing accordingly. Thus simple dispute resolution may become legalistic dispensation of justice before developing into proactive legislative activity. Some leadership careers parallel this sort of progression: today's school-board chairperson may become tomorrow's city councillor, then take in (say) a mayordom before graduating to nation-wide politics. Compare the cursus honorum in ancient Rome.

Those who sing the praises of leadership or of certain types of leadership may encounter problems in implementing consistent leadership structures. For example, a pyramidical structure in which authority consistently emanates from the summit can stifle initiative and leave no path for grooming future leaders in the ranks of subordinate levels. Similarly, a belief in universal direct democracy may become unwieldy, and a system consisting of nothing but representative leaders may well become stymied in committees.

Thus many leadership systems promote different rules for different levels of leadership. Hereditary autocrats meet in the United Nations on equal representative terms with elected governments in a collegial leadership. Or individual local democracies may assign some of their powers to temporary dictators in emergencies, as in ancient Rome. Hierarchies intermingle with equality of opportunity at different levels.

Though advocates of the "big man" school of visionary leadership would have us believe that charisma and personality alone can work miracles, most leaders operate within a structure of supporters and executive agents who carry out and monitor the expressed or filtered-down will of the leader. This undercutting of the importance of leadership may serve as a reminder of the existence of the follower: compare followership. A more or less formal bureaucracy (in the Weberian sense) can throw up a colourless nonentity as an entirely effective leader: this phenomenon may occur (for example) in a politburo environment. Bureaucratic organizations can also raise incompetent people to levels of leadership.

In modern dynamic environments formal bureaucratic organizations have started to become less common because of their inability to deal with fast-changing circumstances. Most modern business organizations (and some government departments) encourage what they see as "leadership skills" and reward identified potential leaders with promotions. According to B. Nanus, the forces that shape today's leading-edge organizations and their implications provide the key to visionary leadership. To underline his point we can examine the success-story of Bill Gates: in brief he built Microsoft from the start as a twenty-first-century organization, and he allegedly runs it with a highly-developed sense of visionary leadership.

In a potential down-side to this sort of development, a big-picture grand-vision leader may foster another sort of hierarchy: a fetish of leadership amongst subordinate sub-leaders, encouraged to seize resources for their own sub-empires and to apply to the supreme leader only for ultimate arbitration.

Some leaders build coalitions and alliances: political parties abound with this type of leader. Still others depend on rapport with the masses: they labour on the shop-floor or stand in the front-line of battle, leading by example.

In comparing various leadership styles in many cultures, academic studies have examined the patterns in which leadership emerges and then fades, sometimes by natural succession according to established rules and sometimes by the imposition of brute force.

The simplest way to measure the effectiveness of leadership involves evaluating the size of the following that the leader can muster. By this standard, Adolf Hitler became a very effective leader for a period — even if through delusional promises and coercive techniques. However, this approach may measure power rather than leadership. To measure leadership more specifically, one may assess the extent of influence on the followers, that is, the amount of leading. This may involve testing the results of leadership activities against a goal, vision, or objective.

James MacGregor Burns introduced a normative element: an effective Burnsian leader will unite followers in a shared vision that will improve an organization and society at large. Burns calls leadership that delivers "true" value, integrity, and trust transformational leadership. He distinguishes such leadership from "mere" transactional leadership that builds power by doing whatever will get more followers. But problems arise in quantifying the transformational quality of leadership - evaluation of that quality seems more difficult to quantify than merely counting the followers that the straw man of transactional leadership James MacGregor Burns has set as a primary standard for effectiveness. Thus transformational leadership requires an evaluation of quality, independent of the market demand that exhibits in the number of followers.

Current assessments of transformational and transactional leadership commonly make use of the Multifactor Leadership Questionnaire (MLQ), developed by Bass and Avolio in 1990 and revised in 1995. It measures five dimensions of transformational leadership:

The functional leadership model conceives leadership as a set of behaviours that helps a group perform a task, reach their goal, or perform their function. In this model, effective leaders encourage functional behaviours and discourage dysfunctional ones.

In the path-goal model of leadership, developed jointly by Martin Evans and Robert House and based on the "Expectancy Theory of Motivation", a leader has the function of clearing the path toward the goal(s) of the group, by meeting the needs of subordinates.

Some commentators use the metaphor of an orchestral conductor to describe the quality of the leadership process. An effective leader resembles an orchestra conductor in some ways. He/she has to somehow get a group of potentially diverse and talented people - many of whom have strong personalities - to work together toward a common output. Will the conductor harness and blend all the gifts his or her players possess? Will the players accept the degree of creative expression they have? Will the audience enjoy the sound they make? The conductor may have a clear determining influence on all of these questions.

**Suggested Qualities of Leadership**

Studies of leadership have suggested qualities that people often associate with leadership. They include:

- Guiding others through modeling (in the sense of providing a role model) and through willingness to serve others first (compare followership)
- Talent and technical/specific skill at some task at hand
- Initiative and entrepreneurial drive

- Charismatic inspiration - attractiveness to others and the ability to leverage this esteem to motivate others
- Preoccupation with a role - a dedication that consumes much of leaders' life - service to a cause
- A clear sense of purpose (or mission) - clear goals - focus - commitment
- Results-orientation - directing every action towards a mission - prioritizing activities to spend time where results most accrue
- Optimism - very few pessimists become leaders
- Rejection of determinism - belief in one's ability to "make a difference"
- Ability to encourage and nurture those that report to them - delegate in such a way as people will grow
- Role models - leaders may adopt a persona that encapsulates their mission and lead by example
- Self-knowledge (in non-bureaucratic structures)
- Self-awareness - the ability to "lead" (as it were) one's own self prior to leading other selves similarly
- With regards to people and to projects, the ability to choose winners - recognizing that, unlike with skills, one cannot (in general) teach attitude. Note that "picking winners" ("choosing winners") carries implications of gamblers' luck as well as of the capacity to take risks, but "true" leaders, like gamblers but unlike "false" leaders, base their decisions on realistic insight (and usually on many other factors partially derived from "real" wisdom).
- Understanding what others say, rather than listening to how they say things - this could partly sum this quality up as "walking in someone else's shoes" (to use a common cliché).

The approach of listing leadership qualities, often termed "trait theory", assumes certain traits or characteristics will tend to lead to effective leadership. Although trait theory has an intuitive appeal, difficulties may arise in proving its tenets, and opponents frequently challenge this approach. The "strongest" versions of trait theory see these "leadership characteristics" as innate, and accordingly labels some people as "born leaders" due to their psychological makeup. On this reading of the theory, leadership development involves identifying and measuring leadership qualities, screening potential leaders from non-leaders, then training those with potential.

David McClelland, a Harvard-based researcher in the psychology of power and achievement, saw leadership skills, not so much as a set of traits, but as a pattern of motives. He claimed that successful leaders will tend to have a high need for power, a low need for affiliation, and a high level of what he called activity inhibition (one might call it self-control).

Situational leadership theory offers an alternative approach. It proceeds from the assumption that different situations call for different characteristics. According to this group of theories, no single optimal psychographic profile of a leader exists. The situational leadership model of Hersey and Blanchard, for example, suggest four leadership-styles and four levels of follower-development. For effectiveness, the model posits that the leadership-style must match the appropriate level of followership-development. In this model, leadership behaviour becomes a function not only of the characteristics of the leader, but of the characteristics of followers as well. Other situational leadership models introduce a variety of situational variables. These determinants include:

- The nature of the task (structured or routine)
- Organizational policies, climate, and culture
- The preferences of the leader's superiors
- The expectations of peers
- The reciprocal responses of followers

The contingency model of Vroom and Yetton uses other situational variables, including:

- The nature of the problem
- The requirements for accuracy
- The acceptance of an initiative
- Time-constraints
- Cost constraints

However one determines leadership behaviour, one can categorize it into various leadership styles. Many ways of doing this exist. For example, the Managerial Grid Model, a behavioural leadership-model developed by Robert Blake and Jane Mouton in 1964, suggests five different leadership styles, based on leaders' strength of concern for people and their concern for goal achievement.

Kurt Lewin, Ronald Lipitt, and R. K. White identified three leadership styles: authoritarian, democratic, and laissez-faire, based on the amount of influence and power exercised by the leader.

The Fiedler contingency model bases the leader's effectiveness on what Fred Fiedler called situational contingency. This results from the interaction of leadership style and situational favourableness (later called "situational control").

In 1994 House and Podsakoff attempted to summarize the behaviours and approaches of "outstanding leaders" that they obtained from some more modern theories and research findings. These leadership behaviours and approaches do not constitute specific styles, but cumulatively they probably characterize the most effective style of today's leaders/managers. The listed leadership "styles" cover:

1. Vision. Outstanding leaders articulate an ideological vision congruent with the deeply-held values of followers, a vision that describes a better future to which the followers have an alleged moral right.
2. Passion and self-sacrifice. Leaders display a passion for, and have a strong conviction of, what they regard as the moral correctness of their vision. They engage

in outstanding or extraordinary behaviour and make extraordinary self-sacrifices in the interest of their vision and mission.

3. Confidence, determination, and persistence. Outstanding leaders display a high degree of faith in themselves and in the attainment of the vision they articulate. Theoretically, such leaders need to have a very high degree of self-confidence and moral conviction because their mission usually challenges the status quo and, therefore, may offend those who have a stake in preserving the established order.
4. Image-building. House and Podsakoff regard outstanding leaders as self-conscious about their own image. They recognize the desirability of followers perceiving them as competent, credible, and trustworthy.
5. Role-modeling. Leader-image-building sets the stage for effective role-modeling because followers identify with the values of role models whom they perceived in positive terms.
6. External representation. Outstanding leaders act as spokespersons for their respective organizations and symbolically represent those organizations to external constituencies.
7. Expectations of and confidence in followers. Outstanding leaders communicate expectations of high performance from their followers and strong confidence in their followers' ability to meet such expectations.
8. Selective motive-arousal. Outstanding leaders selectively arouse those motives of followers that the outstanding leaders see as of special relevance to the successful accomplishment of the vision and mission.
9. Frame alignment. To persuade followers to accept and implement change, outstanding leaders engage in "frame alignment". This refers to the linkage of individual and leader interpretive orientations such

that some set of followers' interests, values, and beliefs, as well as the leader's activities, goals, and ideology, becomes congruent and complementary.

10. Inspirational communication. Outstanding leaders often, but not always, communicate their message in an inspirational manner using vivid stories, slogans, symbols, and ceremonies.

Even though these ten leadership behaviours and approaches do not really equate to specific styles, evidence has started to accumulate that a leader's style can make a difference. Style becomes the key to the formulation and implementation of strategy and plays an important role in work-group members' activity and in team citizenship. Little doubt exists that the way (style) in which leaders influence work-group members can make a difference in their own and their people's performance.

**Leadership and Vision**

Many definitions of leadership involve an element of vision — except in cases of involuntary leadership and often in cases of traditional leadership. A vision provides direction to the influence process. A leader (or group of leaders) can have one or more visions of the future to aid them to move a group successfully towards this goal. A vision, for effectiveness, should allegedly:

- Appear as a simple, yet vibrant, image in the mind of the leader
- Describe a future state, credible and preferable to the present state
- Act as a bridge between the current state and a future optimum state
- Appear desirable enough to energize followers
- Succeed in speaking to followers at an emotional or spiritual level (logical appeals by themselves seldom muster a following)

For leadership to occur, according to this theory, some people ("leaders") must communicate the vision to others ("followers") in such a way that the followers adopt the vision as their own. Leaders must not just see the vision themselves, they must have the ability to get others to see it also. Numerous techniques aid in this process, including: narratives, metaphors, symbolic actions, leading by example, incentives, and penalties.

Stacey has suggested that the emphasis on vision puts an unrealistic burden on the leader. Such emphasis appears to perpetuate the myth that an organization must depend on a single, uncommonly talented individual to decide what to do. Stacey claims that this fosters a culture of dependency and conformity in which followers take no pro-active incentives and do not think independently.

## LEADERSHIP IN MANAGEMENT

Some commentators link leadership closely with the idea of management. Some regard the two as synonymous, and others consider management a subset of leadership. If one accepts this premise, one can view leadership as:

- Centralized or decentralized
- Broad or focused
- Decision-oriented or morale-centred
- Intrinsic or derived from some authority

Any of the bipolar labels traditionally ascribed to management style could also apply to leadership style. Hersey and Blanchard use this approach: they claim that management merely consists of leadership applied to business situations; or in other words: management forms a sub-set of the broader process of leadership. They put it this way: "Leadership occurs any time one attempts to influence the behaviour of an individual or group, regardless of the reason. Management is a kind of leadership in which the achievement of organizational goals is paramount."

However, a clear distinction between management and leadership may nevertheless prove useful. This would allow for a reciprocal relationship between leadership and management, implying that an effective manager should possess leadership skills, and an effective leader should demonstrate management skills. One clear distinction could provide the following definition:

- Management involves power by position.
- Leadership involves power by influence.

Abraham Zaleznik, for example, delineated differences between leadership and management. He saw leaders as inspiring visionaries, concerned about substance; while managers he views as planners who have concerns with process. Warren Bennis (1989) further explicated a dichotomy between managers and leaders. He drew twelve distinctions between the two groups:

- Managers administer, leaders innovate
- Managers ask how and when, leaders ask what and why
- Managers focus on systems, leaders focus on people
- Managers do things right, leaders do the right things
- Managers maintain, leaders develop
- Managers rely on control, leaders inspire trust
- Managers have a short-term perspective, leaders have a longer-term perspective
- Managers accept the status-quo, leaders challenge the status-quo
- Managers have an eye on the bottom line, leaders have an eye on the horizon
- Managers imitate, leaders originate
- Managers emulate the classic good soldier, leaders are their own person
- Managers copy, leaders show originality

Paul Birch (1999) also sees a distinction between leadership and management. He observed that, as a broad generalization, managers concerned themselves with tasks while leaders concerned themselves with people. Birch does not suggest that leaders do not focus on "the task." Indeed, the things that characterise a great leader include the fact that they achieve. The difference lies in the leader realising that the achievement of the task comes about through the goodwill and support of others, while the manager may not.

This goodwill and support originates in the leader seeing people as people, not as another resource for deployment in support of "the task". The manager often has the role of organizing resources to get something done. People form one of these resources, and many of the worst managers treat people as just another interchangeable item. A leader has the role of causing others to follow a path he/she has laid out or a vision he/she has articulated in order to achieve a task. Often, people see the task as subordinate to the vision. For instance, an organization might have the overall task of generating profit, but a good leader may see profit as a by-product that flows from whatever aspect of their vision differentiates their company from the competition.

Leadership does not only manifest itself as purely a business phenomenon. Many people can think of an inspiring leader they have encountered who has nothing whatever to do with business: a politician, an officer in the armed forces, a Scout or Guide leader, a teacher, etc. Similarly, management does not occur only as a purely business phenomenon. Again, we can think of examples of people that we have met who fill the management niche in non-business organisations. Non-business organizations should find it easier to articulate a non-money-driven inspiring vision that will support true leadership. However, often this does not occur.

Differences in the mix of leadership and management can define various management styles. Some management styles tend to de-emphasize leadership. Included in this group one could include participatory management, democratic management, and collaborative management styles. Other management styles, such as authoritarian management, micro-management, and top-down management, depend more on a leader to provide direction. Note, however, that just because an organisation has no single leader giving it direction, does not mean it necessarily has weak leadership. In many cases group leadership (multiple leaders) can prove effective. Having a single leader (as in dictatorship) allows for quick and decisive decision-making when needed as well as when not needed. Group decision-making sometimes earns the derisive label "committee-itis" because of the longer times required to make decisions, but group leadership can bring more expertise, experience, and perspectives through a democratic process.

Patricia Pitcher has challenged the bifurcation into leaders and managers. She used a factor analysis technique on data collected over 8 years, and concluded that three types of leaders exist, each with very different psychological profiles. She characterises one group as imaginative, inspiring, visionary, entrepreneurial, intuitive, daring, and emotional, and calls them "artists". In a second grouping she places "craftsmen" as well-balanced, steady, reasonable, sensible, predictable, and trustworthy. Finally she identifies "technocrats" as cerebral, detail-oriented, fastidious, uncompromising, and hard-headed. She speculates that no one profile offers a preferred leadership style. She claims that if we want to build, we should find an "artist leader"; if we want to solidify our position, we should find a "craftsman leader"; and if we have an ugly job that needs to get done (like downsizing), we should find a "technocratic leader." Pitcher also observed that a balanced leader exhibiting all three sets of traits occurs extremely rarely: she found none in her study.

**Leadership by a Group**

In contrast to individual leadership, some organizations have adopted group leadership. In this situation, more than one person provides direction to the group as a whole. Some organizations have taken this approach in hopes of increasing creativity, reducing costs, or downsizing. Others may see the traditional leadership of a boss as costing too much in team performance. In some situations, the maintenance of the boss becomes too expensive - either by draining the resources of the group as a whole, or by impeding the creativity within the team, even unintentionally.

A common example of group leadership involves cross-functional teams. A team of people with diverse skills and from all parts of an organization assembles to lead a project. A team structure can involve sharing power equally on all issues, but more commonly uses rotating leadership. The team member(s) best able to handle any given phase of the project become(s) the temporary leader(s).

For example, the Orpheus orchestra has performed for over thirty years without a conductor — that is, without a sole leader. As a team of over 25 members, it has drawn discriminating audiences, and has produced over 60 recordings for Deutsche Grammophon in successful competition with other world-class orchestras.

Rather than an autocratic or charismatic conductor deciding the overall conception of a work and then dictating how each individual is to perform the individual tasks, the Orpheus team generally selects a different "core group" for each piece of music. The core group provides leadership in working out the details of the piece, and presents their ideas to the whole team. Members of the whole team then participate in refining the final conception, rehearsal, and product, including checking from various places in the auditorium how the sound balances and verifying the quality of the final recording.

At times the entire Orpheus team may follow a single leader, but whom the team follows rotates from task to task, depending on the capabilities of its members.

The orchestra has developed seminars and training sessions for adapting the Orpheus Process to business.

**Co-leadership**

As a compromise between individual leadership and an open group, leadership structures of two or three people or entities occur commonly. Ancient Rome preferred two consuls to a single king, and the Roman Empire grew to accommodate two Emperors - those of the East and of the West - simultaneously. The Middle Ages saw leadership divided between the secular and spiritual realms - between Emperor and Pope. Some groups - often left-wing or Green in orientation - employ a co-leader structure today.

Triumvirates have long served to balance leadership ambitions - notably in Rome in the first century BC, but also as recently as in the Soviet Union troikas of the 20th century. Compare the separation of powers (legislative, judicial and executive) formalised (for example) in the constitution of the United States of America.

## Divided Leadership

Whereas sometimes one can readily and definitively identify the locus of leadership, in other circumstances the situation remains obscured. Pre-modern Japan offers a classical example: the emperors provided symbolic and religious leadership, but the shoguns embodied virtually all political and administrative leadership.

Similar dichotomies appear in many places and in many periods. Any constitutional monarch has a potentially confusing relationship with the day-to-day leader (typically a prime minister) who remains (at least theoretically) subordinate - socially as well as politically. Regents may stand against monarchs (and their supporters) during the minority or absence of those monarchs. Heads of state may operate at cross-purposes with heads of government (see governmental co-habitation). Political leaders may or may not align closely with religious leaders. And in federal-type systems, regional leadership and its potentially different systems may cross swords with national leaders. Not to mention the potentially conflicting leadership manifestations of boards of directors and of Chief Executives.

Greiner's study of the language of U.S. Presidents examined the relationship between leader and followers and observed that changes have taken place in the presidential use of words that define the leader and the community as one. Modern US presidents have an observed tendency to make more use of inclusive words like we, us and our in their inaugural speeches. The use of inclusive words may suggest an effort by these democratically selected leaders to make the community work together to solve problems collectively.

Aristocratic thinkers have postulated that leadership depends on one's blue blood or genes: monarchy takes an extreme view of the same idea, and may prop up its assertions against the claims of mere aristocrats by invoking divine sanction: see the divine right of kings. Contrariwise, more democratically-inclined theorists have pointed to examples of meritocratic leaders, such as the Napoleonic marshals profiting from careers open to talent.

In the autocratic/paternalistic strain of thought, traditionalists recall the role of leadership of the Roman pater familias. Feminist thinking, on the other hand, may damn such models as patriarchal and posit against them emotionally-attuned, responsive, and consensual empathetic guidance and matriarchies.

Comparable to the Roman tradition, the views of Confucianism on "right living" relate very much to the ideal of the (male) scholar-leader and his benevolent rule, buttressed by a tradition of filial piety.

Within the context of Islam, views on the nature, scope and inheritance of leadership have played a major role in shaping sects and their history. See caliphate.

In the 19th century, the elaboration of anarchist thought called the whole concept of leadership into question. (Note that the Oxford English Dictionary traces the word "leadership" in English only as far back as the 19th century.) One response to this denial of élitism came with Leninism, which demanded an élite group of disciplined cadres to act as the vanguard of a socialist revolution, bringing into existence the dictatorship of the proletariat.

Other historical views of leadership have addressed the seeming contrasts between secular and religious leadership. The doctrines of Caesaro-papism have recurred and had their detractors over several centuries. Christian thinking on leadership has often emphasized stewardship of divinely-provided resources - human and material - and their deployment in accordance with a Divine plan. Compare servant leadership.

## SPECIFIC THEORIES OF LEADERSHIP

In State of Exception, Agamben reads Carl Schmitt's theory of sovereignty in the light of Walter Benjamin. Agamben traces Schmitt's definition of sovereignty as the power to decide the state of exception to the Roman concept of auctoritas - the power to declare justitium. Agamben writes: "It is significative that modern specialists were so enclined to admit that auctoritas was inherent to the living person of the pater or the princeps. What was evidently an ideology or a fictio aiming to be the groundwork of auctoritas ' preeminence or, at least, specific rank compared to potestas thus became a figure of right's immanence to life. Although it is evident that there can't be an eternal human type that would incarnate itself each time in Augustus, Napoleon, Hitler, but only more or less similar mechanisms {"dispositif", a term often used by Foucault} - the state of exception, justitium, the auctoritas principis, the Führertum - put in use in more or less different circumstances, in the 1930s - overall, but not only - in Germany, the power that Weber had defined as "charismatic" is related to the concept of auctoritas and elaborated in a Führertum doctrine as the original and personal power of a leader. In 1933, in a short article intending to define the fundamental concepts of national-socialism, Schmitt defines the Führung principal by the "root identity between the leader and his entourage" {"identité de souche entre le chef et son entourage"} (we shall note the use of Weberian concepts)."

James MacGregor Burns wrote that a study of the definition of the word leadership revealed 130 definitions. However, several generally-accepted variations on the definition appear in the management and leadership literature.

Ronald Heifetz described the difference between a descriptive view and a prescriptive view of leadership. A descriptive view describes leadership and how it occurs, and a prescriptive view suggests how it should occur. The notion of "adaptive work" forms a central concept of Heifetz's prescriptive view. Heifetz pointed out (p. 37) that people fail to adapt to new and unsettling situations through six avoidance mechanisms:

1. Blaming others
2. Finding scapegoats (to the extent that this differs from blaming)
3. Externalizing the enemy
4. Denying that a problem exists
5. Jumping to conclusions
6. Finding a distracting issue

In a prescriptive view, the leader would squarely face the problem and avoid the six surface-level solutions of the non-leader. A true leader would help a community face reality and deal with the issues: finding solutions where none previously existed. Using the 1950s television character, the Lone Ranger, as an example, we see the Ranger in a weekly episode, moving from frontier town to frontier town, discovering problems wherever he goes, fixing the problems and riding off into the sunset. In this metaphor, the Ranger fixes the symptom, but not the problem. A Lone Ranger non-leader would catch fish to feed the poor while a true leader would teach the poor how to catch fish and would motivate them to do so. The true leader finds a way to help the community engage the problem and collectively find a solution. For more detail, see Heifetz, R. (1994). Leadership without easy answers. Cambridge, MA: Harvard University Press.

George Terry has defined leadership as: "the activity of influencing people to strive willingly for group objectives". If we define leadership simply as "influencing others to some purpose" and we define followership as "becoming influenced by others to accept (willingly or un willingly) some purpose", then leadership and followership emerge as two sides of the same coin. In this scenario, leadership - whether successful or not - has not occurred until at least one follower joins in.

Likewise, no followership exists without someone or something (not necessarily a leader) to follow. However, in this latter case, a "leader" need not exercise deliberate or even conscious leadership - that is, followers can follow someone who is not trying to lead. Some see "unconscious leadership" as a dubious concept, however. Many, using a different definition of leadership, would claim that it does not classify as leadership at all - simply because no deliberate intention to lead exists. Unconscious "leading by example" (as the phrase has it) may nevertheless exemplify such "leadership".

## CONSCIOUS LEADERSHIP

Dr. James Farr argued not for any one "correct leadership style" but for the style that each situation requires. Great leaders require the use of nearly every leadership style: one must apply the correct style to meet the situation. Farr terms this "Conscious Leadership".

"Conscious Leadership" consists of the art and science of leading change from a self-aware perspective, with clarity of purpose and an acute insight into others' perspectives and state of mind. This fully-aware state uniquely allows leaders to properly inspire motivation in others and to choose the most appropriate course of action both to solve pressing problems and to effectively achieve long-term organizational goals.

Futurist John Renesch has written extensively on conscious leadership, which he advocates for everyone — not only those in positions of authority or holding designated titles. As he wrote in early 2001:

Conscious leaders don't tolerate conditions or processes where people feel the need to compromise their values — to "sell their souls" for the task at hand. Conscious leadership includes conscious discernment, a principle that demands performance, integrity, competence and a noncalloused form of spiritual toughness. The conscious leader does not sit with his or her head in the clouds, dreaming of utopian schemes and professing New Age idealism. The conscious leader walks in the spiritual and physical domains concurrently, remaining simultaneously grounded and comfortable in both.

Renesch also writes about "The Conscious Organization" which he defines as "one which continually examines itself, committed to becoming as conscious as it can. In other words, it has very low tolerance for unconsciousness. It possesses the collective will to be vigilant, the collective commitment to continuous evolution, and the collective courage to act."

### Alternatives to Leadership

Within groups, alternatives to the cult of leadership include using decision-making structures such as co-operative ventures, collegiality, consensus, anarchism and applied democracy. One can down play the ubiquitous idea of leadership by using structures such as information clearing houses or stressing functions such as administration. Note the different implications and connotations of the two phrases "coalition of the willing" and "US-led coalition". The Orpheus Chamber Orchestra, which practises a form of distributed leadership, provides a extbook example of alternative leadership.

## CONTROL AND CO-ORDINATION

A concise and clear general definition is from: "Coordination is the act of managing interdependencies between activities."

Coordination or Co-Ordination is "the ability to reduce all-together, in oder to generate an only one all."

Coordination, co-ordination is the regulation of diverse elements into an integrated and harmonious operation. Coordination means integrating or linking together different parts of an organization to accomplish a collective set of tasks.

New, more "organic" forms or organizations (self-organizing organizations, self-managed teams, network organizations, etc.) allow organizations to be more responsive and adaptable in today's rapidly changing world. These forms also cultivate empowerment among employees, much more than the hierarchical, rigidly structured organizations of the past.

Many people assert that as the nature of organizations has changed, so must the nature of management control. Some people go so far as to claim that management shouldn't exercise any form of control whatsoever. They claim that management should exist to support employee's efforts to be fully productive members of organizations and communities — therefore, any form of control is completely counterproductive to management and employees.

Some people even react strongly against the phrase "management control". The word itself can have a negative connotation, e.g., it can sound dominating, coercive and heavy-handed. It seems that writers of management literature now prefer use of the term "coordinating" rather than "controlling".

Regardless of the negative connotation of the word "control", it must exist or there is no organization at all. In its most basic form, an organization is two or more people working together to reach a goal. Whether an organization is highly bureaucratic or changing and self-organizing, the organization must exist for some reason, some purpose, some mission (implicit or explicit) — or it isn't an organization at all. The organization must have some goal. Identifying this goal requires some form of planning, informal or formal. Reaching the goal means identifying some strategies, formal or informal. These strategies are agreed upon by members of the organization through some form of communication, formal or informal. Then members set about to act in accordance with what they agreed to do. They may change their minds, fine. But they need to recognize and acknowledge that they're changing their minds.

This form of ongoing communication to reach a goal, tracking activities toward the goal and then subsequent decisions about what to do is the essence of management coordination. It needs to exist in some manner — formal or informal.

The following are rather typical methods of coordination in organizations. They are used as means to communicate direction and guide behaviours in that direction. The function of the following methods is not to "control", but rather to guide. If, from ongoing communications among management and employees, the direction changes, then fine. The following methods are changed accordingly.

Note that many of the following methods are so common that we often don't think of them as having anything to do with coordination at all. No matter what one calls the following methods — coordination or control — they're important to the success of any organization.

**Administrative Controls**

Organizations often use standardized documents to ensure complete and consistent information is gathered. Documents include titles and dates to detect different versions of the document. Computers have revolutionized administrative controls through use of integrated management information systems, project management software, human resource information systems, office automation software, etc. Organizations typically require a wide range of reports, e.g., financial reports, status reports, project reports, etc. to monitor what's being done, by when and how.

## DELEGATION

Delegation is an approach to get things done, in conjunction with other employees. Delegation is often viewed as a major means of influence and therefore is categorized as an activity in leading (rather than controlling/coordinating). Delegation generally includes assigning responsibility to an employee to complete a task, granting the employee sufficient authority to gain the resources to do the task and letting the employee decide how that task will be carried out. Typically, the person assigning the task shares accountability with the employee for ensuring the task is completed.

Delegating is a critical skill for supervisors. Delegating involves working with an employee to establish goals, granting them sufficient authority and responsibility to achieve the goals, often giving them substantial freedom in deciding how the goals will be achieved, remaining available as a resource to help them achieve the goals, assessing their performance (the quality of their effort and attainment of the goals), addressing performance issues and/or rewarding their performance. Ultimately, the supervisor retains responsibility for the attainment of the goals, but chooses to achieve the goals by delegating to someone else.

Delegation can sometimes be a major challenge for new supervisors to learn because they are concerned about giving up control or struggle to have confidence in the abilities of others. Supervisors that can effectively delegate can free up a great deal of their own time, help their direct reports to cultivate expertise in learning, and can develop their own leadership skills — skills that are critical for problem solving, goal attainment and learning.

The hallmark of good supervision is effective delegation. Delegation is when supervisors give responsibility and authority to subordinates to complete a task. Effective delegation develops people who are ultimately more fulfilled and productive. Managers become more fulfilled and productive themselves as they learn to count on their staffs and are freed up to attend to more strategic issues.

Delegation is often very difficult for new supervisors, particularly if they have had to scramble to start the nonprofit or start a major new service themselves. Many managers want to remain comfortable, making the same decisions they have always made. They believe they can do a better job themselves. They don't want to risk losing any of their power and stature (ironically, they do lose these if they don't learn to delegate effectively). Often, they don't want to risk giving authority to subordinates in case they fail and impair the organization.

However, there are basic approaches to delegation that, with practice, become the backbone of effective supervision and development. Thomas R. Horton, in Delegation and Team Building: No Solo Acts Please suggests the following general steps to accomplish delegation:

1. Delegate the whole task to one person.

   This gives the person the responsibility and increases their motivation.

2. Select the right person.

   Assess the skills and capabilities of subordinates and assign the task to the most appropriate one.

3. Clearly specify your preferred results.

   Give information on what, why, when, who, where and how. Write this information down.

4. Delegate responsibility and authority

   Assign the task, not the method to accomplish it. Let the subordinate complete the task in the manner they choose, as long as the results are what the supervisor specifies. Let the employee have strong input as to the completion date of the project. Note that you may not even know how to complete the task yourself — this is often the case with higher levels of management.

5. Ask the employee to summarize back to you.

   Ask to hear their impressions of the project and the results that you prefer.

6. Get ongoing non-intrusive feedback about progress on the project.

   This is a good reason to continue to get weekly, written status reports from all direct reports. Reports should cover what they did last week, plan to do next week and any potential issues. Regular staff meetings provide this ongoing feedback, as well.

7. Maintain open lines of communication.

   Don't hover over the subordinate, but sense what they're doing and support their checking in with you along the way.

8. If you're not satisfied with the progress, don't immediately take the project back.

   Continue to work with the employee and ensure they perceive the project as their responsibility.

9. Evaluate and reward performance.

Evaluate results, not methods. Address insufficient performance and reward successes (including the manager's).

## POOR DELEGATION

Signs that you are not borrowing enough brains or that your delegation is failing include:

- Team Motivation / Morale is down
- You are always working late
- Your team is confused / conflicting / tense
- You get questions about delegated tasks too often

### How to Delegate

1. Identify a suitable person for the task.
2. Prepare the person. Explain the task clearly. Make sure that you are understood. Leave room in the task description for ingenuity / initiative.
3. Make sure the person has the necessary authority to do the job properly.
4. Keep in touch with the person for support and monitoring progress. Do not get to close. Accept alternative approaches.
5. Praise / Acknowledge a job well done.

### Responsibility

Even though you have delegated a task to someone else, you are still responsible for making sure the task is done on time and correctly. If the task fails, you can not point the finger. You delegated. It is your fault. You may have picked the wrong person for the job.

### Authority

The amount of authority you delegate is up to you, although it should be enough to complete the task. It is no good giving Bob the task of opening the safe every morning at 10am if you do not give him the authority required to do it. Bob needs the key to open the safe with.

### Tasks you should not delegate

Obviously some aspects of leadership are sensitive and should not be delegated. For example:

- Hiring
- Firing
- Pay issues
- Policy

### Your Task after Delegating

After delegating:

- Plan - goals, meeting, tasks
- Direct - your team, keep them on track
- Encourage - boost morale

## THE ART OF DELEGATION

Delegation is a skill of which we have all heard - but which few understand. It can be used either as an excuse for dumping failure onto the shoulders of subordinates, or as a dynamic tool for motivating and training your team to realize their full potential.

Everyone knows about delegation. Most managers hear about it in the cradle as mother talks earnestly to the baby-sitter: "just enjoy the television... this is what you do if... if there is any trouble call me at"; people have been writing about it for nearly half a millennium; yet few actually understand it.

Delegation underpins a style of management which allows your staff to use and develop their skills and knowledge to the full potential. Without delegation, you lose their full value.

As the ancient quotation above suggests, delegation is primarily about entrusting your authority to others. This means that they can act and initiate independently; and that they assume responsibility with you for certain tasks. If something goes wrong, you remain responsible since you are the manager; the trick is to delegate in such a way that things get done but do not go (badly) wrong.

## OBJECTIVE

The objective of delegation is to get the job done by someone else. Not just the simple tasks of reading instructions and turning a lever, but also the decision making and changes which depend upon new information. With delegation, your staff have the authority to react to situations without referring back to you.

If you tell the janitor to empty the bins on Tuesdays and Fridays, the bins will be emptied on Tuesdays and Fridays. If the bins overflow on Wednesday, they will be emptied on Friday. If instead you said to empty the bins as often as necessary, the janitor would decide how often and adapt to special circumstances. You might suggest a regular schedule (teach the janitor a little personal time management), but by leaving the decision up to the janitor you will apply his/her local knowledge to the problem. Consider this frankly: do you want to be an expert on bin emptying, can you construct an instruction to cover all possible contingencies? If not, delegate to someone who gets paid for it.

To enable someone else to do the job for you, you must ensure that:

- They know what you want
- They have the authority to achieve it
- They know how to do it.

These all depend upon communicating clearly the nature of the task, the extent of their discretion, and the sources of relevant information and knowledge.

## INFORMATION

Such a system can only operate successfully if the decision-makers (your staff) have full and rapid access to the relevant information. This means that you must establish a system to enable the flow of information. This must at least include regular exchanges between your staff so that each is aware of what the others are doing. It should also include briefings by you on the information which you have received in your role as manager; since if you need to know this information to do your job, your staff will need to know also if they are to do your (delegated) job for you.

One of the main claims being made for computerized information distribution is that it facilitates the rapid dissemination of information. Some protagonists even suggest that such systems will instigate changes in managerial power sharing rather than merely support them: that the "enknowledged" workforce will rise up, assume control and innovate spontaneously. You may not believe this vision, but you should understand the premise. If a manager restricts access to information, then only he/she is able to make decisions which rely upon that information; once that access is opened to many others, they too can make decisions - and challenge those of the manager according to additional criteria. The manager who fears this challenge will never delegate effectively; the manager who recognizes that the staff may have additional experience and knowledge (and so may enhance the decision-making process) will welcome their input; delegation ensures that the staff will practise decision-making and will feel that their views are welcome.

**EFFECTIVE CONTROL**

One of the main phobias about delegation is that by giving others authority, a manager loses control. This need not be the case. If you train your staff to apply the same criteria as you would yourself (by example and full explanations) then they will be exercising your control on you behalf. And since they will witness many more situations over which control may be exercised (you can't be in several places at once) then that control is exercised more diversely and more rapidly than you could exercise it by yourself. In engineering terms: if maintaining control is truly your concern, then you should distribute the control mechanisms to enable parallel and autonomous processing.

**STAGGERED DEVELOPMENT**

To understand delegation, you really have to think about people. Delegation cannot be viewed as an abstract technique, it depends upon individuals and individual needs. Let us take a lowly member of staff who has little or no knowledge about the job which needs to be done.

Do you say: "Jimmy, I want a draft tender for contract of the new Hydro Powerstation on my desk by Friday"? No. Do you say: "Jimmy, Jennifer used to do the tenders for me. Spend about an hour with her going over how she did them and try compiling one for the new Hydro Powerstation. She will help you for this one, but do come to me if she is busy with a client. I want a draft by Friday so that I can look over it with you"? Possibly.

The key is to delegate gradually. If you present someone with a task which is daunting, one with which he/she does not feel able to cope, then the task will not be done and your staff will be severely demotivated. Instead you should build-up gradually; first a small task leading to a little development, then another small task which builds upon the first; when that is achieved, add another stage; and so on. This is the difference between asking people to scale a sheer wall, and providing them with a staircase. Each task delegated should have enough complexity to stretch that member of staff - but only a little.

Jimmy needs to feel confident. He needs to believe that he will actually be able to achieve the task which has been given to him. This means that either he must have the sufficient knowledge, or he must know where to get it or where to get help. So, you must enable access to the necessary knowledge. If you hold that knowledge, make sure that Jimmy feels able to come to you; if someone else holds the knowledge, make sure that they are prepared for Jimmy to come to them. Only if Jimmy is sure that support is available will he feel confident enough to undertake a new job.

You need to feel confident in Jimmy: this means keeping an eye on him. It would be fatal to cast Jimmy adrift and expect him to make it to the shore: keep an eye on him, and a lifebelt handy. It is also a mistake to keep wandering up to Jimmy at odd moments and asking for progress reports: he will soon feel persecuted. Instead you must agree beforehand how often and when you actually need information and decide the reporting schedule at the onset. Jimmy will then expect these encounters and even feel encouraged by your continuing support; you will be able to check upon progress and even spur it on a little.

When you do talk to Jimmy about the project, you should avoid making decisions of which Jimmy is capable himself. The whole idea is for Jimmy to learn to take over and so he must be encouraged to do so. Of course, with you there to check his decisions, Jimmy will feel freer to do so. If Jimmy is wrong - tell him, and explain very carefully why. If Jimmy is nearly right - congratulate him, and suggest possible modifications; but, of course, leave Jimmy to decide. Finally, unless your solution has significant merits over Jimmy's, take his: it costs you little, yet rewards him much.

## CONSTRAINED AVAILABILITY

There is a danger with "open access" that you become too involved with the task you had hoped to delegate. One successful strategy to avoid this is to formalize the manner in which these conversation take place. One formalism is to allow only fixed, regular encounters (except for emergencies) so that Jimmy has to think about issues and questions before raising them; you might even insist that he draw-up an agenda. A second formalism is to refuse to make a decision unless Jimmy has provided you with a clear statement of alternatives, pros and cons, and his recommendation. This is my favourite. It allows Jimmy to rehearse the full authority of decision making while secure in the knowledge that you will be there to check the outcome. Further, the insistence upon evaluation of alternatives promotes good decision making practices. If Jimmy is right, then Jimmy's confidence increases - if you disagree with Jimmy, he learns something new (provided you explain your criteria) and so his knowledge increases. Which ever way, he benefits; and the analysis is provided for you.

## OUTCOMES AND FAILURE

Let us consider your undoubtedly high standards. When you delegate a job, it does not have to be done as well as you could do it (given time), but only as well as necessary: never judge the outcome by what you expect you would do (it is difficult to be objective about that), but rather by fitness for purpose. When you delegate a task, agree then upon the criteria and standards by which the outcome will be judged.

You must enable failure. With appropriate monitoring, you should be able to catch mistakes before they are catastrophic; if not, then the failure is yours. You are the manager, you decided that Jimmy could cope, you gave him enough rope to hang himself, you are at fault. Now that that is cleared up, let us return to Jimmy. Suppose Jimmy gets something wrong; what do you want to happen?

Firstly, you want it fixed. Since Jimmy made the mistake, it is likely that he will need some input to develop a solution: so Jimmy must feel safe in approaching you with the problem. Thus you must deal primarily with the solution rather than the cause (look forward, not backwards). The most desirable outcome is that Jimmy provides the solution.

Once that is dealt with, you can analyse the cause. Do not fudge the issue; if Jimmy did something wrong say so, but only is very specific terms. Avoid general attacks on his parents: "were you born this stupid?", and look to the actual event or circumstance which led to the error: "you did not take account of X in your decision". Your objectives are to ensure that Jimmy:

- Understands the problem
- Feels confident enough to resume
- Implements some procedure to prevent recurrence.

The safest ethos to cultivate is one where Jimmy actually looks for and anticipates mistakes. If you wish to promote such behaviour, you should always praise Jimmy for his prompt and wise action in spotting and dealing with the errors rather that castigate him for causing them. Here the emphasis is placed upon checking/testing/monitoring of ideas. Thus you never criticise Jimmy for finding an error, only for not having safe-guards in place.

There is always the question of what to delegate and what to do yourself, and you must take a long term view on this: you want to delegate as much as possible to develop you staff to be as good as you are now.

The starting point is to consider the activities you used to do before you were promoted. You used to do them when you were more junior, so someone junior can do them now. Tasks in which you have experience are the easiest for you to explain to others and so to train them to take over. You thus use your experience to ensure that the task is done well, rather than to actually perform the task yourself. In this way you gain time for your other duties and someone else becomes as good as your once were (increasing the strength of the group).

Tasks in which your staff has more experience must be delegated to them. This does not mean that you relinquish responsibility because they are expert, but it does mean that the default decision should be theirs. To be a good manager though, you should ensure that they spend some time in explaining these decisions to you so that you learn their criteria.

Decisions are a normal managerial function: these too should be delegated - especially if they are important to the staff. In practice, you will need to establish the boundaries of these decisions so that you can live with the outcome, but this will only take you a little time while the delegation of the remainder of the task will save you much more.

In terms of motivation for your staff, you should distribute the more mundane tasks as evenly as possible; and sprinkle the more exciting onces as widely. In general, but especially with the boring tasks, you should be careful to delegate not only the performance of the task but also its ownership. Task delegation, rather than task assignment, enables innovation. The point you need to get across is that the task may be changed, developed, upgraded, if necessary or desirable. So someone who collates the monthly figures should not feel obliged to blindly type them in every first-Monday; but should feel empowered to introduce a more effective reporting format, to use Computer Software to enhance the data processing, to suggest and implement changes to the task itself.

## NEGOTIATION

Since delegation is about handing over authority, you cannot dictate what is delegated nor how that delegation is to be managed. To control the delegation, you need to establish at the beginning the task itself, the reporting schedule, the sources of information, your availability, and the criteria of success. These you must negotiate with your staff: only by obtaining both their input and their agreement can you hope to arrive at a workable procedure.

Once you have delegated everything, what do you do then? You still need to monitor the tasks you have delegated and to continue the development of your staff to help them exercise their authority well.

There are managerial functions which you should never delegate - these are the personal/personnel ones which are often the most obvious additions to your responsibilities as you assume a managerial role. Specifically, they include: motivation, training, team-building, organization, praising, reprimanding, performance reviews, promotion.

As a manager, you have a responsibility to represent and to develop the effectiveness of your group within the company; these are tasks you can expand to fill your available time - delegation is a mechanism for creating that opportunity.

## DELEGATION TIPS

- Delegation helps people grow underneath you in an organization and thus pushes you even higher in management. It provides you with more time, and you will be able to take on higher priority projects.
- Delegate whole pieces or entire job pieces rather than simply tasks and activities.
- Clearly define what outcome is needed, then let individuals use some creative thinking of their own as to how to get to that outcome.

- Clearly define limits of authority that go with the delegated job. Can the person hire other people to work with them? Are there spending constraints?
- Clear standards of performance will help the person know when he or she is doing exactly what is expected.
- When on the receiving end of delegation, work to make your boss' job easier and to get the boss promoted. This wili enhance your promotability also.
- Assess routine activities in which you are involved. Can any of them be eliminated or delegated?
- Never underestimate a person's potential. Delegate slightly more than you think the person is capable of handling. Expect them to succeed, and you will be pleasantly surprised more frequently than not.
- Expect completed staff work from the individuals reporting to you. That is, they will come to you giving you alternatives and suggestions when a problem exists rather than just saying "Boss, what should we do?"
- Do not avoid delegating something because you cannot give someone the entire project. Let the person start with a bite size piece, then after learning and doing that, they can accept larger pieces and larger areas of responsibility.
- Agree on a monitoring or measurement procedure that will keep you informed as to progress on this project because you are ultimately still responsible for it and need to know that it is progressing as it should. In other words-If you can't measure it don't delegate it.

## EVALUATIONS

Evaluation is carefully collecting and analyzing information in order to make decisions. There are many types of evaluations in organizations, for example, evaluation of marketing efforts, evaluation of employee performance, programme evaluations, etc. Evaluations can focus on many aspects of an organization and its processes, for example, its goals, processes and outcomes.

Evaluation, in the context of management activities, is carefully collecting information about something in order to make necessary decisions about it. There are a large number and wide variety of evaluations that can occur in businesses, whether for-profit or nonprofit. Evaluation is closely related to performance management (whether about organizations, groups, processes or individuals), which includes identifying measures to indicate results. Evaluation often includes collecting information around these measures to conclude the extent of performance.

**Financial Statements**

Once the organization has establish goals and associated strategies (or ways to reach the goals), funds are set aside for the resources and labour to the accomplish goals and tasks. As the money is spent, statements are changed to reflect what was spent, how it was spent and what it obtained. Review of financial statements is one of the more common methods to monitor the progress of programmes and plans. The most common financial statements include the balance sheet, income statement and cash flow statement. Financial audits are regularly conducted to ensure that financial management practices follow generally accepted standards, as well.

Performance management focuses on the performance of the total organization, including its processes, critical subsystems (departments, programmes, projects, etc.) and employees. Most of us have some basic impression of employee performance management, including the role of performance reviews. Performance reviews provide an opportunity for supervisors and their employees to regularly communicate about goals, how well those goals should be met, how well the goals are being met and what must be done to continue to meet (or change) those goals. The employee is rewarded in some form for meeting performance standards, or embarks on a development plan with the supervisor in order to improve performance.

Policies help ensure that behaviours in the workplace conform to federal and state laws, and also to expectations of the organization. Often, policies are applied to specified situations in the form of procedures. Personnel policies and procedures help ensure that employee laws are followed (e.g., laws such as the Americans with Disabilities Act, Occupational Health and Safety Act, etc.) and minimize the likelihood of costly litigation. A procedure is a step-by-step list of activities required to conduct a certain task. Procedures ensure that routine tasks are carried out in an effective and efficient fashion.

## QUALITY CONTROL AND OPERATIONS IN MANAGEMENT

The concept of quality control has received a great deal of attention over the past twenty years. Many people recognize phrases such as "do it right the first time, "zero defects", "Total Quality Management", etc. Very broadly, quality includes specifying a performance standard (often by benchmarking, or comparing to a well-accepted standard), monitoring and measuring results, comparing the results to the standard and then making adjusts as necessary. Recently, the concept of quality management has expanded to include organization-wide programmes, such as Total Quality Management, ISO9000, Balanced Scorecard, etc. Operations management includes the overall activities involved in developing, producing and distributing products and services.

# Chapter 3

# Basics of Hotel Management

## HOTEL BUSINESS ORGANISATIONS CATEGORIES

### HOTEL MANAGER

The Hotel manager oversees all of a hotel's daily operations, from staffing to coordinating fresh-cut flowers for the lobby. Many, over time, are given long-term responsibility for negotiating contracts with vendors (such as maintenance supplies), negotiating leases with on-site shops, and physically upgrading the hotel. Hotel managers usually relish "the ability to put your own distinctive style on the [hotel] experience." While managing a hotel and giving it your unique flair are wonderful, they come with full responsibility for failure. "The better you are at what you do, the more responsibilities you are given, the more chances you have to fail," mentioned one hotel manager. When things fall apart, "no one is a hotel manager's friend."

Hotel managers can feel great about their positions, create strong relationships with regular customers, and maintain an amicable working environment. But should the bottom line waver and financial woes occur, the first neck on the chopping block is the hotel manager's. Those in the hotel management industry say that sometimes it seems that you need "to be born on the planet Krypton" to be a good hotel manager because only Superman could juggle the administrative, aesthetic, and financial decisions which constitute daily life on the job. Over

70 percent of the respondents said that tired was an understatement about how they felt at the end of the day or night.

A hotel manager's position as a liaison between the ownership and the staff can be difficult and isolating. But those who can put up with the long hours, the high degree of responsibility, and the variety of tasks emerge with a solid degree of satisfaction and a desire to continue in the profession. The average tenure of a hotel manager is 6.7 years, though this figure doesn't represent the number of managers who work for two years and those who work for decades. Many work at a variety of hotels, build up their resumes, and then find positions that allow them the freedom to operate their own establishments.

Aspiring hotel managers used to begin at the reception desk, as part of the wait staff, or as members of the cleaning staff, then work their way up the ladder. As hotels have become more commercial properties and the duties of hotel managers have expanded, this avenue of advancement has closed off. Now hotel manager hopefuls go to hotel management school, and those who don't should garner as much practical hotel experience as possible. Each chain or specific hotel puts new employees through their own training programmes, so those applying for jobs should learn all they can about the scope and functioning of the specific hotels where they wish to work. Part of life as a hotel manager can be similar to the life of a doctor, as managers can be called to duty at any time of the day or night. Hotel managers must handle any and all emergencies, and those who wish to remain in the profession and maintain respect must be quick-thinking and decisive. Candidates should have a good organizational and financial background, excellent communication and interpersonal skills, and strong self-discipline. They should also be extremely detail-oriented; when running a hotel, there is no such thing as an unimportant detail. The good manager drives himself to improve and upgrade the hotel at every available opportunity.

A hotel manager is responsible for the day-to-day management of a hotel and its staff and has commercial accountability for planning, organising and directing all hotel services, including front-of-house (reception, concierge, reservation), banqueting and housekeeping. In larger hotels, managers often have a specific remit (guest services, accounting, marketing) and make up a general management team.

Financial management - preparing budgets and marketing strategies and achieving targets for the business - plays a major role. The manager must strike a balance between customer satisfaction and effective business management, ensuring financial viability, and facilitate a smooth-running customer service, whilst ensuring staff work together as a team.

**Typical Work Activities**

Typical work activities vary depending on the size and type of hotel, but may include:

- Planning and organising accommodation, catering and other hotel services;
- Promoting and marketing the business;
- Managing budgets and financial plans;
- Maintaining statistical and financial records;
- Achieving profit targets;
- Recruiting, training and monitoring staff;
- Planning work schedules;
- Meeting and greeting customers;
- Dealing with customer complaints and comments;
- Addressing problems and troubleshooting;
- Ensuring events and conferences run smoothly;
- Supervising maintenance, supplies and furnishings;
- Dealing with contractors and suppliers;
- Ensuring security is effective;
- Carrying out inspections of property and services;

- Ensuring compliance with licensing laws, health and safety and other statutory regulations.

The manager of a large hotel may have less contact with guests but will spend time meeting heads of department and planning and monitoring the progress of business strategies. In a smaller establishment, the manager is much more involved in the hands-on day-to-day running of the hotel, which may include carrying out reception duties or serving meals if the need arises.

A significant number of hotel managers are self-employed and this can lead to a more general management experience, from greeting guests to managing finances.

**How to Become a Hotel Manager**

- Ask yourself if you have excellent interpersonal, communication and organizational skills. They are necessary for a successful hotel management career.
- Obtain a college degree in hotel management or restaurant management. Remember that a food services department contributes greatly to the profits of a hotel; a successful restaurant manager can see his or her career advance quickly.
- Take advantage of work-study programmes offered by many colleges so that you will gain solid experience working in hotels.
- Expect to go through a hotel's training programme once you are hired after college. During the first couple of years you will be handling only relatively mundane duties, instead of providing your input on issues such as staffing, hotel decor or conventions.
- Understand that you might be offered a position as a front office manager, a food and beverage manager, a convention services manager, or any of a number of administrative positions after your training period. If you are successful at different managerial positions, your career will benefit in the long run.

- Be aware that a promotion might require you to relocate for a few years if you work for a hotel chain that has properties throughout the country.
- You will need to quickly become proficient with computers because of their widespread use in hotel reservations, billing and overall management operations.
- Consider working for hotels in warm tourist destinations or snowy mountains, depending on your preferred lifestyle.
- Be prepared for long hours, night and weekend work, and the occasional unhappy guest.

Different managerial personnel working as hotel managers —

Catering managers plan, organise and manage the food and beverage services of organisations and businesses, both inside and outside the hospitality industry, with the aim of achieving good quality at low cost and maintaining high standards of hygiene and customer satisfaction.

There is a range of jobs in catering management, along with a number of different routes into the industry. Roles include: managing restaurants, bars and other outlets in hotels, resorts or liners; providing catering services at events; and running catering operations at hospitals, schools and other organisations.

With ongoing growth in the service industry, opportunities in this demanding but rewarding area continue to grow.

The role varies according to the size and nature of the establishment: in a small operation, the catering manager has more of a 'hands on' role and will be involved in the day-to-day running of the operation; in contract catering, the catering manager will spend time negotiating with the client organisation, assessing its requirements and ensuring that it is satisfied with the service delivered.

Typical tasks will include:

- Recruiting and training permanent and casual staff;
- Organising, leading and motivating the catering team;
- Planning menus in consultation with chefs;
- Ensuring health and safety regulations are strictly observed;
- Budgeting and establishing financial targets;
- Monitoring the quality of the product and service provided;
- Keeping financial and administrative records;
- Managing the payroll and monitoring spending levels;
- Maintaining stock levels and ordering new supplies as required;
- Interacting with customers if involved with 'front of house' work;
- Liaising with suppliers and clients;
- Negotiating contracts with customers (in contract catering).

In more senior posts, principal tasks will involve:

- Setting and agreeing budgets;
- Monitoring quality standards;
- Overseeing the management of the facilities, for example checking events bookings and the allocation of resources and staff;
- Planning new promotions and initiatives, and contributing to business development;
- Dealing with staffing and client issues, as they arise.

## FOOD AND RESTAURANT MANAGER

Fast food restaurant managers are responsible for the provision of standardised food and customer service in outlets based in the high street, motor service areas, stations, airports or multiplexes.

Drawing on all the operational functions of a business, the work involves applying financial, marketing and operational know-how, and supervising and training staff.

Managers plan, organise, and co-ordinate all resources and activities in a store. The work involves: setting targets, planning budgets, and controlling stock; recruiting, training and inspiring restaurant teams; creating and driving marketing campaigns; and building bridges with the local community.

Ultimately, it is the manager's ideas, initiative and personality that shape the restaurant.

Tasks typically involve:

- Organising the store in terms of products, equipment and people;
- Planning and checking work schedules;
- Carrying out audits to check health safety, food safety and quality of service in the restaurant;
- Making sure the fast-track audit is completed daily to check the safety of equipment and that food is properly cooked, only in-date stock is used, and all other products are discarded;
- Carrying out work outside the restaurant, including 'mystery shopping' at other restaurants within the chain;
- Attending weekly meetings with senior managers;
- Dealing with problems, queries, complaints, staff and customers in the store;
- Monitoring and maintaining high standards of food, service and hygiene;
- Ensuring the company's required standards of customer care are met;
- Administering payrolls;
- Checking and securing cash receipts;
- Budgeting to ensure maximum profitability;
- Achieving set profit and loss targets;

- Maintaining and securing equipment and buildings and all company assets contained within the unit;
- Publicising and marketing restaurants in the locality;
- Motivating restaurant teams;
- Recruiting, selecting and training new staff and fully inducting the restaurant team in accordance with company policy;
- Developing all team members to their fullest potential using the performance management/review system and identifying individual training needs;
- Ensuring the implementation and maintenance of legislation, company standards and procedures;
- Recognising new trends and implementing action plans accordingly;
- Acting as a communication link between senior teams and the restaurant team;
- Leading by example, acting as a role model for the restaurant team.

A successful manager will strike the right balance between creating both a good service for restaurant customers and a fun work environment for members of staff.

## CATERING MANAGER

Catering managers plan, organise and manage the food and beverage services of organisations and businesses, both inside and outside the hospitality industry, with the aim of achieving good quality at low cost and maintaining high standards of hygiene and customer satisfaction.

There is a range of jobs in catering management, along with a number of different routes into the industry. Roles include: managing restaurants, bars and other outlets in hotels, resorts or liners; providing catering services at events; and running catering operations at hospitals, schools and other organisations.

With ongoing growth in the service industry, opportunities in this demanding but rewarding area continue to grow.

## Typical Work Activities

The role varies according to the size and nature of the establishment: in a small operation, the catering manager has more of a 'hands on' role and will be involved in the day-to-day running of the operation; in contract catering, the catering manager will spend time negotiating with the client organisation, assessing its requirements and ensuring that it is satisfied with the service delivered.

Typical tasks will include:

- Recruiting and training permanent and casual staff;
- Organising, leading and motivating the catering team;
- Planning menus in consultation with chefs;
- Ensuring health and safety regulations are strictly observed;
- Budgeting and establishing financial targets;
- Monitoring the quality of the product and service provided;
- Keeping financial and administrative records;
- Managing the payroll and monitoring spending levels;
- Maintaining stock levels and ordering new supplies as required;
- Interacting with customers if involved with 'front of house' work;
- Liaising with suppliers and clients;
- Negotiating contracts with customers (in contract catering).

In more senior posts, principal tasks will involve:

- Setting and agreeing budgets;
- Monitoring quality standards;
- Overseeing the management of the facilities, for example checking events bookings and the allocation of resources and staff;

- Planning new promotions and initiatives, and contributing to business development;
- Dealing with staffing and client issues, as they arise.

## HUMAN RESOURCES

Human resources has at least two meanings depending on context. The original usage derives from political economy and economics, where it was traditionally called labour, one of three factors of production. The more common usage within corporations and businesses refers to the individuals within the firm, and to the portion of the firm's organization that deals with hiring, firing, training, and other personnel issues.

Modern analysis emphasizes that human beings are not predictable commodity "resources" with definitions totally controlled by contract, but are creative and social beings that make contributions beyond "labour" to a society and to civilization. The broad term human capital has evolved to contain the complexity of this term, and in macro-economics the term "firm-specific human capital" has evolved to represent the original meaning of term "human resources".

Advocating the central role of "human resources" or human capital in enterprises and societies has been a traditional role of socialist parties, who claim that value is primarily created by their activity, and accordingly justify a larger claim of profits or relief from these enterprises or societies. Critics say this is just a bargaining tactic which grew out of various practices of medieval European guilds into the modern trade union and collective bargaining unit.

A contrary view, common to capitalist parties, is that it is the infrastructural capital and (what they call) intellectual capital owned and fused by "management" that provides most value in financial capital terms. This likewise justifies a bargaining position and a general view that "human resources" are interchangeable.

A significant sign of consensus on this latter point is the ISO 9000 series of standards which requires a "job description" of every participant in a productive enterprise. In general, heavily unionized nations such as France and Germany have adopted and encouraged such descriptions especially within trade unions. One view of this trend is that a strong social consensus on political economy and a good social welfare system facilitates labour mobility and tends to make the entire economy more productive, as labour can move from one enterprise to another with little controversy or difficulty in adapting.

An important controversy regarding labour mobility illustrates the broader philosophical issue with usage of the phrase "human resources": governments of developing nations often regard developed nations that encourage immigration or "guest workers" as appropriating human capital that is rightfully part of the developing nation and required to further its growth as a civilization. They argue that this appropriation is similar to colonial commodity fiat wherein a colonizing European power would define an arbitrary price for natural resources, extracting which diminished national natural capital.

The debate regarding "human resources" versus human capital thus in many ways echoes the debate regarding natural resources versus natural capital. Over time the United Nations have come to more generally support the developing nations' point of view, and have requested significant offsetting "foreign aid" contributions so that a developing nation losing human capital does not lose the capacity to continue to train new people in trades, professions, and the arts.

An extreme version of this view is that historical inequities such as African slavery must be compensated by current developed nations, which benefitted from stolen "human resources" as they were developing. This is an extremely controversial view, but it echoes the general theme of converting human capital to "human resources" and thus greatly diminishing its value to the host society, i.e. "Africa", as it is put to narrow imitative use as "labour" in the using society.

In the very narrow context of corporate "human resources", there is a contrasting pull to reflect and require workplace diversity that echoes the diversity of a global customer base. Foreign language and culture skills, ingenuity, humor, and careful listening, are examples of traits that such programmes typically require. It would appear that these evidence a general shift to the human capital point of view, and an acknowledgement that human beings do contribute much more to a productive enterprise than "work": they bring their character, their ethics, their creativity, their social connections, and in some cases even their pets and children, and alter the character of a workplace. The term corporate culture is used to characterize such processes.

The traditional but extremely narrow context of hiring, firing, and job description is considered a 20th century anachronism. Most corporate organizations that compete in the modern global economy have adopted a view of human capital that mirrors the modern consensus as above. Some of these, in turn, deprecate the term "human resources" as useless.

As the term refers to predictable exploitations of human capital in one context or another, it can still be said to apply to manual labour, mass agriculture, low skill "McJobs" in service industries, military and other work that has clear job descriptions, and which generally do not encourage creative or social contributions.

In general the abstractions of macro-economics treat it this way - as it characterizes no mechanisms to represent choice or ingenuity. So one interpretation is that "firm-specific human capital" as defined in macro-economics is the modern and correct definition of "human resources" - and that this is inadequate to represent the contributions of "human resources" in any modern theory of political economy.

In terms of recruitment and selection it is important to consider carrying out a thorough job analysis to determine the level of skills/technical abilities, competencies, flexibility of the employee required etc. At this point it is important to consider both the internal and external factors that can have an impact on the recruitment of employees. The external factors are those out-with the powers of the organization and include issues such as current and future trends of the labour market e.g. skills, education level, government investment into industries etc. On the other hand internal influences are easier to control, predict and monitor, for example management styles or even the organizational culture.

In order to know the business environment in which any organization operates, three major trends should be considered:

- Demographics – the characteristics of a population/ workforce, for example, age, gender or social class. This type of trend may have an effect in relation to pension offerings, insurance packages etc.
- Diversity – the variation within the population/ workplace. Changes in society now mean that a larger proportion of organizations are made up of female employees in comparison to thirty years ago. Also over recent years organizations have become more culturally diverse and have increased the number of working patterns (part-time, casual, seasonal positions) to cope with the changes in both society and the global market. It is important to note here that an organisation must consider the ethic and legal implications of their decisions in relation to the HRM policies they enact to protect employees. Employers have to be acutely aware of the rise in discrimination, unfair dismissal and sexual/racial harassment cases in recent years and the detrimental effects this can have on the employees and the organisation. Anti-discrimination legislation over the past 30 years has provided a foundation for an increasing interest in diversity at work which is "about creating a working culture that seeks respects and values difference."
- Skills and qualifications – as industries move from manual to a more managerial professions so does the

need for more highly skilled graduates. If the market is 'tight' i.e. not enough staff for the jobs, employers will have to compete for employees by offering financial rewards, community investment etc.also the political issues

In regards to how individuals respond to the changes in a labour market the following should be understood:

- Geographical spread – how far is the job from the individual? The distance to travel to work should be in line with the pay offered by the organization and the transportation and infrastructure of the area will also be an influencing factor in deciding who will apply for a post.
- Occupational structure – the norms and values of the different careers within an organization. Mahoney 1989 developed 3 different types of occupational structure namely craft (loyalty to the profession), organization career (promotion through the firm) and unstructured (lower/unskilled workers who work when needed).
- Generational difference –different age categories of employees have certain characteristics, for example their behaviour and their expectations of the organisation.

Recruitment methods are wide and varied, it is important that the job is described correctly and any personal specifications stated. Job recruitment methods can be through job centres, employment agencies/consultants, headhunting, and local/national newspapers. It is important that the correct media is chosen to ensure an appropriate response to the advertised post.

## HUMAN RESOURCES WITHIN FIRMS

Though human resources have been part of business and organizations since the first days of agriculture, the modern concept of human resources began in reaction to the efficiency focus of Taylorism in the early 1900s. By 1920, psychologists and employment experts in the United States started the human relations movement, which viewed workers in terms of their psychology and fit with companies, rather than as interchangeable parts. This movement grew throughout the middle of the 20th century, placing emphasis on how leadership, cohesion, and loyalty played important roles in organizational success. Although this view was increasingly challenged by more quantitatively rigorous and less "soft" management techniques in the 1960s and beyond, human resources had gained a permanent role within the firm.

Facing mankind's problems it is opportune to mobilize as many intellectual resources as possible in order to resolve the emerging troubles. The students have to be trained to construct pertinent knowledge together (for example using the method Learning by teaching). Students can be trained in constructing knowledge outside the classroom too. They have to adopt following attitudes:

- Be aware that they are bearing resources
- Be aware that they have to increase their own resources in order to be more attractive inside the community
- Be aware that they can increase their own resources if they communicate
- Be aware that they can increase their own resources if they share their knowledge with other people
- Ability to identify resource from other community members and to make this resource available for all the group
- Ability to search for pertinent resources outside the group
- Ability to connect people looking for proposing resources
- Ability to organize collective thinking in networks

## EMPLOYEE ENGAGEMENT

Employee engagement is a concept that is generally viewed in terms of employees feeling a strong emotional bond to the organization that employs them. (Robinson) This is associated with people demonstrating a willingness to recommend the organization to others and commit time and effort to help the organization succeed. (Harter) It suggests that people are motivated by intrinsic factors (e.g. personal growth, working to a common purpose, being part of a larger process) rather than simply focusing on extrinsic factors (e.g. pay / reward). (Ryan) The concept has gained popularity as various studies have demonstrated links with productivity.

In 1999, The Gallup Organization published research that showed that engaged employees are more productive, more profitable, more customer-focused, safer, and less likely to leave their employer. The review stated that "engagement with employees within a firm has shown to motivate the employee to work beyond personal factors and work more for the success of the firm." (Harter) Watson Wyatt found that high-commitment organizations (one with loyal and dedicated employees) out-performed those with low commitment by 47% in the 2000 study and by 200% in the 2002 study. (Wyatt) In a study of professional service firms, the Hay Group found that offices with engaged employees were up to 43% more productive, based on a comparison of revenue generation.

Recent research has focused on developing a better understanding of how variables such as quality of work relationships and values of the organization interact and their link to important work outcomes. From the perspective of the employee, "outcomes" range from strong commitment to the isolation of oneself from the organization. The study done by the Gallup Management Journal has shown that only 29 percent of employees are actively engaged in their jobs. Those "engaged" employees work with passion and feel a strong connection to their company. Moreover, 54 percent of employees are not engaged meaning that they go through each workday putting time but no passion into their work. Also, Seventeen percent of employees are actively disengaged, meaning that they are busy acting out of their own personal unhappiness, which undermines what their engaged co-workers are trying to accomplish.

Access to a reliable model enables organizations to conduct validation studies to establish the relationship of employee engagement to productivity/performance and other measures linked to effectiveness.

It is an important principle of occupational psychology (i.e. the application of psychological theories, research methods, and intervention strategies involving workplace issues) that validation studies should be anchored in reliable scales (i.e. organized and related groups of items) and not simply focus on individual elements in isolation. To understand how high levels of employee engagement affect organizational performance/productivity it is important to have an a priori model that demonstrates how the scales interact. (Konrad) There is also overlap between this concept and those relating to well-being at work and the psychological contract.

As employee productivity is clearly connected with employee engagement, creating an environment that encourages employee engagement is considered to be essential in the effective management of human capital.

Employee engagement will be influenced by:

1. Employee perceptions of job importance. This study has found that "...an employees attitude toward the job['s importance] and the company had the greatest impact on loyalty and customer service then all other employee factors combined."
2. Employee clarity of job expectations. "If expectations are not clear and basic materials and equipment not provided, negative emotions such as boredom or resentment may result, and the employee may then become focused on surviving more then thinking about how he can help the organization succeed."
3. Career advancement/improvement opportunities. "Plant supervisors and managers indicated that many plant improvements were being made outside the suggestion system, where employees initiated

changes in order to reap the bonuses generated by the subsequent cost savings."

4. Regular feedback and dialogue with superiors. "Feedback is the key to giving employees a sense of where they're going, but many organizations are remarkably bad at giving it." (Hay Group) "'What I really wanted to hear was 'Thanks. You did a good job.' But all my boss did was hand me a check."
5. Quality of working relationships with peers, superiors, and subordinates. "...if employee's relationship with their managers is fractured, then no amount of perks will persuade the employees to perform at top levels. Employee engagement is a direct reflection of how employees feel about their relationship with the boss."
6. Perceptions of the ethos and values of the organization. "'Inspiration and values' is the most important of the six drivers in our Engaged Performance model. Inspirational leadership is the ultimate perk. In its absence, [it] is unlikely to engage employees."

As additional research becomes available, the significance of the various factors will become more evident.

## HUMAN INTERACTION MANAGEMENT

Human Interaction Management (HIM) is the set of principles and patterns for structuring, supporting and controlling human work practices proposed by Keith Harrison-Broninski in his 2005 book "Human Interactions".

Current mainstream techniques and tools for work support, whether categorized as Workflow or as Business Process Management (BPM), deal only with "mechanistic" business processes. In such business processes, human involvement is limited to key data entry and decision points. Workflow/BPM techniques and tools deal with only the externally-observable aspects of work - tasks, that are visible from outside.

HIM extends this to include support for "human-driven" processes focused on human creativity and collaboration. To achieve this, HIM deals not only with tasks, but also with those aspects of work visible from inside - information, interaction and innovation.

In HIM, a business process requiring human knowledge, judgement and experience is divided into Roles, which are then assigned to the appropriate members of an organization via a Human Interaction Management System (HIMS). A HIMS is also used to manage the work and integrate it with organizational strategy/tactics, via separation into "levels of control".

The main focus of HIM is currently on the integration of organizational objectives with human work practices, in order to implement strategy/tactics and fulfil requirements for compliance. However, HIM has application beyond the improvement of organizational efficiency, since it provides a rich set of patterns for structuring and managing collaborative work that are also finding application in spheres such as social/political negotiation, law enforcement and healthcare.

## ACCOUNTING MANAGEMENT

Accounting Management (Business) is the practical application of management techniques to control and report on the financial health of the organization. This involves the analysis, planning, implementation, and control of programmes designed to provide financial data reporting for managerial decision making. This includes the maintenance of bank accounts, developing financial statements, cash flow and financial performance analysis. Accounting management is a mandatory knowledge module of any MBA programme.

## COST MANAGEMENT

Cost management is the process whereby companies use cost accounting to report or control the various costs of doing business. The term CM is widely used in business today. Unfortunately there is no uniform definition. We use CM to describe the approaches and activities of managers in short run and long run planning and control decisions that increase value for customers and lower costs of products and services. For example, managers make decisions regarding the amount and kind of material being used, changes of plant processes, and changes in product designs. Information from accounting systems helps managers make such decisions, but the information and the accounting systems themselves are not cost management.

Cost management has a broad focus. It includes – but is not confined to – the continuous reduction of costs. The planning and control of costs is usually inextricably linked with revenue and profit planning. For instance, to enhance revenues and profits, managers often deliberately incur additional costs for advertising and product modifications.

Cost management is not practiced in isolation. It's an integral part of general management strategies and their implementation. Examples include programme that enhance customer satisfaction and quality as well as programmes that promote blockbuster new product development.

## CUSTOMER RELATIONSHIP MANAGEMENT

Customer relationship management (CRM) covers methods and technologies used by companies to manage their relationships with clients. Information stored on existing customers (and potential customers) is analyzed and used to this end. Automated CRM processes are often used to generate automatic personalized marketing based on the customer information stored in the system.

Customer relationship management is a corporate level strategy, focusing on creating and maintaining relationships with customers. Several commercial CRM software packages are available which vary in their approach to CRM. However, CRM is not a technology itself, but rather a holistic approach to an organisation's philosophy, placing the emphasis firmly on the customer.

CRM governs an organization's philosophy at all levels, including policies and processes, front-of-house customer service, employee training, marketing, systems and information management. CRM systems are integrated end-to-end across marketing, sales, and customer service.

A CRM system should:

- Identify factors important to clients.
- Promote a customer-oriented philosophy
- Adopt customer-based measures
- Develop end-to-end processes to serve customers
- Provide successful customer support
- Handle customer complaints
- Track all aspects of sales
- Create a holistic view of customers' sales and services information

There are three fundamental components in CRM:

- Operational - automation of basic business processes (marketing, sales, service)
- Analytical - analysis of customer data and behaviour using business intelligence
- Collaborative - communicating with clients

Operational CRM provides automated support to "front office" business processes (sales, marketing and service). Each interaction with a customer is generally added to a customer's history, and staff can retrieve information on customers from the database as necessary.

According to Gartner Group operational CRM typically involves three general areas:

**Sales force automation (SFA):** SFA automates some of a company's critical sales and sales force management tasks, such as forecasting, sales administration, tracking customer preferences and demographics, performance management, lead management, account management, contact management and quote management.

**Customer service and support (CSS):** CSS automates certain service requests, complaints, product returns and enquiries.

**Enterprise marketing automation (EMA) :** EMA provides information about the business environment, including information on competitors, industry trends, and macroenvironmental variables. EMA applications are used to improve marketing efficiency.

Integrated CRM software is often known as a "front office solution", as it deals directly with customers.

Many call centers use CRM software to store customer information. When a call is received, the system displays the associated customer information (determined from the number of the caller). During and following the call, the call center agent dealing with the customer can add further information.

Some customer services can be fully automated, such as allowing customers to access their bank account details online or via a WAP phone.

**Analytical CRM**

Analytical CRM analyses data (gathered as part of operational CRM, or from other sources) in an attempt to identify means to enhance a company's relationship with its clients. The results of an analysis can be used to design targeted marketing campaigns, for example:

- Acquisition: Cross-selling, up-selling
- Retention: Retaining existing customers (antonym: customer attrition)
- Information: Providing timely and regular information to customers

Other examples of the applications of analyses include:

- Contact optimization
- Evaluating and improving customer satisfaction
- Optimizing sales coverage
- Fraud detection
- Financial forecasts
- Price optimization
- Product development

- Programme evaluation
- Risk assessment and management
- Strategic Marketing
- Operational marketing

Data collection and analysis is viewed as a continuing and iterative process. Ideally, business decisions are refined over time, based on feedback from earlier analyses and decisions. Most analytical CRM projects use a data warehouse to manage data.

**Collaborative CRM**

Collaborative CRM focuses on the interaction with customers (personal interaction, letter, fax, phone, Internet, e-mail etc.)

Collaborative CRM includes:

- Providing efficient communication with customers across a variety of communications channels
- Providing online services to reduce customer service costs
- Providing access to customer information while interacting with customers

Driven by authors from the Harvard Business School (Kracklauer/Mills/Seifert), Collaborative CRM also seems to be the new paradigma to succeed the leading Efficient Consumer Response and Category Management concept in the industry/ trade relationship.

In its broadest sense, CRM covers all interaction and business with customers. A good CRM programme allows a business to acquire customers, provide customer services and retain valued customers.

Customer services can be improved by:

- Providing online access to product information and technical assistance around the clock
- Identifying what customers value and devising appropriate service strategies for each customer

- Providing mechanisms for managing and scheduling follow-up sales calls
- Tracking all contacts with a customer
- Identifying potential problems before they occur
- Providing a user-friendly mechanism for registering customer complaints
- Providing a mechanism for handling problems and complaints
- Providing a mechanism for correcting service deficiencies
- Storing customer interests in order to target customers selectively
- Providing mechanisms for managing and scheduling maintenance, repair, and on-going support
- Scalability: the system should be highly scalable, as the volume of data stored in the system grows over time
- Communication channels: CRM can interface with a variety of different channels (phone, WAP, Internet etc.)
- Workflow - a company's business processes need to be represented by the system with the ability to track the individual stages and transfer information between steps
- Assignment - the ability to assign requests, such as service requests, to a person or group.
- Database - the means of storing customer data and histories (in a data warehouse)
- Customer privacy considerations, such as data encryption and legislation.

**Improving Customer Relationships**

CRM applications often track customer interests and requirements, as well as their buying habits. This information can be used to target customers selectively. Furthermore, the products a customer has purchased can be tracked throughout the product's life cycle, allowing customers to receive information concerning a product or to target customers with information on alternative products once a product begins to be phased out.

Repeat purchases rely on customer satisfaction, which in turn comes from a deeper understanding of each customer and their individual needs. CRM is an alternative to the "one size fits all" approach. In industrial markets, the technology can be used to coordinate the conflicting and changing purchase criteria of the sector.

The data gathered as part of CRM raises concerns over customer privacy and enables persuasive sales techniques (see persuasion technology). However, CRM does not necessarily involve gathering new data, but also includes making better use of customer information gathered as a result of routine customer interaction.

The privacy debate generally focuses on the customer information stored in the centralized database itself, and fears over a company's handling of this information. For example, there is virtually no way a consumer can determine if the company shares private (personally identifiable) data with third parties. Furthermore, companies may not always accurately declare to the consumer the types of information collected by CRM systems and the specific purposes for which the information is used.

CRM is also important to non-profit organizations, which sometimes use the terms "constituent relationship management", "contact relationship management" or "community relationship management" to describe their information systems for managing donors, volunteers and other supporters. salesforce.com, a popular CRM service that is on demand, offers its products for free to nonprofit organizations

## FINANCIAL MANAGEMENT

New business leaders and managers have to develop at least basic skills in financial management. Expecting others in the organization to manage finances is clearly asking for trouble. Basic skills in financial management start in the critical areas of cash management and bookkeeping, which should be done according to certain financial controls to ensure integrity in the bookkeeping process. New leaders and managers should soon go on to learn how to generate financial statements (from bookkeeping journals) and analyze those statements to really understand the financial condition of the business. Financial analysis shows the "reality" of the situation of a business — seen as such, financial management is one of the most important practices in management. This topic will help you understand basic practices in financial management, and build the basic systems and practices needed in a healthy business.

If your small business is a corporation, you would do well to find someone experienced in financial management and encourage them to be your board treasurer (your board chair has this responsibility to find someone suitable, as well). Therefore, it's important to understand the role of the board treasurer.

New, more "organic" forms or organizations (self-organizing organizations, self-managed teams, network organizations, etc.) allow organizations to be more responsive and adaptable in today's rapidly changing world. These forms also cultivate empowerment among employees, much more than the hierarchical, rigidly structured organizations of the past.

Many people assert that as the nature of organizations has changed, so must the nature of management control. Some people go so far as to claim that management shouldn't exercise any form of control whatsoever. They claim that management should exist to support employee's efforts to be fully productive members of organizations and communities — therefore, any form of control is completely counterproductive to management and employees.

Some people even react strongly against the phrase "management control". The word itself can have a negative connotation, e.g., it can sound dominating, coercive and heavy-handed. It seems that writers of management literature now prefer use of the term "coordinating" rather than "controlling".

Regardless of the negative connotation of the word "control", it must exist or there is no organization at all. In its most basic form, an organization is two or more people working together to reach a goal. Whether an organization is highly bureaucratic or changing and self-organizing, the organization must exist for some reason, some purpose, some mission (implicit or explicit) — or it isn't an organization at all. The organization must have some goal. Identifying this goal requires some form of planning, informal or formal. Reaching the goal means identifying some strategies, formal or informal. These strategies are agreed upon by members of the organization through some form of communication, formal or informal. Then members set about to act in accordance with what they agreed to do. They may change their minds, fine. But they need to recognize and acknowledge that they're changing their minds.

This form of ongoing communication to reach a goal, tracking activities toward the goal and then subsequent decisions about what to do is the essence of management coordination. It needs to exist in some manner — formal or informal.

The following are rather typical methods of coordination in organizations. They are used as means to communicate direction and guide behaviours in that direction. The function of the following methods is not to "control", but rather to guide. If, from ongoing communications among management and employees, the direction changes, then fine. The following methods are changed accordingly.

Note that many of the following methods are so common that we often don't think of them as having anything to do with coordination at all. No matter what one calls the following methods — coordination or control — they're important to the success of any organization.

## ADMINISTRATIVE CONTROLS

Organizations often use standardized documents to ensure complete and consistent information is gathered. Documents include titles and dates to detect different versions of the document. Computers have revolutionized administrative controls through use of integrated management information systems, project management software, human resource information systems, office automation software, etc. Organizations typically require a wide range of reports, e.g., financial reports, status reports, project reports, etc. to monitor what's being done, by when and how.

Delegation is an approach to get things done, in conjunction with other employees. Delegation is often viewed as a major means of influence and therefore is categorized as an activity in leading (rather than controlling/coordinating). Delegation generally includes assigning responsibility to an employee to complete a task, granting the employee sufficient authority to gain the resources to do the task and letting the employee decide how that task will be carried out. Typically, the person assigning the task shares accountability with the employee for ensuring the task is completed. Evaluation is carefully collecting and analyzing information in order to make decisions. There are many types of evaluations in organizations, for example, evaluation of marketing efforts, evaluation of employee performance, programme evaluations, etc. Evaluations can focus on many aspects of an organization and its processes, for example, its goals and processes, outcomes.

## FINANCIAL STATEMENTS

Once the organization has establish goals and associated strategies (or ways to reach the goals), funds are set aside for the resources and labour to the accomplish goals and tasks. As the money is spent, statements are changed to reflect what was spent, how it was spent and what it obtained. Review of financial statements is one of the more common methods to monitor the progress of programmes and plans. The most common financial statements include the balance sheet, income statement and cash flow statement. Financial audits are regularly conducted to ensure that financial management practices follow generally accepted standards, as well.

Performance management focuses on the performance of the total organization, including its processes, critical subsystems (departments, programmes, projects, etc.) and employees. Most of us have some basic impression of employee performance management, including the role of performance reviews. Performance reviews provide an opportunity for supervisors and their employees to regularly communicate about goals, how well those goals should be met, how well the goals are being met and what must be done to continue to meet (or change) those goals. The employee is rewarded in some form for meeting performance standards, or embarks on a development plan with the supervisor in order to improve performance.

Policies help ensure that behaviours in the workplace conform to federal and state laws, and also to expectations of the organization. Often, policies are applied to specified situations in the form of procedures. Personnel policies and procedures help ensure that employee laws are followed (e.g., laws such as the Americans with Disabilities Act, Occupational Health and Safety Act, etc.) and minimize the likelihood of costly litigation. A procedure is a step-by-step list of activities required to conduct a certain task. Procedures ensure that routine tasks are carried out in an effective and efficient fashion.

## QUALITY CONTROL AND OPERATIONS MANAGEMENT

The concept of quality control has received a great deal of attention over the past twenty years. Many people recognize phrases such as "do it right the first time, "zero defects", "Total Quality Management", etc. Very broadly, quality includes specifying a performance standard (often by benchmarking, or comparing to a well-accepted standard), monitoring and measuring results, comparing the results to the standard and then making adjusts as necessary. Recently, the concept of quality management has expanded to include organization-wide programmes, such as Total Quality Management, ISO9000, Balanced Scorecard, etc. Operations management includes the overall activities involved in developing, producing and distributing products and services.

## RISK, SAFETY AND LIABILITIES

For a variety of reasons (including the increasing number of lawsuits), organizations are focusing a great deal of attention to activities that minimize risk, avoid liabilities and ensure safety of employees. Several decades ago, it was rare to hear of an organization undertaking contingency planning, disaster recovery planning or critical incident analysis. Now those activities are becoming commonplace.

## EVALUATION ACTIVITIES IN ORGANIZATIONS

Evaluation, in the context of management activities, is carefully collecting information about something in order to make necessary decisions about it. There are a large number and wide variety of evaluations that can occur in businesses, whether for-profit or nonprofit. Evaluation is closely related to performance management (whether about organizations, groups, processes or individuals), which includes identifying measures to indicate results. Evaluation often includes collecting information around these measures to conclude the extent of performance.

# ADVERTISING AND PROMOTIONS

Before you learn more about advertising, you should get a basic impression of what advertising is. Advertising is a major "phase" of overall product or service development and management. Advertising is specifically part of the "outbound" marketing activities, or activities geared to communicate to the market, eg, advertising, promotions, public relations, etc. Inbound" marketing activities are geared to communicate from the market, and include, eg, market research about the market.

Although your use of the latest hot marketing and sales strategies may improve the bottom line of your business, you may get into hot "legal waters" if you do not exercise the proper restraints. This article discusses the boundaries beyond which you do not want to stray lest you run afoul of the laws governing false advertising.

Two conflicting principles are involved in advertising law. On the one hand, the First Amendment, which is part of the U.S. Constitution and grants us the right of free speech, protects all forms of communication, including advertising (referred to by lawyers as "commercial speech"). On the other hand, the U.S. Constitution gives the federal government the power to regulate interstate commerce. Most state constitutions similarly give state governments the power to regulate commerce conducted solely within that state.

In exercising its power over interstate commerce, the Congress has enacted two statutes that have the greatest effect on advertising. These are the Federal Trade Commission (FTC) Act and the Lanham Act.

The FTC Act states that false advertising is a form of unfair and deceptive commerce. The term "false advertising" has been broadly construed. As you might expect, the term includes advertisements that are in fact untrue. However, the term false advertising extends well beyond untrue advertisements. It also includes advertisements that make representations that the advertiser has no reasonable basis to believe, even if the representations turn out to be true. An example would be an advertisement for a photocopier machine which stated that the machine used less toner than any comparable machine. The advertiser would have committed false advertising if it had no reasonable basis to believe the truth of this claim (such as through comparative tests), even if it turned out to be true.

The FTC Act gives the FTC broad authority to regulate advertising. Under this broad mandate, the FTC has issued regulations barring advertisements that could be misleading even if they are true. A famous example involves Anacin, a brand of aspirin. The maker of Anacin ran ads claiming that clinical tests showed that Anacin delivered the same headache relief as the leading pain relief prescription. The ad did not mention that aspirin itself is the leading pain medicine. The FTC determined that the ad was misleading. The ad implied that Anacin was more effective than aspirin, when in fact, Anacin is really just aspirin.

In addition to barring advertisements, the FTC also has the power to order corrective ads. Corrective advertising requires a business to run ads that alert future consumers to certain unfavorable facts about a product not revealed in past advertising campaigns. Another famous example involved Listerine mouthwash. For years, Listerine was touted as a cold and sore throat remedy. The FTC forced the manufacturer to run ads stating that Listerine would not cure colds or relieve sore throats. Surely, this is not part of a desirable marketing strategy.

The FTC has a further power, known as "fencing in." This enables the FTC to bar misleading ads with respect to a particular product and across all of a business's other unrelated product lines. For example a testimonial constituting false advertising regarding product A could lead purchasers to believe that products B and c must also be great. In that case, the FTC could bar use of the ad for products A, B, and C.

Only the FTC has the authority to enforce the FTC Act. Private parties, such as consumers or competitors, can bring a legal action regarding false advertising under the Lanham Act.

To establish a violation under the Lanham Act, consumers and competitors must prove the following: (1) the advertiser made false statements of fact about its product; (2) the false advertisements actually deceived or had the capacity to deceive a substantial segment of the target population; (3) the deception was material; (4) the falsely advertised product was sold in interstate commerce; and (5) the party bringing the lawsuit (known as the "plaintiff") was injured as a result of the deception.

Actual loss is not required to show an injury. All that is needed is a reasonable basis for the belief that the plaintiff is likely to be damaged as a result of the advertising. An example of such damage would include ads that deceive consumers who are the target population of both the advertiser and the plaintiff. The penalties for a Lanham Act violation include the plaintiff's lost profits, the additional profits to the advertiser resulting from the deceptive ad, treble damages, and attorneys' fees.

In addition to the FTC Act and the Lanham Act, which are federal statutes, most states, including Illinois, also have laws proscribing false advertising. Illinois is one of many states that has enacted the Uniform Deceptive Trade Practices Act. Under the Act, a "deceptive trade practice" includes such practices as "palming off," misrepresentation, product disparagement, and bait-and-switch advertising.

Palming off occurs when an advertiser creates the impression that its goods or services are those that are furnished by a competitor. For example, this could occur if you set up a hamburger stand that looked like a McDonalds restaurant. Misrepresentation occurs when an advertiser makes false or misleading claims about its goods or services, as under the FTC Act and the Lanham Act. Product disparagement occurs when an advertiser intentionally makes false or misleading negative remarks about competing goods or services, causing its competitor to lose sales. Bait-and-switch advertising occurs when the advertised goods or services are withdrawn from the market and substitute goods or services are instead offered for sale.

The laws regulating false advertising present many traps for the unwary. If you engage a marketing or advertising agent to assist you in your marketing and sales campaign, you might want to get your agent to guarantee that your ads are lawful. Of course, if you are in the business of preparing marketing or advertising campaigns, you might want to get your client to guarantee that the information he or she provides is true. In either case, when in doubt, you should consult with an attorney.

Advertising and promotions is bringing a service to the attention of potential and current customers. Advertising and promotions are best carried out by implementing an advertising and promotions plan. The goals of the plan should depend very much on the overall goals and strategies of the organization, and the results of the marketing analysis, including the positioning statement.

The plan usually includes what target markets you want to reach, what features and benefits you want to convey to them, how you will convey it to them (this is often called your advertising campaign), who is responsible to carry the various activities in the plan and how much money is budgeted for this effort. Successful advertising depends very much on knowing the preferred methods and styles of communications of the target markets that you want to reach with your ads. A media plan and calendar can be very useful, which specifies what advertising methods are used and when.

For each service, carefully consider: What target markets are you trying to reach with your ads? What would you like them to think and perceive about your products (this should be in terms of benefits to them, not you)? How can you get them to think and perceive that? What communications media do they see or prefer the most? Consider TV, radio, newsletters, classifieds, displays/signs, posters, word of mouth, press releases, direct mail, special events, brochures, neighbourhood newsletters, etc.

What media is most practical for you to use in terms of access and affordability (the amount spent on advertising is often based on the revenue expected from the product or service, that is, the sales forecast)?

You can often find out a lot about your customers preferences just by conducting some basic market research methods. The following closely related links might be useful in preparation for your planning.

Far too often, we think we know what our customers think and want because — well, we just know, that's all. Wrong! Businesses can't be successful if they don't continue to meet the needs of their customers. Period. There should be few activities as important as finding out what your customers want for products and services and finding out what they think of yours. Fortunately, there are a variety of practical methods that businesses can use to feedback from customers.

The methods you choose and how you use them depend on what the type of feedback that you want from customers, for example, to find out their needs in products and services, what they think about your products and services, etc.

**Employees**

Your employees of usually the people who interact the most with your customers. Ask them about products and services that customers are asking for. Ask employees about what the customers complain about.

**Comment Cards**

Provide brief, half-page comment cards on which they can answer basic questions such as: Were you satisfied with our services? How could we provide the perfect services? Are there any services you'd like to see that don't exist yet?

**COMPETITION**

What is your competition selling? Ask people who shop there. Many people don't notice sales or major items in stores. Start coaching those around you to notice what's going on with your competition.

**Customers**

One of the best ways to find out what customers want is to ask them. Talk to them when they visit your facility or you visit theirs.

**Documentation and Records**

Notice what customers are buying and not buying from you. If you already know what customers are buying, etc., then is this written down somewhere? It should be so that you don't forget, particularly during times of stress or when trying to train personnel to help you out.

**Focus Groups**

Focus groups are usually 8-10 people that you gather to get their impressions of a product or service or an idea.

**Surveys by Mail**

You might hate answering these things, but plenty of people don't — and will fill our surveys especially if they get something in return. Promise them a discount if they return the completed form to your facility.

## COMPETITIVE ANALYSIS

Marketing should include competitor analysis. Who are your competitors? What customer needs and preferences are you competing to meet? What are the similarities and differences between their products/services and yours? What are the strengths and weaknesses of each of their products and services? How do their prices compare to yours? How are they doing overall? How do you plan to compete? Offer better quality services? Lower prices? More support? Easier access to services? How are you uniquely suited to compete with them?

### Competitive Intelligence for Business Success

Some businesses think it is best to get on with their own plans and ignore the competition. Others become obsessed with tracking the actions of competitors (often using underhand or illegal methods). Many businesses are happy simply to track the competition, copying their moves and reacting to changes.

Competitor analysis has several important roles in strategic planning:

- To help management understand their competitive advantages/disadvantages relative to competitors
- To generate understanding of competitors' past, present (and most importantly) future strategies
- To provide an informed basis to develop strategies to achieve competitive advantage in the future
- To help forecast the returns that may be made from future investments (e.g. how will competitors respond to a new product or pricing strategy?

### Questions to Ask

What questions should be asked when undertaking competitor analysis? The following is a useful list to bear in mind:

- Who are our competitors?
- What threats do they pose?
- What is the profile of our competitors?
- What are the objectives of our competitors?
- What strategies are our competitors pursuing and how successful are these strategies?
- What are the strengths and weaknesses of our competitors?
- How are our competitors likely to respond to any changes to the way we do business?

**Sources of Information for Competitor Analysis**

Davidson describes how the sources of competitor information can be neatly grouped into three categories:

- Recorded data: this is easily available in published form either internally or externally. Good examples include competitor annual reports and product brochures;
- Observable data: this has to be actively sought and often assembled from several sources. A good example is competitor pricing;
- Opportunistic data: to get hold of this kind of data requires a lot of planning and organisation. Much of it is "anecdotal", coming from discussions with suppliers, customers and, perhaps, previous management of competitors.

The table below lists possible sources of competitor data using Davidson's categorisation:

| Recorded Data | Observable Data | Opportunistic Data |
|---|---|---|
| Annual report and accounts | | Pricing / price lists<br>Meetings with suppliers |
| Press releases | Advertising campaigns | Trade shows |
| Newspaper articles | Promotions | Sales force meetings |

| | | |
|---|---|---|
| Analysts reports | Tenders | Seminars / conferences |
| Regulatory reports | Patent applications | Recruiting ex-employees |
| Government reports | | Discussion with shared distributors |
| Presentations / speeches | | Social contacts with competitors |

In his excellent book *Even More Offensive Marketing,* Davidson likens the process of gathering competitive data to a jigsaw puzzle. Each individual piece of data does not have much value. The important skill is to collect as many of the pieces as possible and to assemble them into an overall picture of the competitor. This enables you to identify any missing pieces and to take the necessary steps to collect them.

**What Businesses Need to Know about their Competitors**

The tables below lists the kinds of competitor information that would help businesses complete some good quality competitor analysis.

You can probably think of many more pieces of information about a competitor that would be useful. However, an important challenge in competitor analysis is working out how to obtain competitor information that is reliable, up-to-date and available legally.

| What businesses probably already know their competitors |
|---|
| Overall sales and profits |
| Sales and profits by market |
| Sales by main brand |
| Cost structure |
| Market shares (revenues and volumes) |
| Organisation structure |
| Distribution system |
| Identity / profile of senior management |
| Advertising strategy and spending |
| Customer / consumer profile and attitudes |
| Customer retention levels |

| What businesses would really like to know about competitors |
|---|
| Sales and profits by product |
| Relative costs |
| Customer satisfaction and service levels |
| Customer retention levels |
| Distribution costs |
| New product strategies |
| Size and quality of customer databases |
| Advertising effectiveness |
| Future investment strategy |
| Contractual terms with key suppliers |
| Terms of strategic partnerships |

## COMPETITOR ARRAY

One common and useful technique is constructing a competitor array. The steps include:

- Define your industry - scope and nature of the industry
- Determine who your competitors are
- Determine who your customers are and what benefits they expect
- Determine what the key success factors are in your industry
- Rank the key success factors by giving each one a weighting - The sum of all the weightings must add up to one.
- Rate each competitor on each of the key success factors - this can best be displayed on a two dimensional matrix - competitors along the top and key success factors down the side.
- Multiply each cell in the matrix by the factor weighting.
- Sum columns for a weighted assessment of the overall strength of each competitor relative to each other.

An example of a competitor array follows:

| Key Industry Success Factors | Weighting | Competitor # 1 rating | Competitor #1 weighted | Competitor #2 rating | Competitor #2 weighted |
|---|---|---|---|---|---|
| 1 - Extensive distribution | .4 | 6 | 2.4 | 3 | 1.2 |
| 2 - Customer focus | .3 | 4 | 1.2 | 5 | 1.5 |
| 3 - Economies of scale | .2 | 3 | .6 | 3 | .6 |
| 4 - Product innovation | .1 | 7 | .7 | 4 | .4 |
| **Totals** | 1.0 | 20 | 4.9 | 18 | 3.7 |

Based on material presented in "Beat the Competition: How to Use Competitive Intelligence to Develop Winning Business Strategies", Ian Gordon, Basil Blackwell Publishers, Oxford, UK, 1989.

In this example competitor #1 is rated higher than competitor #2 on product innovation ability (7 out of 10, compared to 4 out of 10) and distribution networks (6 out of 10), but competitor #2 is rated higher on customer focus (5 out of 10). Overall, competitor #1 is rated slightly higher than competitor #2 (20 out of 40 compared to 18 out of 40). When the success factors are weighted according to their importance, competitor #1 gets a far better rating (4.9 compared to 3.7).

## COMPETITOR PROFILING

Another common technique is to create detailed profiles on each of your major competitors. These profiles give an in-depth description of the competitor's background, finances, products, markets, facilities, personnel, and strategies. This involves:

- Background
  - Location of offices, plants, and online presences
  - History - key personalities, dates, events, and trends
  - Ownership, corporate governance, and organizational structure

- Financials
  - P-E ratios, dividend policy, and profitability** various financial ratios, liquidity, and cash flow
  - Profit growth profile; method of growth (organic or acquisitive)
- Products
  - Products offered, depth and breadth of product line, and product portfolio balance
  - New products developed, new product success rate, and R&D strengths
  - Brands, strength of brand portfolio, brand loyalty and brand awareness
  - Patents and licenses
  - Quality control conformance
  - Reverse engineering
- Marketing
  - Segments served, market shares, customer base, growth rate, and customer loyalty
  - Promotional mix, promotional budgets, advertising themes, ad agency used, sales force success rate, online promotional strategy
  - Distribution channels used (direct and indirect), exclusivity agreements, alliances, and geographical coverage
  - Pricing, discounts,and allowances
- Facilities
  - Plant capacity, capacity utilization rate, age of plant, plant efficiency, capital investment
  - Location, shipping logistics, and product mix by plant
- Personnel
  - Number of employees, key employees, and skill sets
  - Strength of management, and management style
  - Compensation, benefits, and employee morale and retention rates

- Corporate and marketing strategies
  - Objectives, mission statement, growth plans, acquisitions, and divestitures
  - Marketing strategies

## MEDIA SCANNING

We can learn a lot about the competitive environment by scanning our competitors' ads. Changes in a competitor's advertising message can reveal new product offerings, new production processes, a new branding strategy, a new positioning strategy, a new segmentation strategy, line extensions and contractions, problems with previous positions, insights from recent marketing or product research, a new strategic direction, a new source of sustainable competitive advantage, or value migrations within the industry. It might also indicate a new pricing strategy such as penetration, price discrimination, price skimming, product bundling, joint product pricing, discounts, or loss leaders. It may also indicate a new promotion strategy such as push, pull, balanced, short term sales generation, long term image creation, informational, comparative, affective, reminder, new creative objectives, new unique selling proposition, new creative concepts, appeals, tone, and themes, or a new advertising agency. It might also indicate a new distribution strategy, new distribution partners, more extensive distribution, more intensive distribution, a change in geographical focus, or exclusive distribution. Little of this intelligence is definitive : additional information is needed before conclusions should be drawn.

A competitor's media strategy reveals budget allocation, segmentation and targeting strategy, and selectivity and focus. From a tactical perspective, it can also be used to help a manager implement his/her own media plan. By knowing the competitor's media buy, media selection, frequency, reach, continuity, schedules, and flights, the manager can arrange his/her own media plan so that they do not coincide.

Other sources of corporate intelligence include trade shows, patent filings, mutual customers, annual reports, and trade associations.

Some firms hire competitor intelligence professionals to obtain this information.

## NEW COMPETITORS

In addition to analysing current competitors, it is necessary to estimate future competitive threats. The most common sources of new competitors are:

- Companies competing in a related product/market
- Companies using related technologies
- Companies already targeting your prime market segment but with unrelated products
- Companies from other geographical areas and with similar products
- New start-up companies organised by former employees and/or managers of existing companies

The entrance of new competitors is likely when:

- There are high profit margins in the industry
- There is unmet demand (insufficient supply) in the industry
- There are no major barriers to entry
- There is future growth potential
- Competitive rivalry is not intense
- Gaining a competitive advantage over existing firms is feasible

# MARKETING

Marketing is a social and managerial function that attempts to create, expand and maintain a collection of customers. It attempts to deliver demand satisfying output through profitable exchanges.

- Marketing, as suggested by the American Marketing Association, is "an organizational function and a set of processes for creating, communicating and delivering value to customers and for managing customer relationships in ways that benefit the organization and its stakeholders".

- Philip Kotler, in his earlier books, defines marketing as: "human activity directed at satisfying needs and wants through exchange processes". Still another marketing definition, coined by Brian Norris: "The process of repeatedly moving people closer to making a decision to purchase, use, follow, refer, upload, download, obey, reject, conform, become complacent to another person's, society's or organization's value. Simply, if it doesn't facilitate a "sale" then it's not marketing."
- Identifying needs/wants and finding and implimenting solutions that satisfy those needs and wants.
- Add to Kotler's and Norris' definitions, a response from the Chartered Institute of Marketing (CIM). The association's definition claims marketing to be the "management process of anticipating, identifying and satisfying customer requirements profitably". Thus, operative marketing involves the processes of market research, market segmentation, new product development, product life cycle management, pricing, channel management as well as promotion.
- Marketing-"taking actions to define, create, grow, develop, maintain, defend and own markets".
- An approach to business that seeks to identify, anticipate and satisfy customers needs.
- Al Ries and Jack Trout defined marketing as simply "war" between competitors.
- Any activity that connects producers with consumers.
- At a macro level, marketing is the process of raising the standards of living, by identifying the existing problems and unsatisfied needs of people and then satisfying that need with a product/service that delivers value to the customer.

The practice of marketing is almost as old as humanity itself. Whenever a person has an item or is capable of performing a service, and he or she seeks another person who might want that item or service, that person is involved in marketing. A Market was originally simply a gathering place where people with a supply of items or capacity to perform a service could meet with those who might desire the items or services, perhaps at a pre-arranged time.

Such meetings embodied all the aspects of today's marketing methods, although in an informal way. Sellers and buyers sought to understand each other's needs, capacities, and psychology, all with the goal of getting the exchange of items or services to take place. Open air markets throughout the world, with buyers and sellers freely mingling, are today's example of this basic activity. Today's New York Stock Exchange had its humble beginnings as an open air market located at Wall Street in New York City.

The rise of Agriculture undoubtedly influenced markets as the earliest means of 'mass production' of an item, namely foodstuffs. As agriculture allowed one to grow more food than could be eaten by the grower alone, and most food is perishable, there was likely motivation to seek out others who could use the excess food, before it spoiled, in exchange for other items.

Prior to the advent of market research, most companies were product-focused, employing teams of salespeople to push their products into or onto the market, regardless of market desire. A market-focused, or customer-focused, organization instead first determines what its potential customers desire, and then builds the product or service. Marketing theory and practice is justified on the belief that customers use a product/service because they have a need, or because a product/service has a perceived benefit.

Two major factors of marketing are the recruitment of new customers (acquisition) and the retention and expansion of relationships with existing customers (base management).

Once a marketer has converted the prospective buyer, base management marketing takes over. The process for base management shifts the marketer to building a relationship, nurturing the links, enhancing the benefits that sold the buyer in the first place, and improving the product/service continuously to protect her business from competitive encroachments.

Marketing methods are informed by many of the social sciences, particularly psychology, sociology, and economics. Anthropology is also a small, but growing, influence. Market research underpins these activities. Through advertising, it is also related to many of the creative arts.

For a marketing plan to be successful, the mix of the four "Ps" must reflect the wants and desires of the consumers in the target market. Trying to convince a market segment to buy something they don't want is extremely expensive and seldom successful. Marketers depend on marketing research, both formal and informal, to determine what consumers want and what they are willing to pay for. Marketers hope that this process will give them a sustainable competitive advantage. Marketing management is the practical application of this process. The offer is also an important addition to the 4P's theory.

Within most organizations the activities encompassed by the marketing function are led by a Chief Marketing Officer, or an equivalent executive. Most often the CMO position reports to the Chief Executive Officer.

The big debate in the marketing discipline is whether marketing is an art or a science. Marketing is a technology or set of technologies. Marketing can be neither an art nor a science because arts and sciences only seek to explain natural phenomena. The objective of marketing is to manipulate and influence natural phenomena to create practical unnatural outcomes, specifically to manufacture, grow, sustain and defend markets. Marketers use their knowledge of economics, psychology, sociology, anthropology and strategy to arrange and control the external environment to their advantage and lock in profit. To understand what marketing is one must understand that marketing operates on three different levels.

## CORPORATE LEVEL MARKETING

Marketing at the corporate levels asks this question as 'What business should we be in and what opportunities should we pursue?' This is marketing before we even have a business, idea or product. This is what is known as entreprenuership. This level of marketing strategy is where the Ted Turners, Bill Gates' and Michael Dells of the world make market changing decisions. This level is also where corporate management of existing companies decide to branch off into new uncharted territories and opportunities.

## BUSINESS LEVEL MARKETING

Marketing at the business level asks this question as 'How are we going to compete against the competition?' When Jack Trout says that marketing is 'the war between competitors' and 'the conflict between companies' what he is really doing is defining marketing at the business level. Business level marketing deals with high level strategic marketing concerns. This level deals with long term sustainable advantages and business models.

## FUNCTIONAL LEVEL MARKETING

Marketing at the functional level (also known as the operating level) ask this question as 'How do we create and keep customers?' This level deals with marketing tactics and the '4ps' of the marketing mix. This level of marketing defines and develops products, prices them, promotes them and then distributes them in a way that helps a company create and sustain demand for their products.

In popular usage, "marketing" is the promotion of products, especially advertising and branding. However, in professional usage the term has a wider meaning which recognizes that marketing is customer centered. Products are often developed to meet the desires of groups of customers or even, in some cases, for specific customers. E. Jerome McCarthy divided marketing into four general sets of activities. His typology has become so universally recognized that his four activity sets, the Four Ps, have passed into the language.

The four Ps are:

- Product: The Product management and Product marketing aspects of marketing deal with the specifications of the actual good or service, and how it relates to the end-user's needs and wants.
- Pricing: This refers to the process of setting a price for a product, including discounts.
- Promotion: This includes advertising, sales promotion, publicity, and personal selling, and refers to the various methods of promoting the product, brand, or company.
- Placement or distribution refers to how the product gets to the customer; for example, point of sale placement or retailing. This fourth P has also sometimes been called Place, referring to the channel by which a product or service is sold (e.g. online vs. retail), which geographic region or industry, to which segment (young adults, families, business people), etc.

These four elements are often referred to as the marketing mix. A marketer can use these variables to craft a marketing plan. The four Ps model is most useful when marketing low value consumer products. Industrial products, services, high value consumer products require adjustments to this model. Services marketing must account for the unique nature of services. Industrial or B2B marketing must account for the long term contractual agreements that are typical in supply chain transactions. Relationship marketing attempts to do this by looking at marketing from a long term relationship perspective rather than individual transactions.

As a counter to this, Morgan, in Riding the Waves of Change (Jossey-Bass, 1988), adds "Perhaps the most significant criticism of the 4 Ps approach, which you should be aware of, is that it unconsciously emphasizes the inside–out view (looking from the company outwards), whereas the essence of marketing should be the outside–in approach". Even so, having made this important caveat, the 4 Ps offer a memorable and quite workable guide to the major categories of marketing activity, as well as a framework within which these can be used.

As well as the standard four Ps (Product, Pricing, Promotion and Place), services marketing calls upon an extra three, totalling seven and known together as the extended marketing mix. These are:

- People: Any person coming into contact with customers can have an impact on overall satisfaction. Whether as part of a supporting service to a product or involved in a total service, people are particularly important because, in the customer's eyes, they are generally inseparable from the total service. As a result of this, they must be appropriately trained, well motivated and the right type of person. Fellow customers are also sometimes referred to under 'people', as they too can affect the customer's service experience, (e.g., at a sporting event).
- Process: This is the process(es) involved in providing a service and the behaviour of people, which can be crucial to customer satisfaction.
- Physical evidence: Unlike a product, a service cannot be experienced before it is delivered, which makes it intangible. This, therefore, means that potential customers could perceive greater risk when deciding whether or not to use a service. To reduce the feeling of risk, thus improving the chance for success, it is often vital to offer potential customers the chance to see what a service would be like. This is done by providing physical evidence, such as case studies, or testimonials.

As well as the other 7 Packaging has been added to this list by some people. The rationale is that it is very important how the product is presented to the customer, and the packaging is often the first contact that a customer has with a product. Although some disagree because packaging is seen as a subfield of promotion.

"Philosophy" is the potential 8th P of marketing. Products (or services) should reflect the underlying philosophy or ethos of the organization. It should also be clear what the philosophy behind the introduction of the particular product is, as well. In his book, "Meeting Need", Ian Bruce explains this concept as it relates to marketing for charities. It also applies to other products and services

## RESOURCES, RELATIONSHIPS, OFFERINGS AND BUSINESS MODELS

Marketing in the past focused mainly on basic concepts like the 4 Ps, and primarily on the psychological and sociological aspects of marketing. Competitive advantage was created by directly appealing to the needs, wants and behaviours of customers, better than the competition. Successful marketing was based on who could create the better brand or the lowest price or the most hype. Marketing in the future will be based on a more strategic approach to competitive marketing success. Marketers will consciously build and allocate resources, relationships, offerings and business models that other companies find hard to match.

Companies with a greater amount of resources than their competitors will have an easier time competing in the marketplace. Resources include: financial (cash and cash reserves), physical (plant and equipment), human (knowledge and skill), legal (trademarks and patents), organizational (structure, competencies, policies), and informational (knowledge of consumers and competitors). Small companies usually have a harder time competing with larger corporations because of their disadvantage in resource allocation.

Success in business, as in life, is based on the relationships you have with people. Marketers must aggressively build relationships with consumers, customers, distributors, partners and even competitors if they want to have success in today's competitive marketplace.

Most companies sell a mix of products and/or services. Today's marketplace is often too competitive for "one-trick ponies". Companies that sell the right mix products and services can have a competitive advantage over companies that sell just one product or service.

The concept of product vs. product in competitive marketing is dying. It's slowly becoming business model vs. business model. Business model innovation can make the competition's product superiority irrelevant. Business model innovation allows a marketer to change the game instead of competing on a level playing field.

## CUSTOMER FOCUS

Most companies today have a customer orientation (also called customer focus). This implies that the company focuses its activities and products on ever changing consumer demands. Generally there are tthree ways of doing this: the customer-driven approach, the sense of identifying market changes and the product innovation approach.

In the consumer-driven approach, consumer wants are the drivers of all strategic marketing decisions. No strategy is pursued until it passes the test of consumer research. Every aspect of a market offering, including the nature of the product itself, is driven by the needs of potential consumers. The starting point is always the consumer. The rationale for this approach is that there is no point spending R&D funds developing products that people will not buy. History attests to many products that were commercial failures in spite of being technological breakthroughs.

The next big thing is a concept in marketing that refers to a product or idea that will allow for a high amount of sales for that product and related products. Marketers believe that by finding or creating the next big thing they will spark a cultural revolution that results in this sales increase.

## PRODUCT FOCUS

In a product innovation approach, the company pursues product innovation, then tries to develop a market for the product. Product innovation drives the process and marketing, research is conducted primarily to ensure that a profitable market segment(s) exists for the innovation. The rationale is that customers may not know what options will be available to them in the future so we should not expect them to tell us what they will buy in the future. However, marketers can aggressively over pursue product innovation and try to overcapitalize on a niche. When pursuing a product innovation approach, marketers must ensure that they have a varied and multi-tiered approach to product innovation. It is claimed that if Thomas Edison depended on marketing research he would have produced larger candles rather than inventing light bulbs. Many firms, such as research and development focused companies, successfully focus on product innovation. Many purists doubt whether this is really a form of marketing orientation at all, because of the ex post status of consumer research. Some even question whether it is marketing.

## OTHER ASPECTS

- An emerging area of study and practice concerns internal marketing, or how employees are trained and managed to deliver the brand in a way that positively impacts the acquisition and retention of customers (employer branding).
- Diffusion of innovations research explores how and why people adopt new products, services and ideas.
- A relatively new form of marketing uses the Internet and is called internet marketing or more generally e-marketing, affiliate marketing or online marketing. It typically tries to perfect the segmentation strategy used in traditional marketing. It targets its audience more precisely, and is sometimes called personalized marketing or one-to-one marketing.
- With consumers' eroding attention span and willingness to give time to advertising messages, marketers are turning to forms of Permission marketing such as Branded content and Reality marketing.
- The use of herd behaviour in marketing.

Some aspects of marketing, especially promotion, are treated as the subject of criticism. It is especially problematic in classical economic theory, which is based on the assumption that supply and demand are independent. However, product promotion is an attempt coming from the supply side to influence demand. In this way producer market power is attained as measured by profits that would not be realized under a free market. Then the argument follows that non-free markets are imperfect and lead to production and consumption of suboptimal amounts of the product.

Critics acknowledge that marketing has legitimate uses in connecting goods and services to the consumers who want them. Critics also point out that marketing techniques have been used to achieve morally dubious ends by businesses, governments and criminals. Critics see a systemic social evil inherent in marketing. Marketing is accused of creating ruthless exploitation of both consumers and workers by treating people as commodities whose purpose is to consume.

Most marketers believe that marketing, like any other technology, is amoral. It can be used for good or evil purposes, but the technique itself is ethically neutral.

The Observer's survey among 1'206 UK adult consumers in 2001 highlighted some of the stark changes our society has gone through in the last two decades. This raises a question on the effectiveness of the CIM's definition of marketing (anticipating, identifying and satisfying customer needs profitably), mainly in consumer marketing. There are similar concerns in industrial markets, also known as business-to-business or B2B.

Core marketing elements such as segmentation, targeting and positioning are still relevant in the modern (or post-modern) world. However, they are complex topics that need a high level of effort, intelligent thinking as well as resources to be implemented successfully. A definitive statement cannot be made whether the conventional marketing concept is applicable in today's environment. Its relevance is very much situational and depends on many factors such as the product, the segment, time, location, political and economic conditions and the inner workings of a company.

However, some scholars such as Stephen Brown challenge the marketing concept in an extreme language. Their statements, though self-contradicting and sometimes unfair, are relevant, which is why Post Modern Marketing 2 was chosen as a key reference point for this chapter.

On the one hand Brown makes positive statements about marketing, e.g. marketing is endowed with considerable personal charm and has enjoyed more than its fair share of conquests; and indeed, the increasing academic attention that is being devoted to marketing and consumption-related phenomena by non-business disciplines such as sociology, anthropology and history; far from being the second-hand rose of the scholarship, marketing is now something of a fashion leader.

On the other hand, he condemns marketing by saying "marketing has to decide whether to expose its intellectual nakedness or press itself against the searing heat of postmodernism"; and using quotes such as "mid-life crisis"; "in decline; failing; anachronistic; being abandoned; no longer appropriate; in an unprecedented state of crisis; delivered nothing of value; failure; confusion; misunderstanding; occasional inexplicable hitting of the jackpot".

This apparent love-hate relationship is proof in itself that even a sceptic Mr Brown cannot deny the contribution that marketing has made and can make to customer satisfaction and economic value. It has contributed to both customers' and suppliers' quality of life by selecting profitable customer satisfaction as its sole objective. The marketing concept, together with other business disciplines, helped the UK to make the transition from a 19th-century manufacturing economy to a modern model of success in the service industry, creating an economic growth period never seen in UK history before.

It is marketing that has helped create value through customised products, no-questions-asked refund policies, comfortable cars, environmental attention, shopkeepers' smile, and guaranteed delivery dates. Even some government departments address the public not as 'the Queen's subjects' or 'the applicants' any more but as 'customers'. Of course all of the above is done for economic or political gain, for better or worse. Despite all this achievement, to dismiss marketing as a failure is unfair.

Marketing also helps companies avoid unnecessary R&D, operational and sales costs by helping to develop products because customers want them, not for the sake of innovation. Another success is the now commonly implemented value-pricing principle, whereby a product or service is sold for the price the customer is willing to pay, not on a cost-plus basis. This way, both suppliers and customers get a fair deal.

In the context of segmentation, Brown suggests that "the traditional, linear, step-by-step marketing model of analysis, planning, implementation and control no longer seems applicable, appropriate or even pertinent to what is actually happening on the ground". If Mr. Brown had studied "the ground" before making his statement, he would have realised that companies are successful the world over precisely because they implement this model.

They segment their markets, relate their products and services to them, define their value proposition and serve their customers accordingly. Examples are GE, HSBC, PriceWaterhouseCoopers, Smiths Aerospace, BAE Systems, BOC Edwards, Weir Group and BT to name but a few. A brief visit to their websites can make this point clear.

Brown also has a constructive suggestion: "I reckon we need more passion in marketing, not less; it is time we banished banishing passion from works of marketing scholarship" (p. 256). This refers mainly to promotion, which is only one element within the marketing concept. The truth is that marketing today leads the way in segmentation, innovation, pricing, product management, distribution, and last but not least, promotion.

After all the contribution as well as further potential, to deny its successes and try to reduce it to only promotion is a great injustice to the marketing profession as well as to academic insight. Contrary to Brown's suggestion in his final paragraph, we need objectivity, rigour, quantification, models, relationships, paradigm shifts and (some application of) science.

Marketing is not full of holes, but a management process that has helped generate wealth and satisfied millions of customers for the most part of the 20th century. It can do even better in the 21st provided practitioners and scholars do not loose faith and focus. Kotler is not dead, but very much alive, and still kicking.

## ADVERTISING

Advertising is typically paid communication through a non-personal medium in which the sponsor is identified and the message is controlled. However, it can also include variations, such as publicity, public relations, personal selling, product placement, sponsorship, underwriting, and sales promotion. Major advertisers are typically corporations, but may also include schools, the military, political candidates, advocacy groups, churches, and other organizations that pay to have their message delivered to an audience. The media through which the message is delivered are varied: they include network and cable TV, radio, magazines, newspapers, the internet, billboards, handmade signs, sky writing, and bumper stickers; the list is almost endless.

Strictly speaking, word-of-mouth is not advertising because it is not paid, the message is not controlled, and it is delivered by a personal rather than non-personal medium. Ironically, word-of-mouth communications are often far more effective than advertising campaigns that may have cost many millions of dollars. "Buzz advertising" is a recent term used to describe an attempt by advertisers to simulate word-of-mouth communications.

In ancient times, commercial messages and political campaign displays have been found in the ruins of Pompeii. Egyptians used papyrus to create sales messages and wall posters, while lost-and-found advertising on papyrus was common in Greece and Rome. Wall or rock painting for commercial advertising is another manifestation of an ancient media advertising form, which is present to this day in many parts of Asia, Africa, and South America. For instance, the tradition of wall painting can be traced back to Indian rock-art paintings that goes back to 4000 BC. As printing developed in the 15th and 16th century, advertising expanded to include handbills. In the 17th century advertisements started to appear in weekly newspapers in England.

These early print ads were used mainly to promote books,and newspapers which became increasingly affordable thanks to the printing press, and medicines, which were increasingly sought after as disease ravaged Europe. However, false advertising and so-called "quack" ads became a problem, which ushered in regulation of advertising content.

As the economy was expanding during the 19th century, the need for advertising grew at the same pace. In the United States, classified ads became popular, filling pages of newspapers with small print messages promoting all kinds of goods. The success of this advertising format led to the growth of mail-order advertising such as the Sears Catalog, at one time referred to as the "Farmer's Bible". In 1843 the first advertising agency was established by Volney Palmer in Philadelphia. At first the agencies were just brokers for ad space in newspapers, but it wasn't until N.W. Ayer & Son came along, advertising agencies started to take over responsibility for the content as well. N.W. Ayer and Son was the first full service Ad Agency. They were also the first agency to start to charge commission on ads.

When commercial radio stations began broadcasting in the early 1920's, the programmes were aired without advertising. Many radio stations were established by radio equipment manufacturers and retailers. Programming was provided to sell radio transmitters and receivers.

The radio station owners soon realized they could earn more money by selling sponsorship rights to other businesses. In those days, each show was usually sponsored by a single business, in exchange for a brief mention of the sponsor at the beginning and end of the show. This practice was carried over to televsion in the late 1940's and early 1950's.

In the early 1950's, the Dumont television network began the modern trend of selling advertisement time to multiple sponsors. Dumont had trouble finding sponsors for many of their programmes and compensated by selling smaller blocks of advertising time to several businesses. This eventually became the norm for the commercial television industry in the United States.

The 1960s saw advertising transform into a modern, more scientific approach in which creativity was allowed to shine, producing unexpected messages that made advertisements more tempting to consumers' eyes. The Volkswagen ad campaign featuring such headlines as "Think Small" and "Lemon" ushered in the era of modern advertising by promoting a "position" or "unique selling proposition" designed to associate each brand with a specific idea in the reader or viewer's mind.

The late 1980s and early 1990s saw the introduction of cable television and particularly MTV. Pioneering the concept of the music video, MTV ushered in a new type of advertising: the consumer tunes in for the advertisement, rather than it being a byproduct or afterthought. As cable (and later satellite) television became increasingly prevalent, "specialty" channels began to emerge, and eventually entire channels, such as QVC and Home Shopping Network and ShopTV, devoted to advertising merchandise, where again the consumer tuned in for the ads.

Marketing through the Internet opened new frontiers for advertisers and led to the "dot-com" boom of the 1990s. Entire corporations operated solely on advertising revenue, offering everything from coupons to free Internet access. At the turn of the 21st century, the search engine Google revolutionized online advertising by emphasizing contextually relevant, unobtrusive ads intended to help, rather than inundate, users. This has led to a plethora of similar efforts and an increasing trend of interactive advertising.

The share of advertising spending relative to total economic output (GDP) has changed little across large changes in media. For example, in the U.S. in 1925, the main advertising media were newspapers, magazines, signs on streetcars, and outdoor posters. Advertising spending as a share of U.S. GDP was about 2.6% in 1925. By 1998, television and radio had become major advertising media. Nonetheless, advertising spending as a share of GDP was slightly lower — about 2.4%.

A recent advertising innovation is "guerrilla promotions", which involve unusual approaches such as staged encounters in public places, giveaways of products such as cars that are covered with brand messages, and interactive advertising where the viewer can respond to become part of the advertising message. This reflects an increasing trend of interactive and "embedded" ads, such as via product placement, having consumers vote through text messages, and various innovations utilizing social networking sites (e.g. Myspace).

## PRODUCT ADVERTISING

Certain products use a specific form of advertising known as "Custom publishing". This form of advertising is usually targeted at a specific segment of society, but may also "draw" the attention of others.

The same advertising techniques used to promote commercial goods and services can be used to inform, educate and motivate the public about non-commercial issues, such as AIDS, political ideology, energy conservation, religious recruitment, and deforestation.

Advertising, in its non-commercial guise, is a powerful educational tool capable of reaching and motivating large audiences. "Advertising justifies its existence when used in the public interest - it is much too powerful a tool to use solely for commercial purposes." - Attributed to Howard Gossage by David Ogilvy

Public service advertising, non-commercial advertising, public interest advertising, cause marketing, and social marketing are different terms for (or aspects of) the use of sophisticated advertising and marketing communications techniques (generally associated with commercial enterprise) on behalf of non-commercial, public interest issues and initiatives.

In the United States, the granting of television and radio licenses by the FCC is contingent upon the station broadcasting a certain amount of public service advertising. To meet these requirements, many broadcast stations in America air the bulk of their required Public Service Announcements during the late night or early morning when the smallest percentage of viewers are watching, leaving more day and prime time commercial slots available for high-paying advertisers.

Public service advertising reached its height during World Wars I and II under the direction of several governments. Commercial advertising media can include wall paintings, billboards, street furniture components, printed flyers, radio, cinema and television ads, web banners, web popups, skywriting, bus stop benches, magazines, newspapers, town criers, sides of buses, taxicab doors and roof mounts, musical stage shows, subway platforms and trains, elastic bands on disposable diapers, stickers on apples in supermarkets, the opening section of streaming audio and video, posters, chicken niblets, and the backs of event tickets and supermarket receipts. Any place an "identified" sponsor pays to deliver their message through a medium is advertising.

Covert advertising embedded in other entertainment media is known as product placement. A more recent version of this is advertising in film, by having a main character use an item or other of a definite brand - an example is in the movie Minority Report, where Tom Cruise's character Tom Anderton owns a computer with the Nokia logo clearly written in the top corner, or his watch engraved with the Bulgari logo.

Another example of advertising in film is in I, Robot, where main character played by Will Smith mentions his Converse shoes several times, calling them "classics," because the film is set far in the future. Cadillac chose to advertise in the movie The Matrix Reloaded, which as a result contained many scenes in which Cadillac cars were used. Similarly, product placement for Omega Watches, BMW and Aston-Martin cars are featured in recent James Bond films, most notably, Casino Royale.

The TV commercial is generally considered the most effective mass-market advertising format and this is reflected by the high prices TV networks charge for commercial airtime during popular TV events. The annual Super Bowl football game in the United States is known as much for its commercial advertisements as for the game itself, and the average cost of a single thirty-second TV spot during this game has reached $2.5 million (as of 2006).

Virtual advertisements may be inserted into regular television programming through computer graphics. It is typically inserted into otherwise blank backdrops or used to replace local billboards that are not relevant to the remote broadcast audience. More controversially, virtual billboards may be inserted into the background where none existing in real-life. Virtual product placement is also possible. Increasingly, other mediums such as those discussed below are overtaking television due to a shift towards consumer's usage of the Internet as well as devices such as TiVo.

Advertising on the World Wide Web is a recent phenomenon. Prices of Web-based advertising space are dependent on the "relevance" of the surrounding web content and the traffic that the website receives.

E-mail advertising is another recent phenomenon. Unsolicited bulk E-mail advertising is known as "spam".

Some companies have proposed to place messages or corporate logos on the side of booster rockets and the International Space Station. Controversy exists on the effectiveness of subliminal advertising (see mind control), and the pervasiveness of mass messages.

Unpaid advertising (also called word of mouth advertising), can provide good exposure at minimal cost. Personal recommendations ("bring a friend", "sell it"), spreading buzz, or achieving the feat of equating a brand with a common noun ("Xerox" = "photocopier", "Kleenex" = tissue, and "Vaseline" = petroleum jelly) — these are the pinnacles of any advertising campaign. However, some companies oppose the use of their brand name to label an object.

The most common method for measuring the impact of mass media advertising is the use of the rating point (rp) or the more accurate target rating point (trp). These two measures refer to the percentage of the universe of the existing base of audience members that can be reached by the use of each media outlet in a particular moment in time. The difference between the two is that the rating point refers to the percentage to the entire universe while the target rating point refers to the percentage to a particular segment or target. This becomes very useful when focusing advertising efforts on a particular group of people.

- For example, think of an advertising campaign targeting a female audience aged 25 to 45. While the overall rating of a TV show might be well over 10 rating points it might very well happen that the same show in the same moment of time is generating only 2.5 trps (being the target: women 25-45). This would mean that while the show has a large universe of viewers it is not necessarily reaching a large universe of women in the ages of 25 to 45 making it a less desirable location to place an ad for an advertiser looking for this particular demographic. Conversely, a TV show with a low overall rating point may be more successful at selling ads when its target rating points are high. In the United States, networks like the WB and FOX have had success with shows based on this premise; the shows had low overall ratings points, but delivered strong target rating points in the desired demographic.

## ADVERTISEMENT IMPACT

The impact of advertising has been a matter of considerable debate and many different claims have been made in different contexts. During debates about the banning of cigarette advertising, a common claim from cigarette manufacturers was that cigarette advertising does not encourage people to smoke who would not otherwise. The (eventually successful) opponents of advertising, on the other hand, claim that advertising does in fact increase consumption.

According to many media sources, the past experience and state of mind of the person subjected to advertising may determine the impact that advertising has. Children under the age of four may be unable to distinguish advertising from other television programmes, whilst the ability to determine the truthfulness of the message may not be developed until the age of 8.

As advertising and marketing efforts become increasingly ubiquitous in modern Western societies, the industry has come under criticism of groups such as AdBusters via culture jamming which criticizes the media and consumerism using advertising's own techniques. The industry is accused of being one of the engines powering a convoluted economic mass production system which promotes consumption. Recognizing the social impact of advertising, Mediawatch-uk, a British special interest group, works to educate consumers about how they can register their concerns with advertisers and regulators. It has developed educational materials for use in schools. The award-winning book, Made You Look How Advertising Works and Why You Should Know, by former Mediawatch (a feminist organisation founded by Ann Simonton not linked to mediawatch-uk) president Shari Graydon, provides context for these issues for young readers.

Public interest groups are increasingly suggesting that access to the mental space targeted by advertisers should be taxed, in that at the present moment that space is being freely taken advantage of by advertisers with no compensation paid to the members of the public who are thus being intruded upon. This kind of tax would be a Pigovian tax in that it would act to reduce what is now increasingly seen as a public nuisance. Efforts to that end are gathering momentum, with Arkansas and Maine considering bills to implement such taxation. Florida enacted such a tax in 1987 but was forced to repeal it after six months, as a result of a concerted effort by national commercial interests, which withdrew planned conventions, causing major losses to the tourism industry, and cancelled advertising, causing a loss of 12 million dollars to the broadcast industry alone.

An extensively documented effect is the control and vetoing of free information by the advertisers. Any negative information on a company or its products or operations often results in pressures from the company to withdraw such information lines, threatening to cut their ads. This behaviour makes the editors of the media self-censor content that might upset their ad payers. The bigger both companies are, the bigger their relation gets, maximizing control over a single information.

Advertisers may try to minimize information about or from consumer groups, or consumer controlled purchasing initiatives (as joint purchase systems), or consumer controlled quality information systems.

Another indirect effect of advertising is to modify the very nature of the communication media where it is shown. Media that get most of their revenues from publicity try to make their medium a good place for communicating ads before anything else. The most clear example is television, where this means trying to make the public stay for a long time and in a mental state that encourages spectators not to switch the channel through the ads. Programmes that are low in mental stimulus and require light concentration and are varied are best for long sitting times. These make for much easier emotional jumps to ads, which can become more entertaining than regular shows. A simple way to understand the objectives in television programming is to compare contents from channels paid and chosen by the viewer with channels that get their income mainly from advertisements.

There have been increasing efforts to protect the public interest by regulating the content and the reach of advertising. Some examples are the ban on television tobacco advertising imposed in many countries, and the total ban on advertising to children under twelve imposed by the Swedish government in 1991. Though that regulation continues in effect for broadcasts originating within the country, it has been weakened by the European Court of Justice, which has found that Sweden was obliged to accept whatever programming was targeted at it from neighbouring countries or via satellite.

In Europe and elsewhere there is a vigorous debate on whether and how much advertising to children should be regulated. This debate was exacerbated by a report released by the Kaiser Family Foundation in February 2004 which suggested that food advertising targeting children was an important factor in the epidemic of childhood obesity in the United States.

In many countries - namely New Zealand, South Africa, Canada, and many European countries - the advertising industry operates a system of self-regulation. Advertisers, advertising agencies and the media agree on a code of advertising standards that they attempt to uphold. The general aim of such codes is to ensure that any advertising is 'legal, decent, honest and truthful'. Some self-regulatory organizations are funded by the industry, but remain independent, with the intent of upholding the standards or codes (like the Advertising Standards Authority in the UK).

Naturally, many advertisers view governmental regulation or even self-regulation as intrusion of their freedom of speech or a necessary evil. Therefore, they employ a wide-variety of linguistic devices to bypass regulatory laws (e.g. giving English words in bold and French translations in fine print to deal with the Article 12 of the 1994 Toubon Law limiting the use of English in French advertising); see Bhatia and Ritchie 2006:542. The advertising of controversial products such as cigarettes and condoms is subject to government regulation in many countries. For instance, the tobacco industry is required by law in India and Pakistan to display warnings cautioning consumers about the health hazards of their products. Linguistic variation is often used by advertising as a creative device to reduce the impact of such requirement.

With the dawn of the Internet have come many new advertising opportunities. Popup, Flash, banner, advergaming, and email advertisements (the last often being a form of spam) abound.

Each year, greater sums are paid to obtain a commercial spot during the Super Bowl, which is by most measures considered to be the most important football game of the year. Companies attempt to make these commercials sufficiently entertaining that members of the public will actually want to watch them.

Another problem is people recording shows on DVRs (ex. TiVo). These devices allow users to record the programmes for later viewing enabling them to fast forward through commercials. Additionally, as more seasons or "Boxed Sets" come out of Television shows; fewer people are watching their shows on TV. However, the fact that these sets are sold, means that the company will additionally receive profits from the sales of these sets. To counter this effect, many advertisers have opted for product placement on TV shows like Survivor.

Particularly since the rise of "entertaining" advertising, some people may like an advert enough that they wish to watch it later or show a friend. In general, the advertising community has not yet made this easy, although some have used the Internet to widely distribute their adverts to anyone wishing to see or hear them.

Another significant trend to note for the future of advertising is the growing importance of niche or targeted ads. Also brought about by the Internet and the theory of The Long Tail, advertisers will have an increasing ability to reach narrow audiences. In the past, the most efficient way to deliver a message was to blanket the largest mass market audience possible. However, usage tracking, customer profiles and the growing popularity of niche content brought about by everything from blogs to social networking sites, provides advertisers with audiences that are smaller but much better defined, leading to ads that are more relevant to viewers and more effective for companies marketing products. Among others, Comcast Spotlight is one such advertiser employing this method in their video on demand menus. These advertisements are targeted to a specific group and can be viewed by anyone wishing to find out more about a particular business or practice at any time, right from their home. This causes the viewer to become proactive and actually choose what advertisements they want to view.

## ADVERTISING CAMPAIGN

An advertising campaign is a series of advertisement messages that share a single idea and theme which make up an integrated marketing communication (IMC). Advertising campaigns appear in different media across a specific time frame.

The critical part of making an advertising campaign is determining a campaign theme, as it sets the tone for the individual advertisements and other forms of marketing communications that will be used. The campaign theme is the central message that will be communicated in the promotional activities. The campaign themes are usually developed with the intention of being used for a substantial period but many of them are short lived due to factors such as being ineffective or market conditions and/or competition in the marketplace.

## COMMUNICATION DESIGN

Communication design is a sub-discipline of design which is concerned with how media intermission such as printed, crafted, electronic media or presentations communicate with people. A communication design approach is more concerned with messages communicated than aesthetics in media. The distinction between communication design and other applied arts is in the motivation: while the communication design process does involve a certain amount of self-expression and creativity, the goals are often those of the commissioning body rather than the artist's, and the parameters set by the commissioning body are often more constraining.

The term communication design is often used interchangeably with visual communication and more specifically graphic design, but has an alternate broader meaning that includes auditory communications as well as visual. Examples of Communication Design include information architecture, editing, typography, illustration and professional writing skills applied to creative industries.

## ENVIRONMENTAL SCANNING

For a company to gain or maintain a sustainable competitive advantage, it must be ever vigilant, watching for changes in the business environment. It must also be agile enough to alter its strategies and plans when the need arises.

There are three ways of scanning the business environment:

- Ad-hoc scanning - Short term, infrequent examinations usually initiated by a crisis
- Regular scanning - Studies done on a regular schedule (say, once a year)
- Continuous scanning - (also called continuous learning) - continuous structured data collection and processing on a broad range of environmental factors

Most commentators feel that in today's turbulent business environment the best scanning method available is continuous scanning. This allows the firm to act quickly, take advantage of opportunities before competitors do, and respond to environmental threats before significant damage is done.

Environmental scanning usually refers just to the macroenvironment, but it can also include industry and competitor analysis, consumer analysis, product innovations, and the company's internal environment. Macroenvironmental scanning involves analysing:

- The Economy
  - GNP or GDP per capital
  - GNP or GDP growth
  - Unemployment rate
  - Inflation rate
  - Consumer and investor confidence
  - Inventory levels
  - Currency exchange rates
  - Merchandise trade balance
  - Financial and political health of trading partners
  - Balance of payments
  - Future trends
- Government
  - Political climate - amount of government activity
  - Political stability and risk
  - Government debt
  - Budget deficit or surplus
  - Corporate and personal tax rates
  - Payroll taxes
  - Import tariffs and quotas
  - Export restrictions
  - Restrictions on international financial flows
- Legal
  - Minimum wage laws
  - Environmental protection laws
  - Worker safety laws
  - Union laws
  - Copyright and patent laws
  - Anti- monopoly laws
  - Sunday closing laws
  - Municipal licences
  - Laws that favour business investment
- Technology
  - Efficiency of infrastructure, including: roads, ports, airports, rolling stock, hospitals, education,

healthcare, communication, etc.
  - Industrial productivity
  - New manufacturing processes
  - New products and services of competitors
  - New products and services of supply chain partners
  - Any new technology that could impact the company
  - Cost and accessibility of electrical power
- Ecology
  - Ecological concerns that affect the firms production processes
  - Ecological concerns that affect customers' buying habits
  - Ecological concerns that affect customers' perception of the company or product
- Socio-Cultural
  - Demographic factors such as:
    - Population size and distribution
    - Age distribution
    - Education levels
    - Income levels
    - Ethnic origins
    - Religious affiliations
  - Attitudes towards:
    - Materialism, capitalism, free enterprise
    - Individualism, role of family, role of government, collectivism
    - Role of church and religion
    - Consumerism
    - Environmentalism
    - Importance of work, pride of accomplishment
  - Cultural structures including:
    - Diet and nutrition
    - Housing conditions

- Potential Suppliers
  - Labour supply
    - Quantity of labour available
    - Quality of labour available
    - Stability of labour supply
    - Wage expectations
    - Employee turn-over rate
    - Strikes and labour relations
    - Educational facilities
  - Material suppliers
    - Quality, quantity, price, and stability of material inputs
    - Delivery delays
    - Proximity of bulky or heavy material inputs
    - Level of competition among suppliers
  - Service Providers
    - Quantity, quality, price, and stability of service facilitators
    - Special requirements

Scanning these macroenvironmental variables for threats and opportunities requires that each issue be rated on two dimensions. It must be rated on its potential impact on the company, and rated on its likeliness of occurrence. Multiplying the potential impact parameter by the likeliness of occurrence parameter gives us a good indication of its importance to the firm.

## SUSTAINABLE COMPETITIVE ADVANTAGE

Competitive advantage (CA) is a position that a firm occupies in its competitive landscape. Michael Porter posits that a competitive advantage, sustainable or not, exists when a company makes economic rents, that is, their earnings exceed their costs, especially including cost of capital. That means that normal competitive pressures are not able to drive down the firm's earnings to the point where they cover all costs and just provide minimum sufficient additional return to keep capital invested. Most forms of competitive advantage cannot be sustained for any length of time because the promise of economic rents drives competitiors to duplicate the competitive advantage held by any one firm.

A firm possesses a Sustainable Competitive Advantage when it has value-creating processes and positions that cannot be duplicated or imitated by other firms that lead to the production of above normal rents. An SCA is different from a competitive advantage (CA) in that it provides a long-term advantage that is not easily replicated. But these above-normal rents can attract new entrants who drive down economic rents. A CA is a position a firm attains that lead to above-normal rents or a superior financial performance. The processes and positions that engender such a position is not necessarily non-duplicable or inimitable. It is possible for some companies to make profits for a time above the cost of capital without sustainable competitive advantage.

A key difference between CA and SCA is that the processes and positions a firm may hold are non-duplicable and inimitable when a firm possesses a SCA. Hence a sustainable competitive advantage is one that can be maintained for a significant amount of time even in the presence of competition. This brings us to the question what is a "significant amount of time". A CA becomes SCA when all duplication and imitation efforts have ceased and the rival firms have not been able to create the same value that the said firm is creating.

Analysis of the factors of profitability is the subject of numerous theories of strategy including the five forces model pioneered by Michael Porter of the Harvard Business School.

In marketing and strategic management, sustainable competitive advantage is an advantage that one firm has relative to competing firms. The source of the advantage can be something the company does that is distinctive and difficult to replicate, also known as a core competency — for example Procter & Gamble's ability to derive superior consumer insights and implement them in managing its brand portfolio.

It can also be an asset such as a brand (e.g. Coca Cola) or a patent, such as Viagra. It can also simply be a result of the industry's cost structure – for example, the large fixed costs that tend to create natural monopolies in utility industries. To be sustainable, the advantage must be:

1. Distinctive, and
2. Proprietary

## BUILDING SUSTAINABLE COMPETITIVE ADVANTAGE

There are basically three types of assets that help build an SCA. These categories are exhaustive and include all of the company's SCAs:

1. Organization and managerial process
   - Coordination and integration: Coordination among teams in organization is key to organizational success. Interdepartmental coordination and resource sharing to reach a common goal is fundamental to creating "value". Integrating resources is key to the success of firms. Firms that are able to integrate resources see synergistic effects of resources coming together.
   - Learning: Organizational learning is key to the success of a firm. It determines how a firm collects, distributes, interprets and responds to market based information collection and changes in the environment. These changes in the environment could be customer based changes, technological developments, legal and government restrictions. Firms have to develop robust market sensing and spanning capabilities to effectively collect information. Once they collect info they have embed this knowledge in the products they produce.
   - Reconfiguring and transformation: The environment for firms is constantly changing and constant reconfiguring and transformation is key

to forming SCA. A double loop learning and transformation is key to producing innovative products. Innovative capacity of a firm determines how it reacts and learns from market information.

2. Positions: market positions are the assets of a company. Most of them are self-explanatory:
   - Technological assets
   - Financial assets
   - Reputational assets
   - Structural assets: The structure of a company can determine how it performs. The hierarchy of a company can influence its culture, procedure and routines.
3. Paths:
   - Path dependencies: At the birth of a company usually accompanied with certain orientations. The progenitor brings certain orientations and attributes that stay with the company for a long time. The path the company takes then determines the development of its competencies.
   - Technological opportunities: technology development at a time can determine how a firm can exploit opportunities to form SCA. Very often we see the advent of several technological factors converging into a capability that forms a SCA. An example would be the rise of companies such as Genentech at the turn of the previous century with the advent of gene mapping, significant developments in target selection and databases of previous studies and gene pools.

## STRATEGIC MANAGEMENT

Strategic management is that set of managerial decisions and actions that determines the long-run performance of a corporation. It includes environmental scanning, strategy formulation, strategy implementation and evaluation and control.

An organization's strategy must be appropriate for its resources, environmental circumstances, and core objectives. The process involves matching the company's [internal resources (eg IT) and capabilities (eg quality management)] to the external business environment the organization faces. Strategy formulation involves:

- Doing a situation analysis: both internal and external; both micro-environmental and macro-environmental.
- Concurrent with this assessment, objectives are set. This involves crafting vision statements (long term view of a possible future), mission statements (the role that the organization gives itself in society), overall corporate objectives (both financial and strategic), strategic business unit objectives (both financial and strategic), and tactical objectives.
- These objectives should, in the light of the situation analysis, sugsgest a strategic plan. The plan provides the details of how to achieve these objectives.

This three-step strategy formulation process is sometimes referred to as determining where you are now, determining where you want to go, and then determining how to get there. These three questions are the essence of strategic planning. SWOT Analysis: I/O Economics for the external factors and RBV for the internal factors.

Strategy Implementation involves:

- Allocation of sufficient resources (financial, personnel, time, technology support)
- Establishing a chain of command or some alternative structure (such as cross functional teams)
- Assigning responsibility of specific tasks or processes to specific individuals or groups
- It also involves managing the process. This includes monitoring results, comparing to benchmarks and best practices, evaluating the efficacy and efficiency of the process, controlling for variances, and making adjustments to the process as necessary.

- When implementing specific programmes, this involves acquiring the requisite resources, developing the process, training, process testing, documentation, and integration with (and/or conversion from) legacy processes.

Strategy formulation and implementation is an on-going, never-ending, integrated process requiring continuous reassessment and reformation. Strategic management is dynamic; see Strategy dynamics. It involves a complex pattern of actions and reactions. It is partially planned and partially unplanned. Strategy is both planned and emergent, dynamic, and interactive. Some people (such as Andy Grove at Intel) feel that there are critical points at which a strategy must take a new direction in order to be in step with a changing business environment. These critical points of change are called strategic inflection points.

## TIME SCALES

Strategic management operates on several time scales. Short term strategies involve planning and managing for the present. Long term strategies involve preparing for and preempting the future. Marketing strategist Derek Abell (1993), has suggested that understanding this dual nature of strategic management is the least understood part of the process. He claims that balancing the temporal aspects of strategic planning require's the use of dual strategies simultaneously.

Strategic Management is actually a solid foundation or a framework within which all the functionning managerial operations are bundled together. This is the highest level corporate activity that sets the terms and goals for a company that it should follow for prosperity.

In general terms, there are two main approaches to strategic management which are opposite but complement each other in some ways:

- 'The Industrial Organization Approach'
  - Based on economic theory – deals with issues like competitive rivalry, resource allocation, economies of scale

  - Assumptions – rationality, self discipline behaviour, profit maximization
- The Sociological Approach
  - Deals primarily with human interactions
  - Assumptions – bounded rationality, satisficing behaviour, profit sub-optimality. An example of a company that currently operates this way is Google

Strategic management techniques can be viewed as bottom-up, top-down, or collaborative processes. In the bottom-up approach, employees submit proposals to their managers who, in turn, funnel the best ideas further up the organization. This is often accomplished by a capital budgeting process. Proposals are assessed using financial criteria such as return on investment or cost-benefit analysis. The proposals that are approved form the substance of a new strategy, all of which is done without a grand strategic design or a strategic architect. The top-down approach is the most common by far. In it, the CEO, possibly with the assistance of a strategic planning team, decides on the overall direction the company should take. Some organizations are starting to experiment with collaborative strategic planning techniques that recognize the emergent nature of strategic decisions.

In most (large) corporations there are several levels of strategy. Strategic management is the highest in the sense that it is the broadest, applying to all parts of the firm. It gives direction to corporate values, corporate culture, corporate goals, and corporate missions. Under this broad corporate strategy there are often functional or business unit strategies.

Functional strategies include marketing strategies, new product development strategies, human resource strategies, financial strategies, legal strategies, and information technology management strategies. The emphasis is on short and medium term plans and is limited to the domain of each department's functional responsibility. Each functional department attempts to do its part in meeting overall corporate objectives, and hence to some extent their strategies are derived from broader corporate strategies.

Many companies feel that a functional organizational structure is not an efficient way to organize activities so they have reengineered according to processes or strategic business units (called SBUs). A strategic business unit is a semi-autonomous unit within an organization. It is usually responsible for its own budgeting, new product decisions, hiring decisions, and price setting. An SBU is treated as an internal profit centre by corporate headquarters. Each SBU is responsible for developing its business strategies, strategies that must be in tune with broader corporate strategies.

The "lowest" level of strategy is operational strategy. It is very narrow in focus and deals with day-to-day operational activities such as scheduling criteria. It must operate within a budget but is not at liberty to adjust or create that budget. Operational level strategy was encouraged by Peter Drucker in his theory of management by objectives (MBO). Operational level strategies are informed by business level strategies which, in turn, are informed by corporate level strategies. Business strategy, which refers to the aggregated operational strategies of single business firm or that of an SBU in a diversified corporation refers to the way in which a firm competes in its chosen arenas.

Corporate strategy, then, refers to the overarching strategy of the diversified firm. Such corporate strategy answers the questions of "in which businesses should we compete?" and "how does being in one business add to the competitive advantage of another portfolio firm, as well as the competitive advantage of the corporation as a whole?"

Since the turn of the millennium, there has been a tendency in some firms to revert to a simpler strategic structure. This is being driven by information technology. It is felt that knowledge management systems should be used to share information and create common goals. Strategic divisions are thought to hamper this process. Most recently, this notion of strategy has been captured under the rubric of dynamic strategy, popularized by the strategic management textbook authored by Carpenter and Sanders. This work builds on that of Brown and Eisenhart as well as Christensen and portrays firm strategy, both business and corporate, as necessarily embracing ongoing strategic change, and the seamless integration of strategy formulation and implementation. Such change and implementation are usually built into the strategy through the staging and pacing facets.

**Why Strategic Plans Fails**

There are many reasons why strategic plans fail, especially:

- Failure to understand the customer
  - Why do they buy
  - Is there a real need for the product
  - Inadequate or incorrect marketing research
- Inability to predict environmental reaction
  - What will competitors do
    - Fighting brands
    - Price wars
  - Will government intervene
- Over-estimation of resource competence
  - Can the staff, equipment, and processes handle the new strategy
  - Failure to develop new employee and management skills
- Failure to coordinate
  - Reporting and control relationships not adequate
  - Organizational structure not flexible enough
- Failure to obtain senior management commitment
  - Failure to get management involved right from the start
  - Failure to obtain sufficient company resources to accomplish task
- Failure to obtain employee commitment
  - New strategy not well explained to employees
  - No incentives given to workers to embrace the new strategy

- Under-estimation of time requirements
  - No critical path analysis done
- Failure to follow the plan
  - No follow through after initial planning
  - No tracking of progress against plan
  - No consequences for above
- Failure to manage change
  - Inadequate understanding of the internal resistance to change
  - Lack of vision on the relationships between processes, technology and organization
- Poor communications
  - Insufficient information sharing among stakeholders
  - Exclusion of stakeholders and delegates
- Failure to focus
  - Inability or unwillingness to make choices which are true to the strategic mission (i.e. to do fewer things, better), leads to mediocrity, inability to compete

Although a sense of direction is important, it can also stifle creativity, especially if it is rigidly enforced. In an uncertain and ambiguous world, fluidity can be more important than a finely tuned strategic compass. When a strategy becomes internalized into a corporate culture, it can lead to group think. It can also cause an organization to define itself too narrowly. An example of this is marketing myopia.

Most theories of strategic management seem to have a lifespan less than that of the popularity of the latest teen music idol. Many critics claim that this is because most of them generally do not work. Keep in mind that this article describes only the 50 or so most successful theories, thus exhibiting survivorship bias (ironically, itself an area of research in strategic management). For every theory that gets incorporated into strategic management textbooks there are many that are quickly forgotten. Many theories tend either to be too narrow in focus to build a complete corporate strategy on, or too general and abstract to be applicable to specific situations. The low success rate is further fueled by the management lecture circuit in which hundreds of self-appointed gurus, many without serious academic credentials or substantial expertise, attempt to sell books and explain their "revolutionary" and "groundbreaking" theories to audiences of business executives for a sizable fee. While there are undoubtedly inspirational ideas contained in these seminars, the theories expounded therein have not, for the most part, been subjected to serious study.

Some critics take the opposite approach claiming effectively that there are not enough theories, and when they arrive they are too late to help managers make any important decisions. These commentators remind us that the basic, everyday purpose of strategic management is to match a company's strategy with the business environment that the organization is in. Because the environment is constantly changing, effective strategic management requires a continuous flow of new theories suitable for the new circumstances. The problem with most theories is that they solve yesterday's problems, similar to a business Maginot Line. Various approaches to solve this problem have emerged, however, including Mintzberg's ideas of 'emergent strategies' and use of ideas from complexity theory in what is often called complexity strategy.

Gary Hamel coined the term strategic convergence to explain the limited scope of the strategies being used by rivals in greatly differing circumstances. He lamented that strategies converge more than they should, because the more successful ones get imitated by firms that do not understand that the strategic process involves designing a custom strategy for the specifics of each situation.

## Chapter 4

# Management Theories

A business philosophy or popular management theory is any of a range of approaches to accounting, marketing, public relations, operations, training, labour relations, executive time management, investment, and/or corporate governance claimed (by their proponents, and sometimes only by their proponents and selected clients) to improve business performance in some measurable or otherwise provable way.

These management theories often have their own vocabulary (jargon). They sometimes depend on the business insights of a single guru. They rarely have the sophistication or internal consistency to qualify as a school of philosophy in the conventional sense - some (branded "biz-cults") resemble a cult religion. They tend to have in common high-cost consulting fees to consult with the "business gurus" who have created the "philosophy". Only rarely do such schools transmit to any trusted students the capacity to teach others - one of the key requirements of any legitimate non-esoteric school of thought or academic discipline.

Most of these theories tend to experience a limited period of popularity (about 5 to 10 years). Then they disappear from the popular consciousness. Occasionally one has lasting value and gets incorporated into textbooks and into academic management thought. For every theory that gets incorporated into strategic management textbooks about a hundred remain forgotten. Many theories tend either to have too narrow a focus to build a complete corporate strategy on, or appear too general and abstract for applicability to specific situations. The management-talk circuit fuels the low success rate: in that circuit hundreds of self-appointed gurus queue in turn to sell their books and to explain their "revolutionary" and "groundbreaking" theories to audiences of business executives for phenomenal fees.

Note too, however, that management theories often undergo testing in the real world. Disciples apply or attempt to apply such theories, and find them sometimes consistently applicable over time, sometimes merely an "idea du jour". The relevant and valuable principles become recognized, and in this way may get incorporated into academic management thought.

Accountancy (profession) or accounting (methodology) is the measurement, disclosure or provision of assurance about financial information that helps managers, investors, tax authorities and other decision makers make resource allocation decisions. The names come from the use of financial accounts. Financial accounting is one branch of accounting and historically has involved processes by which financial information about a business is recorded, classified, summarized, interpreted, and communicated. Accounting is also widely referred to as the "language of business".

Auditing, a related but separate discipline, has two sub-disciplines: Internal and External auditing. External auditing is the process whereby an independent auditor examines an organization's financial statements and accounting records in order to express an opinion — that conveys reasonable but not absolute assurance — as to the truth and fairness of the statements and the accountant's adherence to Generally Accepted Accounting Principles (GAAP), in all material respects.

Internal auditing is an examination in which management, and not the external public, is the main beneficiary. It is carried out usually by auditors employed by the company, but sometimes by external service providers. The internal auditor's role is broader, and basically depends on what kind of assurance management wants. It usually certifies the efficiency and effectiveness of processes, departments, projects or internal controls. The Institute of Internal Auditors is generally accepted as the custodian of Internal Auditing best practice.

At the heart of accounting is the measurement of financial transactions which are transfers of legal property rights made under contractual relationships. Non-financial transactions are specifically excluded due to conservatism and materiality principles.

Practitioners of accountancy are known as accountants. There are many professional bodies for accountants throughout the world. Many allow their members to use titles indicating their membership. Examples are Chartered Certified Accountant (ACCA or FCCA), Chartered Accountant (FCA, CA or ACA) and Certified Public Accountant (CPA).

Accountancy attempts to create accurate financial reports that are useful to managers, regulators, and other stakeholders such as shareholders, creditors, or owners. The day-to-day record-keeping involved in this process is known as bookkeeping.

At the heart of modern financial accounting is the double-entry bookkeeping system. This system involves making at least two entries for every transaction: a debit in one account, and a corresponding credit in another account. The sum of all debits should always equal the sum of all credits. This provides an easy way to check for errors. This system was first used in medieval Europe, although claims have been made that the system dates back to Ancient Greece.

According to critics of standard accounting practices, it has changed little since. Accounting reform measures of some kind have been taken in each generation to attempt to keep bookkeeping relevant to capital assets or production capacity. However, these have not changed the basic principles, which are supposed to be independent of economics as such. In recent times, the divergence of accounting from economic principles has resulted in controversial reforms to make financial reports more indicative of economic reality.

## OPERATIONS MANAGEMENT

Operations management is an area of business that is concerned with the production of goods and services, and involves the responsibility of ensuring that business operations are efficient and effective. It is also the management of resources and the distribution of goods and services to customers.

Operations also refers to the production of goods and services, the set of value-added activities that transform inputs into many outputs. Fundamentally, these value-adding creative activities should be aligned with market opportunity for optimal enterprise performance.

Historically, the body of knowledge stemming from industrial engineering formed the basis of the first MBA programmes, and is central to operations management as used across diverse business sectors, industry, consulting and non-profit organizations.

## ORGANIZATIONS

A number of professional organizations have been formed to promote operations management profession.

Institute for Operations Research and Management Sciences has a subdivision called The Manufacturing and Service Operations Management Society. This division has the following objective: The Manufacturing and Service Operations Management Society promotes the enhancement and dissemination of knowledge, and the efficiency of industrial practice, related to the operations function in manufacturing and service enterprises.

Another organization, Production and Operations Management Society, is an international professional organization representing the interests of POM professionals from around the world.

A third organization, The Association for Operations Management (APICS - the acronym comes from the original name: American Production and Inventory Control Society) defines operations management as "the field of study that focuses on the effective planning, scheduling, use and control of a manufacturing or service organization through the study of concepts from design engineering, industrial engineering, management information systems, quality management, production management, inventory management, accounting, and other functions as they affect the organization".

## BUSINESS PROCESS REENGINEERING

Business Process Reengineering is a management approach that examines aspects of a business and its interactions, and attempts to improve the efficiency of the underlying processes. It is a fundamental and radical approach by either modifying or eliminating non-value adding activities. The key steps involved in a BPR are: 1. Defining the purpose and goal of the BPR project; 2. Defining the scope of the project so as to include (or exclude) activities; A flowchart of the activities can assist to define the scope of the project; 3. Identifying the requirements that will meet the needs of the clients; 4. Assess the environment - the position of competitors, prospective changes in technology, legislation or socio-economic factors; 5. Redesign the business processes and activities in light of the above; 6. Implement the redesigned processes; 7. Monitor the success/ failure of the redesign.

Business process reengineering is also known as BPR, Business Process Redesign, Business Transformation, Process Change Management.

In 1990, Michael Hammer, a former professor of computer science at the Massachusetts Institute of Technology (MIT), published an article in the Harvard Business Review, in which he claimed that the major challenge for managers is to obliterate non-value adding work, rather than using technology for automating it. This statement implicitly accused managers of having focused the wrong issues, namely that technology in general, and more specifically information technology, has been used primarily for automating existing work. rather than using it as an enabler for making non-value adding obsolete.

Hammer's claim was simple: Most of the work being done does not add any value for customers, and this work should be removed, not accelerated through automation. Instead, companies should reconsider their processes in order to maximize customer value, while minimizing the consumption of resources required for delivering their product or service. A similar idea was advocated by Thomas Davenport and J. Short, at that time a member of the Ernst & Young research center, in a paper published in the Sloan Management Review the same year as Hammer published his paper.

This idea, to unbiased review a company's business processes, was rapidly adopted by a huge number of firms, which were striving for renewed competitiveness, which they had lost due to the market entrance of foreign competitors, their inability to satisfy customer needs, and their insufficient cost structure. Even well established management thinkers, such as Peter Drucker and Tom Peters, were accepting and advocating BPR as a new tool for (re-)achieving success in a dynamic world. During the following years, a fast growing number of publications, books as well as journal articles, was dedicated to BPR, and many consulting firms embarked on this trend and developed BPR methods. However, the critics were fast to claim that BPR was a way to dehumanize the work place, increase managerial control, and to justify downsizing, i.e. major reductions of the work force and a rebirth of Taylorism under a different label.

Despite this critique, reengineering was adopted at an accelerating pace and in 1993, as many as 65% of the Fortune 500 companies claimed to either have initiated reengineering efforts, or to have plans to do so. This trend was fueled by the fast adoption of BPR by the consulting industry, but also by the study Made in America, conducted by the MIT, that showed how companies in many US industries had lagged behind their foreign counterparts in terms of competitiveness, time-to-market and productivity.

While there are almost as many definitions of BPR as there are authors publishing on the topic, we can identify multiple aspects that they have in common. Let us first review a number of definitions.

Hammer and Champy define BPR as"the fundamental rethinking and radical redesign of business processes to achieve dramatic improvements in critical contemporary measures of performance, such as cost, quality, service, and speed".

Thomas Davenport, another well-known BPR theorist, uses the term process innovation, which he says "encompasses the envisioning of new work strategies, the actual process design activity, and the implementation of the change in all its complex technological, human, and organizational dimensions".

Additionally, Davenport points out the major difference between BPR and other approaches to organization development (OD), especially the continuous improvement or TQM movement, when he states:

"Today firms must seek not fractional, but multiplicative levels of improvement – 10x rather than 10%."

Finally, Johansson et. al. (1993) provide a description of BPR relative to other process-oriented views, such as Total Quality Management (TQM) and Just-in-time (JIT), and state:

Business Process Reengineering, although a close relative, seeks radical rather than merely continuous improvement. It escalates the efforts of JIT and TQM to make process orientation a strategic tool and a core competence of the organization. BPR concentrates on core business processes, and uses the specific techniques within the JIT and TQM "toolboxes" as enablers, while broadening the process vision.

In order to achieve the major improvements BPR is seeking for, the change of structural organizational variables, and other ways of managing and performing work is often considered as being insufficient. For being able to reap the achievable benefits fully, the use of information technology is conceived as a major contributing factor. While IT traditionally has been used for supporting the existing business functions, i.e. it was used for increasing organizational efficiency, it now plays a role as enabler of new organizational forms, and patterns of collaboration within and between organizations. BPR derives its existence from different disciplines, and we can identify four major areas being subjected to change in BPR - organization, technology, strategy, and people - where a process view is used as common framework for considering these dimensions. The approach can be graphically depicted by a modification of "Leavitt's diamond".

Business strategy is the primary driver of BPR initiatives and the other dimensions are governed by strategy's encompassing role. The organization dimension reflects the structural elements of the company, such as hierarchical levels, the composition of organizational units, and the distribution of work between them. Technology is concerned with the use of computer systems and other forms of communication technology in the business. In BPR, information technology is generally considered as playing a role as enabler of new forms of organizing and collaborating, rather than supporting existing business functions. The people, or human resources dimension deals with aspects such as education, training, motivation and reward systems. The concept of business processes - interrelated activities aiming at creating an value added output to a customer - is the basic underlying idea of BPR. These processes are characterized by a number of attributes: Process ownership, customer focus, value-adding, and cross-functionality.

### Methodology

Although the names and steps being used differ slightly between the different methodologies, they share the same basic principles and elements.

## BPR - A REBIRTH OF SCIENTIFIC MANAGEMENT

By its critics, BPR is often accused to be a re-animation of Taylor's principles of scientific management, aiming at increasing productivity to a maximum, but disregarding aspects such as work environment and employee satisfaction. It can be agreed that Taylor's theories, in conjunction with the work of the early administrative scientists have had a considerable impact on the management discipline for more than 50 years. However, it is not self-evident that BPR is a close relative to Taylorism and this proposed relation deserves a closer investigation.

In the late 19th century Frederick Winslow Taylor, a mechanical engineer, started to develop the idea of management as a scientific discipline. He applied the premise that work and its organizational environment could be considered and designed upon scientific principles, i.e. that work processes could be studied in detail using a positivist analytic approach. Upon the basis of this analysis, an optimal organizational structure and way of performing all work tasks could be identified and implemented. However, he was not the one to originally invent the concept. In 1886, a paper entitled "The Engineer as Economist", written by Henry Towne for the American Society of Mechanical Engineers, had laid the bedrock for the development of scientific management. The basic idea of scientific management was that work could be studied from an objective scientific perspective and that the analysis of the gathered information could be used for increasing productivity, especially of blue-collar work, significantly. Taylor summarized his observations in the following four principles:

- Observation and analysis through time study to set the optimal production rate. In other words, develop a science for each man's task–a One Best Way.
- Scientifically select the best man for the job and train him in the procedures he is expected to follow.
- Cooperate with the man to ensure that the work is done as described. This means establishing a differential rate system of piece work and paying the man on an incentive basis, not according to the position.

- Divide the work between managers and workers so that managers are given the responsibility for planning and preparation of work, rather than the individual worker.

Scientific management's main characteristic is the strict separation of planning and doing, which was implemented by the use of a functional foremanship system. This means, that a worker, depending on the task his is performing, can report to different foreman, each of them being responsible for a small, specialized area.

Taylor's ideas had a major impact on manufacturing, but also administration. One of the most well-known examples is Ford Motor Co., which adopted the principles of scientific management at an early stage, and built its assembly line for the T-model based on Taylor's model of work and authority distribution, thereby giving name to Fordism.

Later on, Taylor's ideas were extended by the time and motion studies performed by Frank Gilbreth and his wife Lillian. Henry Gantt, a co-worker of Taylor, developed Taylor's idea further, but placed more emphasis on the worker. He developed a reward system that no longer took into account only the output of the work, but was based on a fixed daily wage, and a bonus for completing the task.

Taylor's work can be, and has been, criticized many times for degrading individuals to become machinelike. One of the most famous critiques of the situation that an application of scientific management could result in, is shown in Charles Chaplin's movie "Modern Times". Despite that fact, Taylor was inspired by the vision of creating a workplace that is beneficial to all members of the organization, both management and workers.

When looking at Taylor's ideas retrospectively, we can conclude, that they very well fitted the organizations of the early 20th century. The kind of organization he proposed requires certain pre-conditions, which were satisfied in the technological and socio-economic environment of his time and the heritage from economic individualism and a Protestant view of work. However, despite the good intention of designing organizations where managers and workers could jointly contribute to the common achievements, Taylor missed the fact that he had been building his principles on wrong assumptions. There are some major critical points that can be brought forward against Taylor's concept.

The strict belief in man being totally rational, and the history of protestant ethic, which considered work as being a manifestation of religious grace, made him disregard the crucial issue of human behaviour and the fact that money is insufficient as the single source of motivation.

The lack of considering the organizational environment as a conceivable factor, and the overemphasis on organizational efficiency. As Thompson notes:

"Scientific management, focusing primarily on manufacturing or similar production activities, clearly employs economic efficiency as its ultimate criterion and achieves conceptual closure of the organization by assuming that goals are known, tasks are repetitive, output of the production process somehow disappears, and resources in uniform qualities are available."

If accepting Thompson's critique as valid and relevant, we can conclude that the strict hierarchical organization seems to be unfit to take on the challenges that are imposed by fierce competition and dynamic market structures. Due to the focus on improvement through repetition and resource uniformity, the applicability on organizations and processes without these characteristics, such as pharmaceutical R&D, can be questioned.

Peter Drucker noted a third problem related to scientific management, namely that there was no real concern about technology, i.e. that Taylor considered his theory as being general, and that it could be applied to any organization, independently of the technology used. Drucker stated:

"Scientific management was not concerned with technology. It took tools and technology as givens."

This point brings forward a clear argument against the application of Taylor's principles and methodologies for improving today's organizations. Considering that the rapid development in the IT field actually constitutes a driving force in itself, it appears to be unfit to employ organizational concepts that neglect the changing and enabling role of technology. On the other hand we can argue that the application of scientific management in the early 20st century, as we look at it retrospectively, must be considered as the contemporary use of a concept that would look and be applied in a different way today. Taylor did not neglect technology, he considered it as an important contributor to organizational performance, but given the pace of development, he could not consider it as a major driver of change.

Looking at the suggested relationship between BPR and Taylor's principles we can conclude that primarily Thompson's and Drucker's criticism build a strong case against BPR being a successor of Taylorism. An organizational concept that does not take into account changing business environments and rapid technological advancements is not fit for serving as an improvement method today. Also the BPR literature offers a harsh critique of the continuous application of tayloristic principles in the modern business world, thus rejecting the separation of planning and doing and the strict functional division of labour. BPR proponents claim that taking BPR for Taylorism is a major misunderstanding of the concept, and responsible for a considerable number of reengineering project failures. On the other hand, there is also a similarity which stems from the methodological approach: Both scientific management and BPR have a focus on productivity and efficient use of resources that can be achieved through an optimum process design and its sub-sequent deployment. The following quote, referring to scientific management can equally be used to describe the intention of reengineering:

"To conduct the undertaking toward its objectives by seeking to derive optimum advantage from all available resources."

At the same time it cannot be denied, that the implementation of process-based organizations in practice often is accompanied by massive lay-offs and an emphasis on managerial control. A study by CSC Index from 1994 revealed that 73% of the companies applying BPR reduced their workforce with an average of 21%. Thomas Davenport, an early contributor to the BPR-field, provided a harsh critique against labeling substantial workforce reductions reengineering and in a paper from 1995 he stated that "reengineering didn't start out as a code word for mindless bloodshed. The other thing to remember about the start of reengineering is that the phrase 'massive layoffs' was never part of the early vocabulary."

**Key Targets**

Business Process Redesign/Reengineering can be defined as "the analysis and design of workflow and processes within and between organizations". BPR has three key target categories:

- Customer Friendly: One of the main goals of introducing BPR is to get a competitive edge and that can only be gained by providing the customers more than what the others in the market are asking for. If a customer is looking for products tailored to their needs, for example: a car customized to the customer's taste, then that car-maker would most probably gain more customers over the competition due to the customization option.
- Effectiveness: How effective is the product or service that the business or manufacturing company providing the customer? If whatever product or service the business might be providing to the customer is successful, then the customers would automatically want to buy that product or service again. For example: Japanese made cars like Honda and Toyota, even though they are more expensive compared to the domestic cars, they are very reliable cars causing the customers to continue going back to those brands for generations.

- Efficiency: How efficient is the company that is manufacturing the product before introducing it to the market to minimise costs? This is one of the key categories that is believed to be more important than any others. If a manufacturing company can master the skill of being efficient then they can automatically be more customer friendly and effective. Efficiency is not just about being efficient at the production floor level but the management level also has to be efficient. An example of only the production floor being efficient and not the management level would be the Japanese manufacturing companies. Now they are going through turmoil to repair their problems.

BPR, if implemented properly, can give huge returns. BPR has helped giants like Procter and Gamble Corporation and General Motors Corporation succeed after financial drawbacks due to competition. It helped American Airlines somewhat get back on track from the bad debt that is currently haunting their business practice. BPR is about the proper method of implementation.

General Motors Corporation implemented a 3-year plan to consolidate their multiple desktop systems into one. It is known internally as "Consistent Office Environment". This reengineering process involved replacing the numerous brands of desktop systems, network operating systems and application development tools into a more manageable number of vendors and technology platforms. According to Donald G. Hedeen, director of desktops and deployment at GM and manager of the upgrade programme, he says that the process "lays the foundation for the implementation of a common business communication strategy across General Motors." Lotus Development Corporation and Hewlett-Packard Development Company, formerly Compaq Computer Corporation, received the single largest non-government sales ever from General Motors Corporation. GM also planned to use Novell NetWare as a security client, Microsoft Office and Hewlett-Packard printers. According the Donald G. Hedeen, this saved GM 10% to 25% on support costs, 3% to 5% on hardware, 40% to 60% on software licensing fees, and increased efficiency by overcoming incompatibility issues by using just one platform across the entire company.

Southwest Airlines offers another successful example of reengineering their company and using Information Technology the way it was meant to be implemented. In 1992, Southwest Airlines had a revenue of $1.7 billion and an after-tax profit of $91 million. American Airlines, the largest U.S. carrier, on the other hand had a revenue of $14.4 billion dollars but lost $475 million and has not made a profit since 1989. Companies like Southwest Airlines know that their formula for success is easy to copy by new start-ups like Morris, Reno, and Kiwi Airlines. In order to stay in the game of competitive advantage, they have to continuously reengineer their strategy. BPR helps them be original.

Michael Dell is the founder and CEO of DELL Incorporated, which has been in business since 1983 and has been the world's fastest growing major PC Company. Michael Dell's idea of a successful business is to keep the smallest inventory possible by having a direct link with the manufacturer. When a customer places an order, the custom parts requested by the customer are automatically sent to the manufacturer for shipment. This reduces the cost for inventory tracking and massive warehouse maintenance. Dell's website is noted for bringing in nearly "$10 million each day in sales.

Michael Dell mentions: "If you have a good strategy with sound economics, the real challenge is to get people excited about what you're doing. A lot of businesses get off track because they don't communicate an excitement about being part of a winning team that can achieve big goals. If a company can't motivate its people and it doesn't have a clear compass, it will drift." Dell's stocks have been ranked as the top stock for the decade of the 1990s, when it had a return of 57,282%.

Michael Dell is now concentrating more on customer service than selling computers since the PC market price has pretty much equalized. Michael Dell notes: "The new frontier in our industry is service, which is a much greater differentiator when price has been equalized. In our industry, there's been a pretty huge gap between what customers want in service and what they can get, so they've come to expect mediocre service. We may be the best in this area, but we can still improve quite a bit—in the quality of the product, the availability of parts, service and delivery time. Michael Dell understands the concept of BPR and really recognizes where and when to reengineer his business. Ford reengineered their business and manufacturing process from just manufacturing cars to manufacturing quality cars, where the number one goal is quality. This helped Ford save millions on recalls and warranty repairs. Ford has accomplished this goal by incorporating barcodes on all their parts and scanners to scan for any missing parts in a completed car coming off of the assembly line. This helped them guarantee a safe and quality car. They have also implemented Voice-over-IP (VoIP) to reduce the cost of having meetings between the branches.

A multi-billion dollar corporation like Procter and Gamble Corporation, which carries 300 brands and growing really has a strong grasp in re-engineering. Procter and Gamble Corporation's chief technology officer, G. Gil Cloyd, explains how a company which carry multiple brands has to contend with the "classic innovator's dilemma — most innovations fail, but companies that don't innovate die. His solution, innovating innovation...". Cloyd has helped a company like Procter and Gamble grow to $5.1 billion by the fiscal year of 2004. According to Cloyd's scorecard, he was able to raise the volume by 17%, the organic volume by 10%, sales are at $51.4 billion up by 19%, with organic sales up 8%, earnings are at $6.5 billion up 25% and share earnings up 25%. Procter and Gamble also has a free cash flow of $7.3 billion or 113% of earnings, dividends up 13% annually with a total shareholder return of 24%. Cloyd states: "The challenge we face is the competitive need for a very rapid pace of innovation. In the consumer products world, we estimate that the required pace of innovation has double in the last three years. Digital technology is very important in helping us to learn faster." G. Gil Cloyd also predicts, in the near future, "as much as 90% of

P&G's R&D will be done in a virtual world with the remainder being physical validation of results and options."

The biggest problem that businesses usually face with BPR is overzealous expectations. BPR is a business tool with a high price and gradual returns. BPR is quoted as having a 30% success rate due to the time and cost involved.

BPR has been used by corporations as an excuse for job cuts which has tarnished the name with employees. Specifically, in 1995, Pacific Bell called for 10,000 job cuts, followed by Apple Computer Incorporated. Both used the word reengineering to explain the job cuts.

In addition, Michael Hammer and James Champy have admitted that in their book they did not take into account the human constituent of the business process. In late 1996, Dr. Hammer made a confession on the Wall Street Journal where the article read: "Dr. Hammer points out a flaw: He and the other leaders of the $4.7 billion re-engineering industry forgot about people. 'I wasn't smart enough about that,' he says. 'I was reflecting my engineering background and was insufficient appreciative of the human dimension. I've learned that's critical."

Sometimes BPR implementation was based on generic best practices by a business, not specific to a particular company. One example of using a generic idea to a particular company would be the implementation of a $28,000.00 voicemail system at Winguth, Dohahue and Co., which was later scrapped because of the computer generated voice which sounded a little too cold and clients were tired of going through all the menu prompts to reach the desired person.

Six Sigma and Total Quality Management (TQM) are terms often confused with BPR, and are not its replacements. All are change initiatives, with the main difference being BPR is focused on radical, "big bang" change, and Six Sigma and TQM both focused on continuous, incremental improvement. Methods such as that used by Riggours employ the traditional principles of BPR and acknowledge the contributions made by Six Sigma without the adherence to measurement, which while appropriate for some organisations is not suitable for those at the beginning of the BPR change ladder.

In order to reanalyze BPR, it is being replaced by Business Process Management (BPM). BPM is presently taking a similar road toward many failures by focusing too heavily on automation and failing to consider people in processes.

## BUSINESS PROCESS MANAGEMENT

The term Business Process Management (or BPM) refers to activities performed by businesses to optimize and adapt their processes.

Although it can be said that organizations have always been using BPM, a new impetus based on the advent of software tools (business process management systems or BPMS) which allow for the direct execution of the business processes without a costly and time intensive development of the required software. In addition, these tools can also monitor the execution of the business processes, providing managers of an organization with the means to analyze their performance and make changes to the original processes in real-time. Using a BPMS the modified process can then be merged into the current business process atmosphere.

Where Business Process Reengineering (popular in the 1990s) dealt with one-off changes to the organization, Business Process Management deals with the continuity and embedding of process orientation in the organization. Business Process Management has evolved as technology has caught up with management processes to the point that technology should no longer be the limiting factor in BPM.

The activities which constitute business process management can be grouped into three categories: design, execution and monitoring.

### Process Design

This encompasses either the design or capture of existing processes. In addition the processes may be simulated in order to test them. The software support for these activities consists of graphical editors to document the processes and repositories to store the process models.

An emphasis on getting the design of the process right will logically lead to better results as the flow on effect of problems at the design stage logically affects a large number of parts in an integrated system.

Evolution of business processes requires a change to the process design to flow on into the live system. Integrating business process is also a current research area. Integration of software for process design to be used both for creating graphical representations of workflows and implementing and maintaining these workflows makes evolution of business processes less stressful, given that requirements are not as static as information systems.

**Process Execution**

The traditional way to achieve the automatic execution of processes is that an application is developed or purchased which executes the steps required. However, in practice, these applications only execute a portion of the overall process. Execution of a complete business process can also be achieved by using a patchwork of interfacing software with human intervention needed where applications are not able to automatically interface. In addition, certain process steps can only be accomplished with human intervention (for example, deciding on a major credit application). Due to the complexity that this approach engenders, changing a process is costly and an overview of the processes and their state is difficult to obtain.

As a response to these problems, the Business Process Management System (BPMS) category of software has evolved. BPMS allows the full business process (as developed in the process design activity) to be defined in a computer language which can be directly executed by the computer. The BPMS will either use services in connected applications to perform business operations (e.g. calculating a repayment plan for a loan) or will send messages to human workers requesting they perform certain tasks which necessitate a human attribute such as intuition as opposed to automated processes. As the process definition is directly executable, changes in the process can be (in comparison to the traditional approach of application development or maintenance) relatively quickly moved into operation. In order to work effectively a BPMS often requires that the underlying software is constructed according to the principles of a service-oriented architecture. Thus, it is often difficult to make a suite of existing legacy systems fit with a BPMS.

The commercial BPMS software market has focused on graphical process model development, rather than text-language based process models, as a means to reduce the complexity of model development. Visual programming using graphical metaphors has increased productivity in a number of areas of computing and is well accepted by users.

Business rules are a growing area of importance in BPMS as these rules provide governing behaviour to the BPMS, and a business rule engine can be used to drive process execution and resolution.

**Process Monitoring**

This monitoring encompasses the tracking of individual processes so that information on their state can be easily seen and the provision of statistics on the performance of one or more processes. An example of the tracking is being able to determine the state of a customer order (e.g. ordered arrived, awaiting delivery, invoice paid) so that problems in its operation can be identified and corrected. In addition, this information can be used to work with customers and suppliers to improve their connected processes. Examples of the statistics are the generation of measures on how quickly a customer order is processed, how many orders were processed in the last month etc.. These measures tend to fit into three categories: cycle time, defect rate and productivity.

Although such functions may be within the scope of current applications, the use of a BPMS is expected to ease the development of such reporting. Manufacturers of BPMSs will often offer process monitoring software as well as MIS and execution.

Business Process Management is an automated process to handle the complex business policy of any organisation. There are so many tools and programming languages to handle this process and customize the already existing tools, sometimes it's really a challenge to realize the complex business process of an organisation to automate.

The degree of monitoring depends on what information the business wants to evaluate and analyze and how business wants it to be monitored, in real-time or ad-hoc. Here, business activity monitoring (BAM) extend and expand the monitoring tools in BPMS. BAM will not only monitor a process but also monitor and analyze all processes in the business in real-time. BPM monitoring has been always ad-hoc/on-demand monitoring, and BAM compliments this feature with real-time monitoring, analysis and reporting.

Although the initial focus of BPM was on the automation of mechanistic business processes, this has since been extended to integrate human-driven processes in which human interaction takes place in series or parallel with the mechanistic processes. A common form is where individual steps in the business process which require human intuition or judgement to be performed are assigned to the appropriate members of an organization (as with workflow systems). More advanced forms are in supporting the complex interaction between human workers in performing a workgroup task. In the latter case an emerging class of BPM software known as the Human Interaction Management System is used to support and monitor these processes as well as to permit their ongoing redefinition at runtime.

BPMS can be used to understand organizations through expanded views that would not otherwise be available to organise and present. These views include the relationships of processes to each other which, when included in the process model, provide for advanced reporting and analysis that would not otherwise be available. BPM is regarded to be the crucial backbone of enterprise content management.

Not all activities in business can be modelled into business process management modelling. As activities in business varies from the simplest of acquiring stationeries to complex procurement process which includes cross-countries which dealt with various legal laws and regulations.

Some processes in a business are best to be kept as it is for not to add complexity might be occurs when bringin business process management. Too dynamic changes of rules in a business process will not get the most of business process management benefit as time will be wasted on adapating the busines process to the tools.

BPMS is more to a tools or platform which can be used to setup rules and define how business should be executed according to the rules. Thus, if both the rules and the business are too dynamics, it is pointless to implement business process management.

In practice, organizations often start with an objective where management have identified an area for improvement. A project team is tasked to perform Business Process Mapping and use of a common technique such as IDEF or BPMN to depict the processes as they exist before the intended changes. The team will progress to identify desired changes in work practices which will often be implemented by another team, using Kaizen or other approaches.

And to successfully implements the business process management, the initiative must be a top down initiatives.

## BUSINESS PROCESS

A business process is a set of linked activities that create value by transforming an input into a more valuable output. Both input and output can be artefacts and/or information and the transformation can be performed by human actors, machines, or both.

There are three types of business processes:

1. Management processes - the processes that govern the operation. Typical management processes include "Corporate Governance" and "Strategic Management".
2. Operational processes - these processes create the primary value stream, they are part of the core business. Typical operational processes are Purchasing, Manufacturing, Marketing, and Sales.
3. Supporting processes - these support the core processes. Examples include Accounting, Recruitment, IT-support.

A business process can be decomposed into several sub-processes, which have their own attributes, but also contribute to achieving the goal of the super-process. The analysis of business processes typically includes the mapping of processes and sub-processes down to activity level.

Activities are parts of the business process that do not include any decision making and thus are not worth decomposing (although decomposition would be possible), such as "Answer the phone", "produce an invoice".

A business process is usually the result of a business process design or business process reengineering activity. Business process modeling is used to capture, document and reengineer business processes. To visualize a business process, one of the graphical notations can be used such as Business Process Modeling Notation.

The concept of processes is not new. Laying out inter-related activities in a sequence and creating a flow of work has been part of organization design for more than 300 years. On of the first to describe a processes was Adam Smith (1776) in the famous example of an English pin factory. He described the production of a pin in the following way:

"One man draws out the wire, another straights it, a third cuts it, a fourth points it, a fifth grinds it at the top for receiving the head: to make the head requires two or three distinct operations: to put it on is a particular business, to whiten the pins is another... and the important business of making a pin is, in this manner, divided into about eighteen distinct operations, which in some manufactories are all performed by distinct hands, though in others the same man will sometime perform two or three of them."

Smith also first recognized how the organizational outcome could be increased through the use of advanced labour division. Previously, in a society where production was dominated by handcrafted goods, one man would perform all the activities required during the production process, while Smith described how work in a pin factory was divided into a set of simple tasks, which would be performed by specialized workers. The result of labour division in Smith's example resulted in productivity increasing by 24.000 percent (sic!), i.e. that the same number of workers made 240 times as many pins as they had been producing before the introduction of labour division.

It is worth to notice that Smith did not advocate labour division at any price and per se. He observed and noted that, under certain conditions, several tasks could very well be integrated into one, which a single worker would then perform. However, Smith did not provide any guidance for criteria that could be used for finding the optimum level of task division or integration and the determination of the appropriate level took place through experimental design of the production process. This approach to integration could be considered as an implicit proposition of a process-oriented approach, but there is one aspect that constitutes a significant difference to the idea of business processes as it is perceived today. The integration in accordance with the idea of Smith would take place only within the same functional domain and comprise activities that are in direct sequence in the manufacturing process, whereas today's process concept includes cross-functionality as an important characteristic. It is also interesting to note that while Smith is generally accepted as the first to discuss labour division and specialization, only the division of labour was widely adopted, while the integration of tasks into functional, or cross-functional, processes was not considered as an alternative option to increase performance and productivity.

## FURTHER SUPPORTING THEORIES AND CONCEPTS

Frederick Winslow Taylor developed the concept of scientific management. The concept contains aspects on the division of labour being relevant to the theory and practice around business processes. The business process related aspects of Taylor's scientific management concept are discussed in the article on Business Process Reengineering.

### The Span of Control

The span of control is the number of sub-ordinates a supervisor manages within a structural organization. Introducing a business process concept has a considerable impact on the structural elements of the organization and thus also on the span of control. The implications are discussed in the Span of control article.

Large organizations that are not organized as markets need to be organized in smaller units - departments - which can be defined according to different principles. In the context of business processes, process and purpose departmentalization, as defind by Gulick and Urwick, are discussed in the departmentalization article.

## INFORMATION MANAGEMENT CONCEPTS

Information Management and the organization design strategies being related to it, are a theoretical cornerstone of the business process concept.

In the early 1990s, US corporations, and subsequently companies all over the world, started to adopt the concept of reengineering in an attempt to re-achieve the competitiveness that they had lost during the previous decade. A key characteristic of BPR is the focus on business processes. Let us start our investigations with reviewing several business process definitions, as they are used in the reengineering literature. Davenport defines a (business) process as "a structured, measured set of activities designed to produce a specific output for a particular customer or market. It implies a strong emphasis on how work is done within an organization, in contrast to a product focus's emphasis on what. A process is thus a specific ordering of work activities across time and space, with a beginning and an end, and clearly defined inputs and outputs: a structure for action... Taking a process approach implies adopting the customer's point of view. Processes are the structure by which an organization does what is necessary to produce value for its customers."

This definition contains certain characteristics a process must possess. These characteristics are achieved by a focus on the business logic of the process (how work is done), instead of taking a product perspective (what is done). Following Davenports definition of a process we can conclude that a process must have clearly defined boundaries, input and output, that it consists of smaller parts, activities, which are ordered in time and space, that there must be a receiver of the process outcome- a customer - and that the transformation taking place within the process must add customer value.

Hammer & Champy's definition can be considered as a subset of Davenport's. They define a process as "a collection of activities that takes one or more kinds of input and creates an output that is of value to the customer." As we can note, Hammer & Champy have a more transformation oriented perception, and put less emphasis on the structural component–process boundaries and the order of activities in time and space.

Rummler & Brache use a definition that clearly encompasses a focus on the organization's external customers, when stating that "a business process is a series of steps designed to produce a product or service. Most processes are cross-functional, spanning the 'white space' between the boxes on the organization chart. Some processes result in a product or service that is received by an organization's external customer. We call these primary processes. Other processes produce products that are invisible to the external customer but essential to the effective management of the business. We call these support processes."

The above definition distinguishes two types of processes, primary and support processes, depending on whether a process is directly involved in the creation of customer value, or concerned with the organization's internal activities. In this sense, Rummler and Brache's definition follows Porter's value chain model, which also builds on a division of primary and secondary activities. According to Rummler and Brache, a typical characteristic of a successful process-based organization is the absence of secondary activities in the primary value flow that is created in the customer oriented primary processes. The characteristic of processes as spanning the white space on the organization chart indicates that processes are embedded in some form of organizational structure. Also, a process can be cross-functional, i.e. it ranges over several business functions.

Finally, let us consider the process definition of Johansson. They define a process as "a set of linked activities that take an input and transform it to create an output. Ideally, the transformation that occurs in the process should add value to the input and create an output that is more useful and effective to the recipient either upstream or downstream."

This definition also emphasizes the constitution of links between activities and the transformation that takes place within the process. Johansson et.al. also include the upstream part of the value chain as a possible recipient of the process output. Summarizing the four definitions above, we can compile the following list of characteristics for a business process.

1. Definability: It must have clearly defined boundaries, input and output.
2. Order: It must consist of activities that are ordered according to their position in time and space.
3. Customer: There must be a recipient of the process' outcome, a customer.

4. Value-adding: The transformation taking place within the process must add value to the recipient, either upstream or downstream.
5. Embeddedness: A process can not exist in itself, it must be embedded in an organizational structure.
6. Cross-functionality: A process regularly can, but not necessarily must, span several functions.

Frequently, a process owner, i.e. a person being responsible for the performance and continuous improvement of the process, is also considered as a prerequisite.

## PROCESS MODELING

The term process model (usually business process model) is used in different contexts. Process models are concepts which can belong in the area of Process Engineering.

A description of what process models are is provided by Colette Rolland: "Processes of the same nature are classified together into a process model. Thus, a process model is a description of a process at the type level. Since the process model is at the type level, a process is an instantiation of it. The same process model is used repeatedly for the development of many applications and thus, has many instantiations. One possible use of a process model is to prescribe 'how things must/should/could be done' in contrast to the process itself which is really what happens. A process model is more or less a rough anticipation of what the process will look like. What the process shall be will be determined during actual system development."

### Main Aims

- Descriptive
  - Traces what actually happens during a process
  - Takes the point of view of an external observer who looks at the way a process has been performed and determines the improvements that have to be made to make it perform more effectively or efficiently

- Prescriptive
  - Defines desired processes and how they should/could/might be performed
  - Lays down rules, guidelines, and behaviour patterns which, if followed, would lead to the desired process performance. They range from strict enforcement to flexible guidance.
- Explanatory
  - Provides explanations about the rationale of processes
  - Explores and evaluates several possible courses of action based on rational arguments
  - Establishes an explicit link between processes and the requirements that they are to fulfill

"From a theoretical point of view, the Process Meta-Model explains which are the key concepts needed to describe what happens in the development process, on what, when it happens and why. From an operational point of view, the Process Meta-Model is aimed at providing guidance for method engineers and application developers."

The activity of modeling a business process usually predicates a need to change processes or identify issues to be corrected. This transformation may or may not require IT involvement, although that is common driver for the need to model a business process. Change management programmes are desired to put the processes into practice. With advances in technology from larger platform vendors, the vision of BPM models becoming fully executable (and capable of round-trip engineering) is coming closer to reality every day.

Process Modeling addresses the process aspects an Enterprise Business Architecture, leading to an all encompassing Enterprise Architecture. The relationships of a business processes in the context of the rest of the enterprise systems, data, org structure, strategies etc. create greater capabilities in analyzing and planning a change. One real world example is in corporate mergers and acquisitions; understanding the processes in both companies in detail, allowing management to identify redundancies resulting in a smoother merger.

## CLASSIFICATION OF PROCESS MODELS

### Classification by Coverage

Dowson distinguishes four types of coverage where the term process model has been defined differently:

- Activity-oriented: related set of activities conducted for the specific purpose of product definition; a set of partially ordered steps intended to reach a goal
- Product-oriented: series of activities that cause successive product transformations to reach the desired product
- Decision-oriented: set of related decisions conducted for the specific purpose of product definition
- Context-oriented: sequence of contexts causing successive product transformations under the influence of a decision taken in a context

### Classification by Alignment

With regard to Rolland, processes can be of different kinds. These definitions "correspond to the various ways in which a process can be modelled".

- Strategic processes
  - Investigate alternative ways of doing a thing and eventually produce a plan for doing it
  - Are often creative and require human co-operation; thus, alternative generation and selection from an alternative are very critical activities
- Tactical processes
  - Help in the achievement of a plan
  - Are more concerned with the tactics to be adopted for actual plan achievement than with the development of a plan of achievement

- Implementation processes
  - Are the lowest level processes
  - Are directly concerned with the details of the what and how of plan implementation

**Classification by Granularity**

Granularity refers to the detail level of the process model. "Granularity affects the kind of guidance, explanation and trace that can be provided. High granularity limits these to a rather coarse level of detail whereas fine granularity provides more detailed capability. The nature of granularity needed is dependent on the situation at hand."

Project manager, customer representatives, the general, top-level, or middle management require rather large-grained process description as they want to gain an overview over time, budget, and resource planning for their decisions. In contrast, software engineers, users, testers, analysts, or software system architects will prefer a fine-grained process model for the details of the model deliver them with instructions and important execution dependencies such as the dependencies between people.

While notations for fine-grained models exist, most traditional process models are large-grained descriptions. Process models should, ideally, provide a wide range of granularity.

**Classification by Flexibility**

It was found that "even though process models were prescriptive, in actual practice departures from the prescription occurred". Thus, frameworks for adopting methods evolved so that systems development methods match specific organizational situations and thereby improve their usefulness. Method construction approaches can be organized in a spectrum ranging from 'low' flexibility, to 'high'.

"At the 'low' end of this spectrum are rigid methods whereas at the 'high' end is modular method construction. Rigid methods are completely pre-defined and leave little scope for adapting them to the situation at hand. On the other hand, modular methods can be modified and augmented to fit a given situation. Selection from rigid methods allows each project to choose its method from a panel of rigid, pre-defined methods whereas selection of paths within a method consists of selecting the appropriate path for the situation at hand. Finally selection and tuning a method permits each project to select methods from different approaches and tune them to the project's needs."

Rolland lists different styles for representing processes: scripts, programmes, and hypertext. "Process scripts are interactively used by humans as against process programmes which are enacted by a machine. They support non determinism whereas process programmes can, at best, support process deviation under pre-defined constraints. The hypertext style of process representation is a network of links between the different aspects of a process, such as product parts, decisions, arguments, issues, etc. Scripts and programmes are two styles which may be applicable to prescriptive purposes whereas hypertext is well suited to descriptive and explanatory purposes. Strict enforcement of the prescriptive purpose can clearly be represented in process programmes whereas flexible guidance requires the process model to be represented in process scripts. Descriptive and explanatory purposes require the establishment of relationships between different elements of a process trace. These relationships are well articulated as hypertext links."

## CAPACITY PLANNING

Capacity planning is the process of adjusting the capacity of an organization to do work in response to changing or predicted demands.

In the context of capacity planning, capacity is taken to mean the amount work that an organization is capable of completing in a given period of time. In a simple model, it might be calculated as (number of machines and/or workers) x (number of shifts) x (utilization) x (efficiency).

The demand for work an organization experiences will vary under many circumstances. Notable events that might cause the demand for work to vary greatly include starting a new organization, extending the operations of an existing business, considering additions or modifications to product lines, and introducing new techniques, equipment and materials.

Discrepancy between capacity of an organization and the demands of its customers results in an inefficiency, either in under-utilized resources or unfulfilled customers. The goal of capacity planning is to therefore minimize this discrepancy.

The broad classes of capacity planning are lead strategy, lag strategy, and match strategy.

The lead capacity strategy is adding capacity in anticipation of an increase in demand. Lead strategy is an aggressive strategy with the goal of luring customers away from the company's competitors. The possible disadvantage to this strategy is that it often results in excess inventory, which is costly and often wasteful.

Lag strategy refers to adding capacity only after the company is running at full capacity or beyond due to increase in demand. This is a more conservative strategy that decreases the risk of waste but may result in the loss of possible customers.

The match strategy (also known as the tracking strategy) is adding capacity in small amounts in response to changing demand in the market. This is a more moderate strategy.

Capacity planning interacts with the discipline of Performance Engineering, both during the requirements and design activities of building a system, and when using performance monitoring as an input for managing capacity of deployed systems.

Chapter 5

# Distribution and Business

Distribution is one of the four aspects of marketing. A distributor is the middleman between the manufacturer and retailer. After a product is manufactured it is typically shipped (and typically sold) to a distributor. The distributor then sells the product to retailers or customers.

The other three parts of the marketing mix are product management, pricing, and promotion.

Traditionally, distribution has been seen as dealing with logistics: how to get the product or service to the customer. It must answer questions such as:

- Should the product be sold through a retailer?
- Should the product be distributed through wholesale?
- Should multi-level marketing channels be used?
- How long should the channel be (how many members)?
- Where should the product or service be available?
- When should the product or service be available?
- Should distribution be exclusive, selective or extensive?
- Who should control the channel (referred to as the channel captain)?
- Should channel relationships be informal or contractual?

- Should channel members share advertising (referred to as co-op ads)?
- Should electronic methods of distribution be used?
- Are there physical distribution and logistical issues to deal with?
- What will it cost to keep an inventory of products on store shelves and in channel warehouses (referred to as filling the pipeline)?

## THE DISTRIBUTION CHANNEL

Frequently there may be a chain of intermediaries, each passing the product down the chain to the next organization, before it finally reaches the consumer or end-user. This process is known as the 'distribution chain' or the 'channel.' Each of the elements in these chains will have their own specific needs, which the producer must take into account, along with those of the all-important end-user.

### Channels

A number of alternate 'channels' of distribution may be available:

- Selling direct, such as via mail order, Internet and telephone sales
- Agent, who typically sells direct on behalf of the producer
- Distributor (also called wholesaler), who sells to retailers
- Retailer (also called dealer), who sells to end customers

Distribution channels may not be restricted to physical products. They may be just as important for moving a service from producer to consumer in certain sectors, since both direct and indirect channels may be used. Hotels, for example, may sell their services (typically rooms) directly or through travel agents, tour operators, airlines, tourist boards, centralized reservation systems, etc.

There have also been some innovations in the distribution of services. For example, there has been an increase in franchising and in rental services - the latter offering anything from televisions through tools. There has also been some evidence of service integration, with services linking together, particularly in the travel and tourism sectors. For example, links now exist between airlines, hotels and car rental services. In addition, there has been a significant increase in retail outlets for the service sector. Outlets such as estate agencies and building society offices are crowding out traditional grocers from major shopping areas.

**Channel Members**

Distribution channels can thus have a number of levels. Kotler defined the simplest level, that of direct contact with no intermediaries involved, as the 'zero-level' channel.

The next level, the 'one-level' channel, features just one intermediary; in consumer goods a retailer, for industrial goods a distributor, say. In small markets (such as small countries) it is practical to reach the whole market using just one- and zero-level channels.

In large markets (such as larger countries) a second level, a wholesaler for example, is now mainly used to extend distribution to the large number of small, neighbourhood retailers.

In Japan the chain of distribution is often complex and further levels are used, even for the simplest of consumer goods.

**Channel Structure**

To the various 'levels' of distribution, which they refer to as the 'channel length', Lancaster and Massingham also added another structural element, the relationship between its members:

- 'Conventional or free-flow - This is the usual, widely recognized, channel with a range of `middle-men' passing the goods on to the end-user.

- Single transaction - A temporary 'channel' may be set up for one transaction; for example, the sale of property or a specific civil engineering project. This does not share many characteristics with other channel transactions, each one being unique.
- Vertical marketing system (VMS) - In this form, the elements of distribution are integrated.

**Channel Management**

The channel decision is very important. In theory at least, there is a form of trade-off: the cost of using intermediaries to achieve wider distribution is supposedly lower. Indeed, most consumer goods manufacturers could never justify the cost of selling direct to their consumers, except by mail order. In practice, if the producer is large enough, the use of intermediaries (particularly at the agent and wholesaler level) can sometimes cost more than going direct.

Many of the theoretical arguments about channels therefore revolve around cost. On the other hand, most of the practical decisions are concerned with control of the consumer. The small company has no alternative but to use intermediaries, often several layers of them, but large companies 'do' have the choice.

However, many suppliers seem to assume that once their product has been sold into the channel, into the beginning of the distribution chain, their job is finished. Yet that distribution chain is merely assuming a part of the supplier's responsibility; and, if he has any aspirations to be market-oriented, his job should really be extended to managing, albeit very indirectly, all the processes involved in that chain, until the product or service arrives with the end-user. This may involve a number of decisions on the part of the supplier:

- Channel membership
- Channel motivation
- Monitoring and managing channels

## Channel Membership

1. Intensive distribution - Where the majority of resellers stock the 'product' (with convenience products, for example, and particularly the brand leaders in consumer goods markets) price competition may be evident.
2. Selective distribution - This is the normal pattern (in both consumer and industrial markets) where 'suitable' resellers stock the product.
3. Exclusive distribution - Only specially selected resellers (typically only one per geographical area) are allowed to sell the 'product'.

## Channel Motivation

It is difficult enough to motivate direct employees to provide the necessary sales and service support. Motivating the owners and employees of the independent organizations in a distribution chain requires even greater effort. There are many devices for achieving such motivation. Perhaps the most usual is 'bribery': the supplier offers a better margin, to tempt the owners in the channel to push the product rather than its competitors; or a competition is offered to the distributors' sales personnel, so that they are tempted to push the product. At the other end of the spectrum is the almost symbiotic relationship that the all too rare supplier in the computer field develops with its agents; where the agent's personnel, support as well as sales, are trained to almost the same standard as the supplier's own staff.

## Monitoring and Managing Channels

In much the same way that the organization's own sales and distribution activities need to be monitored and managed, so will those of the distribution chain.

In practice, of course, many organizations use a mix of different channels; in particular, they may complement a direct salesforce, calling on the larger accounts, with agents, covering the smaller customers and prospects.

## Vertical Marketing

This relatively recent development integrates the channel with the original supplier - producer, wholesalers and retailers working in one unified system. This may arise because one member of the chain owns the other elements (often called 'corporate systems integration'); a supplier owning its own retail outlets, this being 'forward' integration. It is perhaps more likely that a retailer will own its own suppliers, this being 'backward' integration. (For example, MFI, the furniture retailer, owns Hygena which makes its kitchen and bedroom units.) The integration can also be by franchise (such as that offered by McDonald's hamburgers and Benetton clothes) or simple co-operation (in the way that Marks & Spencer co-operates with its suppliers).

Alternative approaches are 'contractual systems', often led by a wholesale or retail co-operative, and 'administered marketing systems' where one (dominant) member of the distribution chain uses its position to co-ordinate the other members' activities. This has traditionally been the form led by manufacturers.

The intention of vertical marketing is to give all those involved (and particularly the supplier at one end, and the retailer at the other) 'control' over the distribution chain. This removes one set of variables from the marketing equations.

Other research indicates that vertical integration is a strategy which is best pursued at the mature stage of the market (or product). At earlier stages it can actually reduce profits. It is arguable that it also diverts attention from the real business of the organization. Suppliers rarely excel in retail operations and, in theory, retailers should focus on their sales outlets rather than on manufacturing facilities (Marks & Spencer, very deliberately provides considerable amounts of technical assistance to its suppliers, but does not own them).

## Horizontal Marketing

A rather less frequent example of new approaches to channels is where two or more non-competing organizations agree on a joint venture - a joint marketing operation - because it is beyond the capacity of each individual organization alone. In general, this is less likely to revolve around marketing synergy.

## GOOD DISTRIBUTION PRACTICE

Good Distribution Practice or GDP deals with the guidelines for the proper distribution of medicinal products for human use. GDP is a quality warranty system, which includes requirements for purchase, receiving, storage and export of drugs, intended for human consumption.

GDP regulates the division and movement of pharmaceutical products from the premises of the manufacturer of medicinal products, or another central point, to the end user thereof, or to an intermediate point by means of various transport methods, via various storage and/or health establishments.

In the USA the Food and Drug Administration wants to deal with the growing public health problem of counterfeit prescription drugs. Counterfeit drugs are not only illegal but are also inherently unsafe. In the near future the FDA will require that the pharmaceutical industry implements full-scale RFID serialization (needed for closed-loop drug tracking) and electronic pedigree (E-Pedigree) applications (needed to find and prosecute violators).

## LOGISTICS

Logistics is the art and science of managing and controlling the flow of goods, energy, information and other resources like products, services, and people, from the source of production to the marketplace. It is difficult to accomplish any marketing or manufacturing without logistical support. It involves the integration of information, transportation, inventory, warehousing, material handling, and packaging. The operating responsibility of logistics is the geographical repositioning of raw materials, work in process, and finished inventories where required at the lowest cost possible.

Logistics can be defined as having the right quantity at the right time for the right price. It is the science of process and incorporates all industry sectors. The goal of logistic work is to manage the fruition of project life cycles, supply chains and resultant efficiencies.

In particular, the logistics profession involves planning, implementing and controlling efficient, effective flow and storage of goods and services from the beginning point of external origin to the company and from the company to the point of consumption for the purpose of conforming to customer requirements. Logistics is generally viewed as within one company, although it manages flows between the company, its suppliers and customers.

On the other hand, supply chain management includes the logistical flows, the customer order management and production processes and the informational flows necessary to monitor all the activities at the supply chain nodes.

Logistics as a concept is considered to evolve from the military's need to supply themselves as they moved from their base to a forward position. In ancient Greek, Roman and Byzantine empires, there were military officers with the title 'Logistikas' who were responsible for financial and supply distribution matters. The Oxford English dictionary defines logistics as: "The branch of military science having to do with procuring, maintaining and transporting material, personnel and facilities."

Logistics as its own concept in business evolved only in the 1950s. This was mainly due to the increasing complexity of supplying one's business with materials and shipping out products in an increasingly globalized supply chain, calling for experts in the field.

Logistics can be defined as having the right quantity at the right time for the right price. It is the science of process and incorporates all industry sectors. The goal of logistic work is to manage the fruition of project life cycles, supply chains and resultant efficiencies.

In particular, the logistics profession involves planning, implementing and controlling efficient, effective flow and storage of goods and services from the beginning point of external origin to the company and from the company to the point of consumption for the purpose of conforming to customer requirements. Logistics is generally viewed as within one company, although it manages flows between the company, its suppliers and customers.

On the other hand, supply chain management includes the logistical flows, the customer order management and production processes and the informational flows necessary to monitor all the activities at the supply chain nodes.

Logistics as a concept is considered to evolve from the military's need to supply themselves as they moved from their base to a forward position. In ancient Greek, Roman and Byzantine empires, there were military officers with the title 'Logistikas' who were responsible for financial and supply distribution matters. The Oxford English dictionary defines logistics as: "The branch of military science having to do with procuring, maintaining and transporting material, personnel and facilities."

Logistics as its own concept in business evolved only in the 1950s. This was mainly due to the increasing complexity of supplying one's business with materials and shipping out products in an increasingly globalized supply chain, calling for experts in the field.

In military logistics, experts manage how and when to move resources to the places they are needed. In military science, maintaining one's supply lines while disrupting those of the enemy is a crucial—some would say the most crucial—element of military strategy, since an armed force without food, fuel and ammunition is defenseless.

The Iraq war was a dramatic example of the importance of logistics. It had become very necessary for the US and its allies to move huge amounts of men, materials and equipment over great distances. Led by Lieutenant General William

Pagonis, Logistics was successfully used for this effective movement. The defeat of the British in the American War of Independence, and the defeat of Rommel in World War II, have been largely attributed to logistical failure. The historical leaders Hannibal Barca and Alexander the Great are considered to have been logistical geniuses.

The term is used for describing logistic processes within an industry. The purpose of production logistics is to ensure that each machine and workstation is being fed with the right product in the right quantity and quality at the right point in time.

The issue is not the transportation itself, but to streamline and control the flow through the value adding processes and eliminate non-value adding ones. Production logistics can be applied in existing as well as new plants. Manufacturing in an existing plant is a constantly changing process. Machines are exchanged and new ones added, which gives the opportunity to improve the production logistics system accordingly. Production logistics provides the means to achieve customer response and capital efficiency.

## THIRD-PARTY LOGISTICS

A third-party logistics provider (abbreviated 3PL) is a firm that provides outsourced or "third party" logistics services to companies for part or sometimes all of their supply chain management function. Third party logistics providers typically specialize in integrated warehousing and transportation services that can be scaled and customized to customer's needs based on market conditions and the demands and delivery service requirements for their products and materials.

## Chapter 6

# Action Research in Hotel Management

Interactive social science research may be regarded as a pragmatic, utilitarian, or user-oriented approach to research and incorporates a value-base that is committed to promoting change through research. It is democratic and participatory by nature and is in sharp contrast to the positivistic 'top-down' approach which has been accused of 'lifting decisions from the village square' and placing them with 'experts or outside agencies' (Bryant, 2001). The practice goes by many names: community-based research, participatory research, collaborative research, and others, but rests on two main principles: democratization of the knowledge process, and social change.

Action research forms part of this genre, and is associated with attempts to bring about emancipation and social justice based on the desires and direct involvement of ordinary people. Its roots may be traced to writers such as Marx, Engels, Gramsci and Freire, and has been used to promote the empowerment of disadvantaged and oppressed groups through the development of common knowledge and critical awareness which are suppressed by the dominant knowledge in a society. Action research is now used within a range of settings and has developed by drawing from pragmatic philosophy, critical thinking, and humanistic and transpersonal psychology, constructionist theory, systems thinking and complexity theory.

An important element of action research is participation by 'informants' who engage in 'collective, self-reflective enquiry...in social situations in order improve the rationality and justice of their own social practices'. A key feature is empowerment through participation. This may, for example, involve the researcher identifying the user group, working in close collaboration with the users, and getting them involved in identifying their needs, setting up research questions, and using the research findings. The practice involves people reflecting on issues and processes during the research, participants as co-researchers, and entails an element of risk given that the process and outcomes are in a state of on-going change. It is transformed by emergent findings, which, in turn, impact upon the process itself, and subsequent outcomes. As the focus becomes redirected, outcomes may not be readily predicted and, for this reason alone, power holders may not be fully at ease with what they are not in control of: the 'knowledge' it produces, the thinking it stimulates, or the action it promotes.

Action research has now found its way into a diverse range of areas, including the experiential learning movement, community development, action learning, humanistic psychology, popular education, organization development, and feminist thinking. Each field has shaped and redefined 'action research' according to its particular requirements. For example, interactive research has been closely associated with the environmental movement, democratic evaluation has links with education, and empowerment evaluation aims to 'help others to help themselves' in areas that include substance abuse prevention, HIV/AIDS prevention, and adult probation.

When commissioning research, an organisation may perceive that subsequent outcomes will take place within specified parameters that will help to further its overall aims, including the need to develop or maintain working relations with other bodies (eg Tackling Drugs to Build a Better Britain,

1998). What they may not realise, however, is that action research has the potential to instigate certain forms of action which undermine the 'collaborative' framework that they seek. Unlike more professionally-directed models of research, action research can be difficult to 'manage' once underway.

In the area of drugs prevention, action research has been used in tandem with an approach that stresses the role of community development and community involvement. As a philosophy, 'community drugs prevention' entails residents gaining access to a range of social, political and economic resources. In this respect, drugs prevention is concerned with wider quality of life issues that residents define as important and will serve to reduce the demand for drug use. Action research has been used to mobilise communities in order to achieve these objectives.

The research used as a case study for the purpose of this paper took place in a locality exhibiting the usual indices of long-term social and economic decline, including widescale drugs-related difficulties. Initially, the commissioning agency (administered by the Home Office) was committed to devising a community-led drugs prevention strategy. Its original intention was that through operationalising action research, community concerns about drug misuse would be elicited alongside residents' perceptions of what 'drugs prevention' should involve, and residents would be encouraged to get involved in setting up projects and lobbying policy makers for relevant change. The commissioning agency perceived that the local urban regeneration agency would be a key funder for any future projects that may result from the research.

Initially, in-depth individual and group interviews became central to the research process. Later, a series of small-scale public meetings occurred, and community newsletters were produced. At the meetings the earlier findings were fed back to residents who, in turn, commented on them and suggested future directions that the project should take. Residents' participation took various forms. Apart from acting as 'informants' during the interviews, they produced articles that appeared in the newsletters, were actively involved in developing and conducting interviews with other residents, initiated and developed an on-going community forum which discussed the issues emerging from the research, and began lobbying local agencies to take part in various working groups in order that their concerns may be addressed. Although the initial research agenda had been more or less professionally-led, as time progressed, residents were changing the agenda and were leading the process through their actions.

The research had stimulated community awareness around 'drugs prevention' issues, had succeeded in producing an action plan for prevention, and a community forum had emerged comprising of local residents and representatives from local agencies. The regeneration agency (which had not become directly involved in the research process) became critical of the agency that had commissioned the research, the researcher, and the 'biased' outlook of residents that was being put forward in the newsletters published by the forum, and through the emerging research findings published in a working paper which was widely distributed within the locality.

According to its view, the research was merely serving to stir-up and magnify unjustified hostility toward its role in the area. The consequence was that other key agencies in the area (and involved with the forum) became reluctant to continue to support the activities of the local residents for fear of producing tensions between themselves and the powerful regeneration agency. Consequently, as the forum lacked backing from certain key voluntary and statutory sector agencies, the regeneration agency felt justified in not providing funding for projects outlined in the action plan. Funding for the action research and for the researcher expired after a six month period and residents were either unable or unwilling to continue their activities through the forum.

In some ways the action research ignited a powder keg that had been waiting to go off. Simmering tensions between sections of the community and the regeneration agency had frequently boiled over during a long period of time prior to the research. The locality traditionally had a strong and vocal community sector, and was predominantly staunchly left-wing in political outlook. They possessed little faith in the overall aims and objectives of the regeneration agency from not long after its inception - perceiving it to be an imposition from central government whose outlook was regarded as having changed little from those of previous Conservative administrations. The action research became part of the local political process and arguably politicized those residents who were previously not very vocal within the area.

At the outset, the commissioning body expressed a commitment toward 'community involvement' in drugs prevention, but it is doubtful whether it fully appreciated the potential implications of the action research. Based on a model used elsewhere, the agency perceived that the research would primarily involve a consultation exercise culminating in greater levels of community representation in existing and potential new projects. The agency perceived that the research would contribute toward an integrated approach for prevention, bringing organisations and residents together.

Residents expressed a strong commitment to the action research, given the emancipatory and participatory background of the paradigm, and viewed it as a welcome change from previous professionally controlled research that they had regarded as having been an end in itself: a mechanism for integrating residents and community groups into government and prevailing structures thereby giving programmes a degree of credibility and legitimacy, but not bringing about the changes for communities and residents that they desire (Todhunter, 2001). However, action research may appear to offer a potential for change, but just how much change may be expected given the wider interests of agencies and organisations that may be juxtaposed to proposed change?

Agencies may (unconsciously) seek to define residents' needs according to their specific remit, and attempt to set a research agenda accordingly - even though they may label it as 'action' research. In the case outlined here, the commissioning body appeared to put into operation their own limited notion of 'action research'. However, through the research residents emphasised a desire for exerting more direct power in order to facilitate their identity and rights as citizens. They were calling for equal participation on the partnership board of the regeneration agency which they felt was slanted against the interests of local people in favour of statutory sector and business interests. In effect, they were challenging the prevailing power structures by questioning the legitimacy of key agencies. Subsequently, the agency that commissioned the research was not able to respond fully to the needs or views of residents once unpacked.

In the shorter term, action research may produce a 'feel good' factor among participants - consciousness raising, 'participation' and mobilisation may instill a self-belief in ordinary people's capacity to bring about change. In the longer term, real and radical change may indeed come about. To do this however, commitment to change must be forthcoming among all local agencies and interest groups. Otherwise, action research may leave a bitter taste in the mouths of residents, whose expectations are raised, and subsequent programmes for change may have to cope with the damage done by previous projects that failed to deliver. Any good faith which may have been present among residents may have drained away leaving an embittered community that is hostile or cynical toward future programmes which come along.

In many respects the pitfalls that emerged in the case study presented here have been somewhat reminiscent of those surrounding the Community Development Projects of the 1970s. Workers in many of the projects came to reject the analysis and strategies of the original project proposals. They sought to organise and research around larger questions of inequality and deindustrialisation Workers who entered the field in the late 1960s and early 1970s exhibited a readiness to take up oppositional positions. By 1974 the Home Office had largely given up on the projects and they were wound up in 1976.

Commissioning bodies need to be fully aware of the potential pitfalls of undertaking action research. They must understand what 'action research' implies, and that it does not sit easily with conventional and easily manageable 'consultation' exercises - thus making it a high risk strategy. By committing to a process of action research, agencies are legitimizing residents' voices and actions, and their participation in social policy. In some respects they will embarking upon a programme that bucks a wider cultural and social trend encouraging 'involvement' which seeks to guarantee consensus and integration rather than change, and may find themselves in uncomfortable situations.

Action research is a tool that research commissioners must not take lightly, and not undertake impulsively. The groundwork has to be prepared thoroughly, given the potential impact. Agencies must give due thought about imposing a standard model of action research applied elsewhere to a different area, as in the study outlined here. They have to decide how feasible action research and change may be, given wider trends and local political situations, and must also prepare the groundwork effectively prior to committing to the research, bringing on board key players who may find themselves bearing the brunt of residents' frustrations and providing them with a chance to negotiate the shifting research agenda in tandem with residents.

For at least seventy years, some researchers around the world have been identifying what they do using terms like 'action research', or 'participatory research', or a combination of these. Some have stressed the action component,1 while others have focused more on the participatory process. Still others have come from the field of social science and have identified it as a means of inquiry or research per se.

This paper came about in response to requests to speak about some of the collective wisdom that has been generated over many decades by people who have identified what they do using the term 'participatory action research'. It is the way I tell the story.

Throughout this account participatory action research is contrasted with formulations of conventional research science. For me, participatory action research is not a different and separate matter from science at all, but constitutes a formulation of how I understand all science in the wake of the wave of thinking that is popularly being called the 'new physics'. This 'new physics' or 'new paradigm science' in the natural physical world seems to me to match a 'new paradigm science' in the social world. I identify 'participatory action research' not as an optional variant or specialist technique, but as one of the more inclusive descriptions of this new understanding of social science.

This short paper sets out to identify some of the main characteristics of participatory action research for me, and to try and show why I have come to the following two conclusions:

- 'Participatory action research' is a description of social research per se (albeit social research which is more conscious of its underlying assumptions, and collectivist nature, its action consequences and its driving values).
- It faces numerous barriers to its practice which mean that, even when we think we might be doing 'it', we often have our doubts! I have come to conclude that pretty much all of the research we are involved in, is more or less an approximation in the direction of 'it'. That is, every piece of research is more or less participatory. It more or less enables action as part of the process. And it all involves more or less critical reflexive, skeptical and imaginative inquiry.

What do we typically do when we 'do a piece of research'? Let's take a couple of everyday examples.

We are going about our business and a piece of equipment fails to work. We are pulled up in our tracks as we experience a discrepancy between our practice and our expectations. Out of our need for it to 'work', a question arises: 'Why is it so?'. We have a look at the piece of equipment: perhaps involving a little piece of hands-on 'participant observation' fieldwork! Perhaps we employ also some 'secondary analysis' as we consult the maker's manual for their theories and advice! We may develop a hunch (hypothesis) and draw some conclusions. Then we try it out in a form of a naturalistic experiment and we 'give it a go'. Again we go about our business. The equipment works and we carry on. Or, it fails to work again and we again stop in our tracks and raise our question again, and try further fieldwork to develop yet another theory and try yet another tack, and so on.

We are looking for our daughter's shoes in the early morning scramble. We review previous 'historical data' (memories of earlier experiences!) as part of planning our 'research design'. We generate several hypotheses and move quickly into the 'field' to involve other participants and gather new data to test them! We use some observational anthropology. Two brief interviews with daughter and sibling result in reports of failed hunches! (they weren't in their cupboards or on the back verandah!); we engage in further open-ended interviews with the entire household population. Then secondary analysis of the previous day's timetable generates a further hunch (Sports Day!: shoes replaced with runners) and an additional round of observation reveals: shoes in school bag!

These trivial microcosms contain a structure which reliably:

- commences - ironically - with stopping. That is, we do not begin to inquire until we actually suspend our current action because of the:
- Raising of a question; which then provokes us to go about:
- Planning ways to get answers - ways which will involve identifying and involving 'questioners', 'the questioned' and an idea of for who or for what we desire answers;
- Engaging in fieldwork about new, current or past action in order to get answers and improve our

experiential understanding of the problematic situation;

- Generating from the 'answers' an imaginative idea of what to do to change and improve our actions;
- The putting into practice of the new actions (followed by further stopping, reflecting and possible 'problematisation').

This is precisely the cycle of action, reflection, raising of questions, planning of 'fieldwork' to review current (and past) actions - its conduct, analysis of experiences encountered, the drawing of conclusions, and the planning of new and transformed actions - that characterizes all research endeavor. If we are to distinguish this cycle in any ways from what we 'do all the time', we find the important distinctions are in degree rather than kind. That is, in participatory action research we are:

- More conscious of 'problematising' an existing action or practice and more conscious of who is problematising it and why we are problematising it;
- More explicit about 'naming' the problem, and more self-conscious about raising an unanswered question and focusing an effort to answer it;
- More planned and deliberate about commencing a process of inquiry and involving others who could or should be involved in that inquiry;
- More systematic and rigorous in our efforts to get answers;
- More carefully documenting and recording action and what people think about it and in more detail and in ways which are accessible to other relevant parties;
- More intensive and comprehensive in our study, waiting much longer before we 'jump' to a conclusion;
- More self-sceptical in checking our hunches;
- Attempting to develop deeper understandings and more useful and more powerful theory about the

matters we are researching, in order to produce new knowledge which can inform improved action or practice; 6 and

- Changing our actions as part of the research process, and then further researching these changed actions.

One of the ways this understanding of research differs from conceptions of conventional research or 'old paradigm science' is revealed in the diagrams below. Conventional research often sees itself as proceeding from point A to point B along a straight line - commencing with a hypothesis and proceeding to a conclusion which may then be published in a journal.

However new paradigm social science (or participatory action research) considers it critical to the success of the inquiry that the hypothesis is relevant and useful and thus asks: Where did the hunches or hypotheses come from? Are they just any old hypotheses? Or have they been carefully constructed and well-grounded, over time, from deep and engaged involvement in the field being studied? Are they plausible? Are they relevant? Are they already well-evidenced and thus already substantiate new action? (rather than having to spend time re-discovering or re-confirming the already-established).

Furthermore, new paradigm science asks: Have they been checked in practice? Findings, 'discoveries' or new ideas are not accepted until tested in action - otherwise they remain merely 'interesting ideas' or 'just academic'.

Instead of a linear model, participatory action research thus proceeds through cycles, 'starting' with reflection on action, and proceeding round to new action which is then further researched. The new actions differ from the old actions - they are literally in different places.

Interestingly, all science seems to me to follow this logic. However many 'old paradigm' scientists are unaware of their implication in this. There is always new action resulting - even if it is just the same as the old (which we might describe as reproducing the 'status quo'). Inquiry inevitably leads somewhere - even if it isn't far from where it started, or only a small number of people are consciously aware of it. Once inquirers are aware of the implications of inquiring, they are faced with a choice. They can ignore it (or treat it as peripheral or of nuisance value), or they can resolve to work with it as a positive feature of their research environment. Action researchers, it seems to me, are really just researchers who have come to understand the practical and ethical implications of the inevitability of the value-driven and action-effects of their inquiry, that is:

- The effects of raising some questions and not others,
- The effects of involving some people in the process (or even apparently only one) and not others,
- The effects of observing some phenomena and not others,
- The effects of making this sense of it and not alternative senses, and
- The effects of deciding to take this action (or 'no' action) as a result of it rather than any other action and so on.

All research involves these kinds of decisions. Participatory action research attempts to make these decisions more consciously and in relation to more clearly-worked out purposes, and using more appropriate designs and techniques for exploring them.

**The Action Element**

All research seems to me to be implicated in action. Not only is research itself an action in and on existing situations, but it also always has consequences. Things inevitably change as a result of research - the mere act of asking questions is an intervention in a situation, and giving and hearing answers and making sense of them inevitably brings about changes in those involved. Whether people then choose to continue as before or to change course means that the new situation will either be different from that before, or it will be the same. To 'not change' is nevertheless action: some might call it inaction!

Participatory action research is aware of its inevitable intervention in the social situations within which it operates and seeks to turn these to consciously-applied effect. Most participatory action research sets out to explicitly study something in order to change and improve it. It most often arises from an unsatisfactory situation that those most affected wish to alter for the better (although it can also arise from the experience of something which works well, which provokes the desire to reproduce or expand it).

The moving to new and improved action involves a creative 'moment' of transformation. 7 This involves an imaginative leap from a world of 'as it is' to a glimpse of a world 'as it could be'. Where existing situations benefit or promote some but disadvantage or subordinate others, then creative change may be construed as 'political'. As well, participatory action research does not conceptualise this as the development of predictive cause-effect theory ('if this, then that'). Instead, as in the slogan: 'the future is made, not predicted', it is more like 'what if we..., then maybe'. Possibility theory rather than predictive theory. That is, human actors are both wilful and capable of thwarting research prediction, and wilful and capable of selecting and implementing theories or probabilities they want to see manifested! Conventional science sees this as undesirable 'contamination' and 'bias'. Participatory action research sees this as a goal, and the stuff of which 'real life' is made or enacted.

Action research, like the discovery phase of any science, knows it is coming from somewhere and going to somewhere, even though it does not know in advance where precisely it is going to end up or what the new state will look like. Participatory action research, unlike conventional science, does not consider this to be an embarrassment! However it can be difficult for researchers (and research funders) accustomed primarily to a formal experimental approach (the verificationist phase of science), since all that can be stated at the outset is that certain parties have noticed certain problematic matters and have planned certain participatory processes in order to try and 'crack it' for a new way to approach the matter. It may be that funders need to fund iterative or emergent research in connecting stages of 'seeding', 'sapling' and 'tree' phases (and not with up to a year's time lapse in between, as at present).

As there is an infinity of 'could be' worlds, then the action phase is crucially guided by the depth and quality of theorising achieved by the research participants. Superficial or trivial research will result in superficial and trivial ideas for practice.

The major challenge for all participatory action researchers (and indeed all researchers) is to design a process which can result in maximum creativity and imagination. Some of the most spectacular ideas have come about because researchers (or self-researchers) were able to draw on unusual sources for ideas, and then submit them to their critical reference group 10 to see if they 'resonated'. If such creative and imaginative efforts have been well-driven by a critical reference group perspective and well-grounded in an understanding of the critical reference group and their context or environment (including the effects of others and of 'structural' matters or opportunities impinging), then they stand a much better chance of 'getting it right' and ideas 'taking off'. Pretty much every initiative we now see around us as A Good Thing happened in this way: as a product of people who 'knew their turf', knew who they were doing it for, and had the imagination to collectively envision a desirable new state and attract others who shared that vision.

In participatory action research, while there is a conceptual difference between the 'participation' 'action' and 'research' elements, in its most developed state these differences begin to dissolve in practice. That is, there is not participation followed by research and then hopefully action. Instead there are countless tiny cycles of participatory reflection on action, learning about action and then new informed action which is in turn the subject of further reflection. Every minute of every hour may see participants absorbing new ways of seeing or thinking in the light of their experience, leading to new related actions being taken on the spot. Often these will pass unnoticed and unrecorded, but with practice these too become the subject of further reflection and group self-understanding. Change does not happen at 'the end' - it happens throughout. A hallmark of a genuine participatory action research process is that it may change shape and focus over time (and sometimes quite unexpectedly) as participants focus and refocus their understandings about what is 'really' happening and what is really important to them.

It is not possible to do any social research without the participation of other human beings. In typical research there might be one or more 'researchers', there might be people who are 'researched', and there might be people who are 'researched for' - such as those who are to be informed or influenced by findings, or, at a more fundamental level, those who have a problem on which the research is to cast light. However even the research that seems to involve 'no-one', such as the most lone and unobtrusive academic researcher, examining written historical records of people long dead, who seems to be isolated from 'real world practice', and is relatively unknown to peers, still exists in a social world peopled by family, friends, fellow academics, academic administrators, tax-payers and politicians, funding bodies, editors of journals or thesis-examiners, as well as by the written representations of the researched (and there may also be some living representatives) which nevertheless must 'speak' and be 'heard' and understood by the researcher. These all impinge on, and 'construct' the research environment and it's findings, regardless of their apparent invisibility.

More usually there are known groups of researchers, people who commission the research, and live populations of 'researched' and 'researched for', many of whom may know of the research and want to have a say about its conduct or contribute a view about its subject-matter.

Various parties to research 'participate', but the questions become 'Who is treated as participants?', 'How much do they participate?', 'In what ways do they participate?', and 'How is their participation taken into account or not taken into account?'.

Indeed the reason why many of us have felt compelled to add the "p" for participation to the "ar" for action research has been because we have noticed that many have taken existing levels of conventional 'participation' for granted. More importantly there may have been a complacency about the adequacy of current input. Here is a chicken and egg. How do existing participants know the limits of their own perceptions without new participants being there to illuminate the relativism of the existing participants' perceptions - and how would the new participants get to be involved, invited (or tolerated) if their value is not known?

It is worth drawing out the differences between the parties to research in more detail to examine the new possibilities for participation.

In a conventional piece of research there may be less apparent participation. For example, management (group iv), is puzzled or uneasy about some existing matter, or under pressure from another group (iii) or (iv) to Do Something. They might typically employ an independent researcher, (i), to go and study some of the people-with-a-problem, (iii) and perhaps also have some informal discussions with staff, (iv). They may limit their involvement to an initial briefing, the receipt of progress reports, attendance at a steering committee, and receipt of a final report. The researcher may be an academic or a private consultant with some other interests in the matter themselves, (i) and (iv). They are constrained to appear to be neutral or perhaps mildly on everyone's side. They may also be on a short term, highly paid contract with high performance expectations. They expect to get into the field, get the data, get out cleanly, write it up, add some recommendations that seem feasible and then move on to the next demanding job.

The people-with-a-problem: 'clients', 'patients', 'students', or other group of disadvantaged people, (iii), may be directly hurt or disadvantaged by the existing problematic matter, and may or may not have questioned whether there might be a reason for it, and/or a better way. This group is frequently part of 'the researched', although sometimes they may not know it. If they do, they may typically find themselves on the receiving end of a questionnaire or an interview. One of their number may be invited to sit on an Advisory Committee. Some other 'stakeholders': staff, carers, providers, (iv), may be indirectly involved. In conventional research, they may also be questionnaire or interviewed about the group-with-the-problem, or about their service to them or care of them, and perhaps even asked what they think should be changed; and they might also be on the Committee. All then await the researchers' announcement of their 'findings'.

What can typically plague the whole process of such conventional research are the consequences of non participation:

- In the first place there can be confusion or lack of agreement regarding the direction and purpose of the inquiry (for whom and for what).
- There is subsequent disagreement about the form the study should take (how, where, when, who should be involved).
- Alternatively the wrong direction is taken and dissent suppressed or ignored. The wrong questions are asked. The data is then irrelevant. And the conclusions useless.
- There can be misunderstandings about participants' perceptions (about the situation being studied).
- There can be conflict over interpretations and analyses (the 'why' and 'how').
- And there can be disagreement about what these imply for change in action (what next).
- And there can be shooting of the messenger! Or of the manager. Or mutinous troops. And critical reference groups' situations left unchanged.

There is an important point to be made here. Over many years I have observed that where the parties (i), (ii), (iii) and (iv) are more distant from each other and from involvement in the process of inquiry, trouble ensues.

Once in the past a place might have been seen for participation by the various parties at the outset on a committee, or at the end as recipients of a report. Increasingly instead they might become contributors to all stages of the research cycle - as designers, selectors of methods, contributors of 'data', 'analysers' and 'concluders', and then 'takers (or monitors) of new actions', and so on. All parties begin to operate much more as both co-researchers and co-subjects.

In participatory action research, the four conceptual categories of participants may thus in practice become much more overlapping depending on the purposes of the research, and who is 'driving' it. For example, there may be more participation, where a self help group (iii), self-researches (i) its own experiences (ii) and those of others (iv), for itself or for others (i or iv).

The arguments for there being more rather than less participation by all four parties are as follows:

- Those commissioning or carrying out the research These usually already participate the most since they choose the questions, decide how they will be answered, interpret the answers and decide what has been 'discovered'. Yet frequently even they feel constrained to disguise, restrict or eliminate their ideas and values, or refrain from putting in their experiences or their views or opinions, on the grounds the research should be 'objective' and 'unbiased', and 'value-free'. In this way, other participants may never be properly informed about the nature and purposes of the research, and the research design may begin way back 'behind the eight ball' instead of where there is a genuine unanswered question. This may truly bias or distort the research. Feminist 13 and other critical theory 14 research as well as so-called fourth generation evaluation 15 has begun to show a way for researchers (and those commissioning the research) to be more genuine and honest participants in and contributors to their own research.

These approaches have shown also how there can be more of a dissolution of the distinction between researcher/s and 'researched for' (the critical reference group).

- Thus, for example, a more participating researcher would be more clear about why they are interested in the research - perhaps describing their own personal experiences that have led to the questions they are wanting to ask. This clarifies the purposes for other participants, and helps each participant know where the other is 'coming from'. Further, the participating researcher/s, having identified the interests they wish to pursue, can see (and be seen in) their relationship to the critical reference group, and pursue more consciously and sceptically, alternative formulations of the situation.
- The critical reference group: This group conventionally participates least since professional and academic research largely researches on and about and speaks for the disadvantaged, or groups with unmet needs the research is meant to benefit. Laura Nader has called this approach 'studying down' (1972). The identification and involvement of the critical reference group, or even broad relevant critical reference 'arenas' or critical reference 'publics' however, I have noticed leads to:
  - Improved relevance of the inquiry to those who share in the problem;
  - Sharper focusing of the research questions;
  - Enhanced relevance of the inquiry to those whose jobs are to do something about the problem (whether as a service provider, a carer, an administrator, a funder, etc.);

- Increased effectiveness of the research design (what is asked, by whom, of whom, when, where and how);
- Improved meaningfulness of the information thus gained (the researched especially have a say in whether any inquiry 'got it right' in regard to the meaning of what they said or did);
- The power and accuracy of the theory developed to understand the problem;
- The relevance, creativity and effectiveness of the new actions decided-on;
- And the commitment to observing the new actions and acting on and researching of them further.

The difficulties in involving critical reference groups and them remaining involved are numerous. The discussion of how to achieve these conditions of mutual involvement, participation and collaboration are very similar to the discussions about how to achieve 'community development'. For example, the more disempowered you are, the less hope you may have about either the value of participating or even the chances of something good coming out of it. If you are radically disempowered you may not even be able to envisage something better, when even a vague or indistinct vision is a prerequisite for pursuing one at all.

Nevertheless, members of critical reference groups who have problematised a situation are in the most strategic position to work on its improvement. Participatory action research, in its most-developed form, works to assist critical reference groups - and those who share their perspective - pursue their inquiries, by themselves and for themselves, as a community-of-interest. The role of 'outsiders' or those who are not members of critical reference groups changes radically. Rather than operating as the independent expert determiner of the truth-of-the-situation (with critical reference groups assisting the researcher in their pursuit of The Truth), the 'researcher' becomes a facilitator of or an assistant to the critical reference group's own pursuit of their truth (or truths).

- Stakeholders other than the researcher/s and the critical reference group (and whether interested or hostile)

  These typically participate only at the outset: perhaps to convene a Committee or allocate a research brief or contribute funds, or just at the end: to receive a research report or hear of its findings. The pitfalls and wastage that can be associated with this level of participation are numerous. A few possible results include:

  - Manipulation of the research process 'off stage' (by powerful parties who never participated in a democratic process around a table with all other parties), and possible ultimate resistance by other parties when their participation proves to be pointless;
  - Rejection of a report by some or all because they simply never went through the same learning process as did the researcher/s and the critical reference group and never reached the same conclusions;
  - Frustration with a process that does not reflect their realities;
  - Inability to see what are the practical consequences of a set of findings or recommendations.

Service providers can specially benefit from full participation so that the link between their 'theory' (why they do what they do) is in closer connection with their 'practice' (what they actually do). Indeed, in much action research in Western countries, the primary participants are service-providers who work in small circles, examining their practice and trying out alternative ways of working. For the value of this to be maximised, participation needs to be organised around the interests of the critical reference group or driven by a critical reference group perspective, or else the research can risk becoming sidetracked.

- The researched: This may typically be the critical reference group, along with some service-providers or their representatives. However, again I have found that the more there is active participation the greater the chances of maximising both the accuracy and meaningfulness of all contributions, and also the sharing of perceptions and of emerging understandings about the value of what new actions should next be taken.

Research which involves the collaboration of people, rarely is sustained without a shared purpose, and this 'shared purpose' stems from what understandings people have together developed about what is of value. If understanding is not for 'its own sake', but directed towards understanding something 'in order to...', then the point of purposeful inquiry is action. As pointed out before, where the categories 'the researched' and 'the researchers' and 'the researched for' begin to become less distinct, this collaboration can become more cohesive.

What kind of action is for the parties to decide - focused by the perspective of the critical reference group. As pointed out earlier, that new action might be the reproduction of the same old action as was taken previously if it involves researchers who believe they neither are contributing (nor want to contribute) to change. This is research which may carefully reproduce the status quo. Other research, which is self-conscious about why it asked the questions it does, wishes instead to head towards a different and improved state of affairs.

Participatory action research is a term that brings together a set of assumptions underlying 'new paradigm' science and in contrast to those of traditional or 'old paradigm' science. These new assumptions underline the importance of social and collective processes in reaching conclusions about 'what is the case', and what the implications are for change which is deemed useful by those whose problematic situation led to the research in the first place.

In 'real life', actual researchers often straddle (more or less uncomfortably) the two paradigms, but the paradigms themselves are coherent bodies of thought that are not theoretically commensurable. But a paradigm addresses the unsolved problems of the previous paradigm. So while positivism arose to bring certainty and verifiability to a world construed as 'irrational', post positivism addresses the inability to handle enormous complexity in large, cybernetic, self-changing human systems. If conventional science wanted to give a group of people the power to determine 'truth' for and on behalf of others, the new science arose from a world of multiple and competing versions of truth and reality as a way of assisting people both come to the truth of their own reality, and also to embrace that of others.

The urgency of such mutual understanding is to be found in the topics selected by PAR practitioners - mostly concerned with difficult situations of social change, the loss of ways to meet human needs, the rise of anxieties and fears as we become strangers to each other, and the threat of dissolution into violence and alienation.

On such big fronts, participatory action research proceeds modestly, but it does proceed! For all these reasons participatory action research is not just research which we hope will be followed by action! It is action which is researched, changed and re-researched, within the research process by participants. Nor is it simply an exotic variant of consultation. Instead, it aims to be active co-research, by and for those to be helped. Nor can it be used by one group of people to get another group of people to do what is thought best for them - whether that is to implement a central policy or an organisational or service change. Instead it tries to be a genuinely democratic or non-coercive process whereby those to be helped, determine the purposes and outcomes of their own inquiry. Paradoxically it is quite close to a common-sense way of 'learning by doing'. But at the same time it is very hard to achieve the ideal conditions for putting it fully into practice.

Essentially participatory action research is research which involves all relevant parties in actively examining together current action (which they experience as problematic) in order to change and improve it. They do this by critically reflecting on the historical, political, cultural, economic, geographic and other contexts which make sense of it.

'Current problematic action' may range from the trivial to the life-threatening. Much participatory action research lies between these ends of the scale, and typically involves yourself; those who share your concerns, experiences and interests; others suffering from the problematic situation; others trying to assist it to change; and those who oversee the material resources needed to underpin the change effort (such as funds, people, salaries, services, office resources, etc.). Bringing these parties together, and absorbing new ones as the action research effort proceeds to unfold and implicate parties further afield, is not merely a side issue of 'entry to the field' but a central focus for achieving understanding and change. As well, action research is not research which sees these as 'contaminating' processes which 'bias' the scientific effort, nor does it have a problem with the 'researcher/s' identifying with 'the researched' and the 'researched for', - seeing this rather as essential to the gaining of engaged understanding.

What 'drives' participatory action research, like any research, is our 'need to know' in order to bring about desired change. We often shorthand term this our 'values' - which are our precious images of valued states or ways of being. Rather than seeing this holding-of-values as subjective and potentially a source of bias, the strength of the values we hold will determine the power and direction of our research efforts. Two key additional factors which will shape what we do is the strength of our imaginations (to theorise more creatively, deeply and imaginatively) and our scepticism (to keep our theory closely in relationship to the practices we are observing). Like any other research, the critical moment is that of 'discovery' or rather: 'invention' of a different and better way of seeing and understanding our realities. The old adage about science being 5% inspiration and 95% perspiration may hold true enough! The hard sweat and toil comprises the long hours of talking and thinking and sharing the results of our 'fieldwork' with one another. The moment of inspired thinking is when collective values are expressed in a new way of connecting ideas or a new way of 'naming' the world, that advances the collective situation of participants.

The field of action research deriving from education (particularly school room practice) and third world development more often have stressed the necessity of moving relatively quickly towards new action.

The post-war British field of action research, drawing on theory about group psychology or group dynamics, stressed the area of process, sometimes involving very diverse interests from the outset.

They include the classical social anthropology-trained sociologist William Foote Whyte who has moved to action research from what he now calls 'participatory research' (eg. his classic 1943 ethnographic study of an inner city immigrant American-Italian community). Another prominent American sociologist Shulamit Reinharz tells her story of moving from disembodied researching 'on' people to humanistic, qualitative and experiential researching 'with' people (1979). I, myself (Yoland Wadsworth), a Monash-trained sociologist have told of a similar trajectory (1985), moving from using standard large-scale random sample surveys analysed by the obligatory SPSS, to embracing interpretivist phhenomonology to working increasingly with and for critical reference groups using a critical constructivist methodology.

Old paradigm social science is often popularly termed 'positivist'. This refers to a school of philosophical thought which saw the world as having a single 'reality' which existed independently of the observer, and which could only be discovered by an objective and uninvolved scientist through acts of pure perception, ideally in a laboratory setting where all variables could be controlled and manipulated, and exact causation determined. This account has been difficult to sustain in practice - as with Newtonian science - given the limitations of such an uninvolved science. Far more engaged research - literally 'going native' - yields far better understanding. As well, when the social world is encountered, it takes as many forms as there are people. That is, understanding the social world depends on the exchange and communication of interpretations about what is going on. These are multiple and may be conflicting. As with post-Einsteinian physics, the 'observed' is importantly constructed by 'the observer' - and in the social world, is then further reconstructed by the observed (sometimes in the light of the observer's observations!). For old paradigm science this is all so much unwanted 'bias' and 'contamination'. For new paradigm science it is the nature of the 'beast', and all so much more material for illuminating inquiry. New paradigm science also grasps the value-driven nature of inquiry and is in a position to focus its research in the interests of those who might problematise their existing undesirable situations. This offers a better chance of 'driving' theory towards better contributing to practice, and also avoiding the unethical and totalitarian consequences of a science which sees itself as 'value free'.

More formal language which is used to describe 'participatory action research' as a particular philosophy of knowledge (theory of how we know, or the grounds for knowledge, i.e. epistemology) also includes 'critical constructivist', 'post positivist' or 'critical interpretive' methodology.

Ironically, conventional experimental science can have its own problems and 'fail' when an ungrounded (irrelevant and wide of the mark) hypothesis is elaborately and expensively tested, only to discover that it was a poor proposition in the first place. Alternatively, in social science, such poor propositions can survive in the literature and even make their researchers famous (and lead to high status positions!) in the absence of participatory processes or testing in practice which would supply the necessary feedback about their faulty or narrow character. The spectacular failure of European sociologists to predict the bringing down of the Berlin Wall testifies in the same way as the failure of meteorologists to predict the weather accurately. Mostly both sociologists and meteorologists (as well as ordinary people who are observant and shrewd, and who can tap their barometers and feel the aches in their bones) pretty much get it right. Newtonian science mainly works. The break downs occur when matters are enormously complex and defy 'control of variables'. Unfortunately these may be precisely the critical times in messy complex changing human societies.

As well, some academic researchers claim with pride that there are no known beneficiaries of research (and not even an arena of potential beneficiaries). This is what they might call 'pure' research, or 'curiosity-driven' research 'for its own sake'. It is very important that there be time and space for curiosity and speculative forays out into unknown waters and apparently 'irrelevant' matters. However even 'idle' curiosity is always historically and socially located (eg. Fleming's noticing of the penicillin mould) and thus shaped by the social world in which the 'idle curious' have grown up, learned language, learned values, and learned to notice some things and not others. 80% of all scientists, 'pure' and 'applied' alike, just happen to be curious in ways helpful to defence establishments all around the world. On the other hand even the most apparently esoteric inquirer frequently has quite well-formed views about the relevance of their line of inquiry (for example the relationship between Jacobin clothing styles and early capitalist modes of economy, and its relevance to late twentieth century post modernity). Where researchers themselves have no insight, someone else might well be able to carry out a little 'archaeology' and suggest something. For most research in the human services area, the critical reference group is very much more readily identified as service users.

Feminist research utilises (more or less sucessfully) a participatory action research methodology and additionally works in a topic area determined by a particular critical reference group: that of women. The kind of feminist theory used will reflect and in turn determine what kind of use is made of the research, and by whom.

Critical theory is a school of social science which developed firstly in Frankfurt and then in the United States of America after its members went into exile before and during the second world war. It has attempted to bring together the insights of Freudian (and now post Freudian) psychology and Marxian economics, in order to understand how the personal and the structural come together into ideological forms from which some benefit at the expense of others. Its better-known theorists include Adorno, Horkheimer, Habermas and Marcuse. It is now used as a term to describe a range of approaches which raise critical questions about the conditions which sustain existing forms of social life that are experienced as problematic by particular groups of people.

Fourth generation evaluation is a term coined by the Americans Egon Guba and Yvonna Lincoln to describe the application of constructivist methodology to evaluation (in the wake of three previous generations of evaluation which they have criticised on the grounds of over-adherence to a positivist epistemology and to managerialist dominance). They argued for the admission of all relevant parties to the process, and recast the evaluator as a facilitator of an essentially self-evaluation process.

For example school-based action research where parents and students may be involved, however the primary questions identified are those of the teachers. See also hospital projects which similarly stem from nurses' concerns in the absence of patients. Or welfare research about youth suicide or single mothers without any representation of these groups in the research team or committee. Where the questions are not necessarily those of the critical reference group, the research relies on disembodied critical theory to illuminate the assumptions behind things and thus reveal new choices of more relevant topics. For example, say psychiatric nurses want to research how to protect themselves from patient violence. They could recommend regular time off for themselves to recover from their stress. The asking of critical question, such as 'what would be also good for patients?' might lead to this particular solution being problematised however, and set in train a further search for a different solution which does not meet the needs of one group at the expense of another. If patients participate in the research, they might give their perceptions of why the violence arises, leading to a different solution which also might not compound patients' existing problems of loss of staff continuity.

## CONSENSUS DECISION-MAKING

Consensus decision-making is a decision-making process that not only seeks the agreement of most participants, but also to resolve or mitigate the objections of the minority to achieve the most agreeable decision. Consensus is usually defined as meaning both: a) general agreement, and b) the process of getting to such agreement. Consensus decision-making is thus concerned primarily with that process.

Decision making is the cognitive process leading to the selection of a course of action among alternatives. Every decision making process produces a final choice. It can be an action or an opinion. It begins when we need to do something but we do not know what. Therefore, decision making is a reasoning process which can be rational or irrational, and can be based on explicit assumptions or tacit assumptions.

Common examples include shopping, deciding what to eat, when to sleep, and deciding whom or what to vote for in an election or referendum.

Decision making is said to be a psychological construct. This means that although we can never "see" a decision, we can infer from observable behaviour that a decision has been made. Therefore, we conclude that a psychological event that we call "decision making" has occurred. It is a construction that imputes commitment to action. That is, based on observable actions, we assume that people have made a commitment to affect the action.

Structured rational decision making is an important part of all science-based professions, where specialists apply their knowledge in a given area to making informed decisions. For example, medical decision making often involves making a diagnosis and selecting an appropriate treatment. Some research using naturalistic methods shows, however, that in situations with higher time pressure, higher stakes, or increased ambiguities, experts use intuitive decision making rather than structured approaches, following a recognition primed decision approach to fit a set of indicators into the expert's experience and immediately arrive at a satisfactory course of action without weighing alternatives.

Due to the large number of considerations involved in many decisions, computer-based decision support systems have been developed to assist decision makers in considering the implications of various courses of thinking. They can help reduce the risk of human errors. The systems which try to realize some human/cognitive decision making functions are called Intelligent Decision Support Systems (IDSS).

According to behaviouralist Isabel Briggs Myers, a person's decision making process depends to a significant degree on their cognitive style. Starting from the work of Carl Jung, Myers developed a set of four bi-polar dimensions, called the Myers-Briggs Type Indicator (MBTI). The terminal points on these dimensions are: thinking and feeling; extroversion and introversion; judgement and perception; and sensing and intuition. She claimed that a person's decision making style is based largely on how they score on these four dimensions. For example, someone that scored near the thinking, extroversion, sensing, and judgement ends of the dimensions would tend to have a logical, analytical, objective, critical, and empirical decision making style.

## COGNITIVE AND PERSONAL BIASES IN DECISION MAKING

It is generally agreed that biases can creep into our decision making processes, calling into question the correctness of a decision. It is not generally agreed, however, which normative models are to be used to evaluate what constitutes an erroneous decision. Nor is the scientific evidence for all of the biases agreed upon. So, while it is agreed that decision making can be biased, how to tell when it is, and specific cases of biases, are often challenged. The issue in general can be quite controverial among scholars in the field. Below is a list of some of the more commonly debated cognitive biases.

- Selective search for evidence - We tend to be willing to gather facts that support certain conclusions but disregard other facts that support different conclusions.
- Premature termination of search for evidence - We tend to accept the first alternative that looks like it might work.
- Inertia - Unwillingness to change thought patterns that we have used in the past in the face of new circumstances.
- Contrariness or rebelliousness - Unwillingness to share a view with a perceived oppressive authority.
- Experiential limitations - Unwillingness or inability to look beyond the scope of our past experiences; rejection of the unfamiliar.
- Selective perception - We actively screen-out information that we do not think is salient.
- Wishful thinking or optimism - We tend to want to see things in a positive light and this can distort our perception and thinking.
- Choice-supportive bias occurs when we distort our memories of chosen and rejected options to make the chosen options seem relatively more attractive.
- Recency - We tend to place more attention on more recent information and either ignore or forget more distant information.

- Repetition bias - A willingness to believe what we have been told most often and by the greatest number of different of sources.
- Anchoring and adjustment - Decisions are unduly influenced by initial information that shapes our view of subsequent information.
- Group think - Peer pressure to conform to the opinions held by the group.
- Source credibility bias - We reject something if we have a bias against the person, organization, or group to which the person belongs: We are inclined to accept a statement by someone we like.
- Incremental decision making and escalating commitment - We look at a decision as a small step in a process and this tends to perpetuate a series of similar decisions. This can be contrasted with zero-based decision making.
- Inconsistency - The unwillingness to apply the same decision criteria in similar situations.
- Attribution asymmetry - We tend to attribute our success to our abilities and talents, but we attribute our failures to bad luck and external factors. We attribute other's success to good luck, and their failures to their mistakes.
- Role fulfillment - We conform to the decision making expectations that others have of someone in our position.
- Underestimating uncertainty and the illusion of control - We tend to underestimate future uncertainty because we tend to believe we have more control over events than we really do. We believe we have control to minimize potential problems in our decisions.
- Faulty generalizations - In order to simplify an extremely complex world, we tend to group things and people. These simplifying generalizations can bias decision making processes.

- Ascription of causality - We tend to ascribe causation even when the evidence only suggests correlation. Just because birds fly to the equatorial regions when the trees lose their leaves, does not mean that the birds migrate because the trees lose their leaves.

## COGNITIVE NEUROSCIENCE OF DECISION MAKING

The anterior cingulate cortex (ACC) and orbitofrontal cortex are brain regions involved in decision making processes. A recent neuroimaging study, Interactions between decision making and performance monitoring within prefrontal cortex, found distinctive patterns of neural activation in these regions depending on whether decisions were made on the basis of personal volition or following directions from someone else.

Another recent study by Kennerly, et al. (2006) found that lesions to the ACC in the macaque resulted in impaired decision making in the long run of reinforcement guided tasks suggesting that the ACC is responsible for evaluating past reinforcement information and guiding future action.

Decision making in groups is sometimes examined separately as process and outcome. Process refers to the interactions group. Some relevant ideas include coalitions among participants as well as influence and persuasion. The use of politics is often judged negatively, but it is a useful way to approach problems when preferences among actors are in conflict, when dependencies exist that cannot be avoided, when there are no super-ordinate authorities, and when the technical or scientific merit of the options is ambiguous.

In addition to the different processes involved in making decisions, group decision support systems (GDSS) may have different decision rules. A decision rule is the GDSS protocol a group uses to choose among scenario planning alternatives.

- Unanimity is commonly used by juries in criminal trials in the United States. Unanimity requires everyone to agree on a given course of action, and thus imposes a high bar for action.

- Majority requires support from more than 50% of the members of the group. Thus, the bar for action is lower than with unanimity and a group of "losers" is implicit to this rule.
- Consensus decision-making tries to avoid "winners" and "losers". Consensus requires that a majority approve a given course of action, but that the minority agree to go along with the course of action. In other words, if the minority opposes the course of action, consensus requires that the course of action be modified to remove objectionable features.
- Gathering involves all participants acknowledging each other's needs and opinions and tends towards a problem solving approach in which as many needs and opinions as possible can be satisfied. It allows for multiple outcomes and does not require agreement from some for others to act.
- Sub-committee involves assigning responsibility for evaluation of a decision to a sub-set of a larger group, which then comes back to the larger group with recommendations for action. Using a sub-committee is more common in larger governance groups, such as a legislature. Sometimes a sub-committee includes those individuals most affected by a decision, although at other times it is useful for the larger group to have a sub-committee that involves more neutral participants.

Less desirable group decision rules are:

- Plurality, where the largest block in a group decides, even if it falls short of a majority.
- Dictatorship, where one individual determines the course of action.

Plurality and dictatorship are less desirable as decision rules because they do not require the involvement of the broader group to determine a choice. Thus, they do not engender commitment to the course of action chosen. An absence of commitment from individuals in the group can be problematic during the implementation phase of a decision.

There are no perfect decision making rules. Depending on how the rules are implemented in practice and the situation, all of these can lead to situations where either no decision is made, or to situations where decisions made are inconsistent with one another over time.

The ethical principles of decision making vary considerably. Some common choices of principles and the methods which seem to match them include:

- The most powerful person/group decides
  - Method: dictatorship or oligarchy
- Everyone participates in a certain class of meta-decisions
  - Method: parliamentary democracy
- Everyone participates in every decision
  - Direct democracy, consensus decision making

There are many decision making levels having a participation element. A common example is that of institutions making decisions that affect those for whom they provide. In such cases an understanding of what participation level is involved becomes crucial to understand the process and power structures dynamics.

Some of the decision making techniques that we use in everyday life include:

- Listing the advantages and disadvantages of each option, popularized by Benjamin Franklin
- Flipping a coin, cutting a deck of playing cards, and other random or coincidence methods
- Accepting the first option that seems like it might achieve the desired result
- Tarot cards, astrology, augurs, revelation, or other forms of divination
- Acquiesce to a person in authority or an "expert"
- Calculating the expected value for each option. For example, a person is considering two jobs. At the first

job option the person has a 60% chance of getting a 30% percent raise in the first year. And at the second job option the person has a 80% chance of getting a 10% raise in the first year. The decision maker would calculate the expected value of each option, calculating the probability multiplied by the increase of value. (0.60*0.30=0.18 [option a] 0.80*0.10=0.08 [option b]) The person deciding on the job would chose the option with the highest expected value, in this example option a.

An alternative may be to apply one of the processes described below, in particular in the Business and Management section.

In the health care field, the steps of making a decision may be remembered with the mnemonic BRAND, which includes

- Benefits of the action
- Risks in the action
- Alternatives to the prospective action
- Nothing: that is, doing nothing at all
- Decision

## DECISION MAKING MODELS

- Economic men and women is a mathematical model used for human behaviour. This model is used to describe three things:

• Decision makers are informed on all possible options for their decisions and know of all possible outcomes

• Decision makers are infinitely sensitive to the small distinctions among their different options. They are capable of knowing all the differences between their options, regardless of how small they are.

• Decision makers are rational in their choices. They are capable of making a choice to maximize or increase value.

- Subjective expected theory. This is the goal of human action to seek happiness and avoid pain.

• Subjective utility – the prospects based on individual's value than on objective criteria.

• Subjective probability – prospects based on individual's estimates of likelihood rather than mathematical equations.

Using the example in Decisions for One's Personal life, a person would use the subjective expected theory to take into account comfort of the job, how the long hours can affect personal time with family and friends, as well as possible job relocation. This theory also people to take into account the many subjective variables.

## PATH DEPENDENCY

It is perhaps pertinent to note that the cost of making no decision at all itself is a factor, and that the benefit of making some decision, even a random choice, can be beneficial in the longer term. Thus the reversibility of an action may be a good way to judge whether or not an action or process is beneficial. A resource can also be viewed as something expendable, or bearing a cost, rather than the implication of selecting something irrevocably.

## DECISION MAKING IN BUSINESS AND MANAGEMENT

In general, business and management systems should be set up to allow decision making at the lowest possible level.

Several decision making models for business include:

- SWOT Analysis - Evaluation by the decision making individual or organization of Strengths, Weaknesses, Opportunities and Threats with respect to desired end state or objective.
- Analytic Hierarchy Process - procedure for multi-level goal hierarchy
- Buyer decision processes - transaction before, during, and after a purchase
- Complex systems - common behavioural and structural features that can be modelled

- Corporate finance:
  - The investment decision
  - The financing decision
  - The dividend decision
  - working capital management decisions
- Cost-benefit analysis - process of weighing the total expected costs vs. the total expected benefits
- Decision trees
  - Programme Evaluation and Review Technique (PERT)
  - critical path analysis
  - critical chain analysis
- Force field analysis - analizing forces that either drive or hinder movement toward a goal
- Grid Analysis - analysis done by compairing the weighted averages of ranked criteria to options. A way of comparing both objective and subjective data.
- Kepner tregoe - A Management Consultancy firm specialising in rational Problem Solving and Decision Making processes
- Linear programming - optimization problems in which the objective function and the constraints are all linear
- Min-max criterion
- Model (economics)- theoretical construct of economic processes of variables and their relationships
- Monte Carlo method - class of computational algorithms for simulating systems
- Morphological analysis - all possible solutions to a multi-dimensional problem complex
- optimization
  - constrained optimization
- Paired Comparison Analysis - paired choice analysis
- Pareto Analysis - selection of a limited of number of tasks that produce significant overall effect

- Scenario analysis - process of analyzing possible future events
- Six Thinking Hats - symbolic process for parallel thinking
- Strategic planning process - applying the objectives, SWOTs, strategies, programmes process
- Ubiquitous command and control is a concept for dynamic decision making based on "agreement between an individual and the world", and "agreements between individuals"

**Decision-makers and Influencers**

In the context of industrial goods marketing, there is much theory, and even more opinion, expressed about how the various 'decision-makers' and 'influencers' (those who can only influence, not decide, the final decision) interact. Decisions are frequently taken by groups, rather than individuals, and the official buyer often does not have authority to take the decision.

Miller & Heiman, for example, offered a more complex view of industrial buying decisions (particularly in the area of 'complex sales' of capital equipment). They see three levels of decision making:

'Economic buying influence' - the decision-maker who can authorize the necessary funds for purchase

'User buying influences' - the people in the buying company who will use the product and will specify what they want to purchase

'Technical buying influence' - the `experts' (including, typically, the buying department) who can veto the purchase on technical grounds

Webster and Wind, in a similar vein, identify six roles within the 'buying centre':

'Users' - who will actually use the product or service

'Influencers' - particularly technical personnel

'Deciders' - the actual decision-makers

'Approvers' - who formally authorize the decision

'Buyers' - the department with formal authority

'Gatekeepers' - those who have the power to stop the sellers reaching other members of the `buying centre'

Some have said that true consensus involves "meeting everyone's needs." Consensus decision-making is intended to deemphasize the role of factions or parties and promote the expression of individual voices. The method also increases the likelihood of unforeseen or creative solutions by juxtaposing dissimilar ideas. Because it seeks to minimize objection, it is popular with voluntary organizations, wherein decisions are more likely to be carried out when they are most widely approved. Consensus methods are desirable when enforcement of the decision is unfeasible, such that every participant will be required to act on the decision independently.

Consensus decision-making is also found in groups where participants have different areas of expertise but are working toward a common goal. Examples of this include high technology project design teams which must integrate the opinions of people with different areas of expertise.

Minority views must be considered to a greater degree than in circumstances where a majority can take the action and enforce the decision without any further consultation with the minority voters. It is often thought that consensus can require more time and effort to achieve. Thus some groups may reserve consensus decision methods for particularly complex, risky or important decisions. However, there are many examples of groups who employ consensus decision-making in ways that enable them to both consider minority views and make decisions in a timely and efficient manner. Consensus decision making could result in group polarization, where team members make more extreme decisions compared to their prior individual positions. This could potentially have beneficial effects on team decisions (enhance commitment and conviction), or detrimental effects (escalate towards greater risk or greater conservative behaviours). Use of computer-mediated communication could further heighten the effects of group polarization.

Rather than simply list known alternatives, debate for a short time, vote, and then accept or reject by some percentage of majority (ex. over 50%, over 2/3), a consensus decision-making process involves identifying and addressing concerns, generating new alternatives, combining elements of multiple alternatives and checking that people understand a proposal or an argument.

This empowers minorities, those with objections that are hard to state quickly, and those who are less skilled in debate. Therefore, consensus decision-making can be seen as a form of grassroots democracy.

Egalitarian groups that seek to reduce the amount of power delegated to leaders, chairpersons or agenda setters often use consensus methods. Such methods can reduce the amount of harm or loss imposed on minorities (or individuals) by a majority. Consensus methods may be appropriate when personal (or emotional) risk to members is high, trust is low, and time is available for a prolonged discussion. Consensus may be used to remedy patterns of decision-making based on habit, subservience or carelessness.

Alternatively, it can be argued that in a situation of abundant trust - in which each party assumes that any objections or reservations regarding a proposal are meaningful - consensus methods may not only be appropriate, but necessary.

Like any group decision-making, consensus decision-making can disempower those not present in the debating forum, as they cannot expect to have input on the new measures that are proposed (whereas they might have had the opportunity for input into the known alternatives prior to the debate). Accordingly, most systems of consensus decision-making place a premium on participation.

Three key issues tend to define a particular type of consensus decision-making:

1. Degree of agreement or unanimity required;
2. Timing of presentation including division of time among urgent versus important matters;
3. Follow-up to action including the monitoring that arises from dissent, and from claims of majority proponents whose preferred course of action is being taken over minority objections.

There is also the question of facilitation or process leadership, which is handled

A healthy consensus decision-making process usually encourages and outs dissent early, maximizing the chance of accommodating the views of all minorities. It also often assigns a role to the dissenter, e.g. the Vatican used to assign the role of Promotor Fidei to a specific priest who argued against beatification of a saint, to ensure the case 'against' remains well represented. After the decision, the dissenting minority may have some role to play in monitoring the decision. In the Supreme Court of the United States, both the majority opinion and minority opinion are equally well documented, as the legal grounds for agreeing with either may exist in some court in the future.

Many groups consider unanimous decisions a sign of agreement, solidarity, and unity. However, there is evidence that unanimous decisions may be a sign of coercion, fear, undue persuasive power or eloquence, inability to comprehend alternatives, or plain impatience with the process of debate. (For example, elections in which 99% or 100% of the voters support the candidate are generally discredited.) When there are concerns about these aspects of unanimity, various alternatives can be pursued. These include the following:

- Unanimity minus one (or U-1), requires all delegates but one to support the decision. The individual dissenter cannot block the decision although they may be able to prolong debate (e.g. via a filibuster). The dissenter may be the ongoing monitor of the implications of the decision, and their opinion of the outcome of the decision may be solicited at some future time. Betting markets in particular rely on the input of such lone dissenters. A lone bettor against the odds profits when his or her prediction of the outcomes proves to be better than that of the majority. This disciplines the market's odds.

- Unanimity minus two (or U-2), does not permit two individual delegates to block a decision, but tends to curtail debate with a lone dissenter more quickly. Dissenting pairs can present alternate views of what is wrong with the decision under consideration. By focusing on a pair of dissenters, and allocating less time to lone wolves or 'consensus thugs', a U-2 system tends to form stronger bonds among those who find themselves "alone on an island" with each other. Pairs of delegates can be empowered to find the common ground that will enable them to convince a third, decision-blocking, voter to join them. If the pair are unable to convince a third party to join them within a set time, their arguments are deemed to be unconvincing, immature or self-interested. If two people dissent against some common measure, it is more likely that the discussion between them can be extended to third parties easily, since it is already verbalized and illustrated. Western European court systems recognize this by strongly encouraging criminal defendants or civil plaintiffs to get an attorney's aid, so that their case can be fully heard out long before the decision.
- Unanimity minus three, (or U-3), and other such systems recognize the ability of three or more delegates to actively block a decision. However, there is controversy over whether a small group of dissenters, (e.g., militants or terrorists), is morally different from a large minority, (e.g., an opposition

party with support of double-digit percentages of the population). Accordingly U-3 and lesser degrees of unanimity are usually lumped in with statistical measures of agreement, such as: 80%, mean plus one sigma, two-thirds, or greater than half (majority) levels of agreement. Such measures do not fit within the definition of consensus given at the beginning of this article.

- The IETF working group process has a tradition of "rough consensus", where there is no specific rule for "how much is enough", but it is left to the judgment of the working group chair. This makes it harder for a small number of disruptors to block a decision, but puts a lot of responsibility on the chair, and has frequently led to angry debates about whether rough consensus has in fact been correctly identified.

The quality of alternatives considered is, all else being equal, proportional to the amount of time spent gathering and comparing and combining them. The term deliberative democracy reflects the deliberation that underlies all good consensus decision-making. Ralph Nader and others have advocated deliberative measures to extend the time for "sober second thought."

A fictional example of deliberative democracy is the Entmoot from J. R. R. Tolkien's novel The Lord of the Rings. The Ents, who are large ancient living intelligent trees, spend days discussing the issue of whether to go to war, in their verbose and many-syllabled language. This is an example of a decision for which the stakes were high, the individual risk also high, and coercive force difficult or lacking; therefore suited to consensus methods.

Timeliness of decisions is an important issue. In some cases, a wrong decision taken in time can be better than a good decision taken later. Key responsibilities of facilitators of any decision making process, but particularly in consensus decision-making, include:

- Establishing measures to place items on the agenda, or deny them time on the agenda.
- Setting deadlines for changes to the agenda (e.g. can the agenda itself be changed during the meeting?).
- Agenda forming and presentation of issues at the right time, when there is sufficient time for their debate.
- Ensuring that less urgent issues are excluded from the debate, but dealt with at another time.

To achieve a balance between urgency and importance, it is common to reserve enough time for matters that are not urgent, but are nevertheless important, (for e.g., the decision process itself, which takes care to maintain). Consensus decision processes tend to accelerate as rising trust over the course of the meeting, combined with fatigue, increase individual tolerance and the cost of dissent. Placing difficult agenda items first tends to speed a meeting, with the risk that important, but less complex decisions will not be achieved before adjournment.

Decisions about when to split up into working groups, how to handle agendas, how to deal with changes to agendas or working groups from the floor, etc., are affected by the allocation of the group's time to urgent versus important matters. These procedural matters are held to be crucial to the survival of a consensus decision process, along with issues of safety, fairness, and closure which arise from their application in practice.

## Action, Monitoring and Follow-up

Action is the point of decision; without action, the decision is just talk. Military leaders from Alexander the Great to the present have emphasized that orders simply do not get carried out unless they are personally followed up by the commander. The same applies to group decisions, perhaps even more so.

One would not expect the opposing minority to do a good job of ensuring that a measure is carried out, but they can ensure that problems resulting from it are well-documented, and that inconveniences of its implementation are contained.

However, they can also take steps to ensure that the inconvenience of implementation is maximized, so as to make the point that the measure was impractical and ill-advised from the beginning. A major issue in consensus decisions is whose view of the actual outcome to trust, and who to permit time to present their view.

Consensus decisions are especially vulnerable to sabotage of all kinds, so the assignment of action roles, monitoring (from the original majority and minority opinion to some future time when the results of both sets of predictions can be debated), and other follow up (e.g. assessing support of the public for a party after it has taken and publicized a particular measure), is a key responsibility of consensus decision leaders.

## QUAKER-BASED CONSENSUS

The model used by the Quakers is effective because it puts in place a simple, time-tested structure that moves a group towards consensus. The Quaker model has been well-received when employed in secular settings because it gives everyone a chance to speak while limiting potential disruptors (e.g., people who want unlimited airtime, or who have a particular axe to grind).

The following aspects of the Quaker model can be effectively applied in any consensus decision-making process:

- Multiple concerns and information are shared until the sense of the group is clear.
- Discussion involves active listening and sharing of information.
- Norms limit number of times one asks to speak to ensure that each speaker is fully heard.
- Norms limit repetition and long speeches.
- Norms include a short silence after every comment so deliberations are truly thoughtful.
- Ideas and solutions belong to the group; no names are recorded.

- Differences are resolved by discussion. The facilitator ("clerk" or "convenor" in the Quaker model) identifies areas of agreement and names disagreements to push discussion deeper.
- The facilitator articulates the sense of the discussion, asks if there are other concerns, and proposes a minute of the decision.
- The group as a whole is responsible for the decision, and the decision belongs to the group.
- The facilitator can discern if one who is not uniting with the decision is acting without concern for the group or in selfish interest.
- Dissenters' perspectives are embraced.

Key components of Quaker-based consensus are: 1) that the guidance of Spirit is available to each participant who honestly seeks the truth, 2) belief in a common humanity, and, 3) the ability to decide together. The goal is "unity, not unanimity." Ensuring that group members speak only once until others are heard encourages a diversity of thought. The facilitator is understood as serving the group rather than acting as person-in-charge. By articulating the emerging consensus, members can be clear on the decision, and, as their views have been taken into account, will be likely to support it.

Many intentional communities use consensus decision-making. In many cases, with cohousing groups, business must be transacted within time constraints. Thus efficiency is important. If the group genuinely wants to make decisions by consensus, a method is needed that is both efficient and effective. An open discussion needs to be animated by a process that moves towards a timely, and sound, decision that is supported by all. Various techniques have been developed whereby this can be achieved.

In some groups, the cards are used in two ways; one for discussion and another for decisions:

A group member who wishes to speak, holds up a card:

- A green card means "I have something to say" or "I have a question." When several group members hold up a green card, they are noted and placed in a "stack" of people waiting to speak. Each person speaks in turn, in a way that is similar to Quaker-based consensus.

- A yellow card means "I can clarify" or "I need clarification (on what was just said)."
- The red card is the process card. A red card, when raised, asks members to look at the process. For example, an individual who displays a red card might say: "Are we getting off track, here?" or "What is our objective in doing this?" or even "How about we take a break?" It gives all members an equal chance to be facilitator.

Following discussion, the facilitator articulates the proposal and calls for a show of cards:

- The green card means: "I agree."
- The yellow card means: "I can live with it." This is often referred to as "standing aside"
- The red card means: "I don't agree, but am willing to work to find a better way, taking into account what has been said by all group members." Thus holding up a red card does not block progress, it signifies that the person who displayed it will work with others on the matter in question and bring it back to a subsequent meeting. This tends to ensure that red cards are not used lightly.

In the Uniting Church of Australia, orange and blue cards are used to mean "I am warm toward this" or "I am cool toward this." The use of orange and blue allows people who are colourblind, and cannot distinguish red and green, to participate in the discussion.

If groups agree to apply methods such as these, and all group members are willing to work at it, consensus decision-making can be both effective in meeting a group's goals, and time-efficient.

A similar method has come to be used in other forums, such as W3C and other computer standards bodies. There, is it known as the Quaker poll.

In lieu of coloured cards, some consensus-based groups use a system of simple hand signals. While the nature, meaning and popularity of such signals changes from group to group, there is a common 'vocabulary':

- Twinkle: Wiggling of the fingers of one or both hands, with palms facing downward. Used by non-speakers to indicate agreement with the speaker. Also often used as a replacement of a raised hand to indicate a 'yea' vote to a proposal.
- Triangle: Forming of a triangle with the thumbs and index fingers of both hands. Used to indicate a point of order or procedure to the facilitator.
- Crossed arms: Forearms crossed with hands in fists. Used to indicate a strong disagreement with the speaker or to cast a 'block' vote to a proposal.

In the Internet Engineering Task Force (IETF), decisions are assumed to be taken by "rough consensus." The IETF has studiously refrained from defining a mechanical method for verifying such consensus, apparently in the belief that any such codification will lead to attempts to "game the system." Instead, a working group (WG) chair or BoF chair is supposed to "recognize it when I see it."

One tradition in support of rough consensus is the tradition of humming rather than (countable) hand-raising; this allows a WG to quickly tell the difference between "one or two objectors" or a "sharply divided community", without making it easy to slip into "majority rule". However, hand-raising is also used, especially in larger meetings, but actual counting is frowned upon.

Much of the business of the IETF is carried out on mailing lists, where all parties can speak their view at all times; the social dynamics of mailing lists is worthy of a study in itself.

## Chapter 7

# Organizational Learning

Organizational learning is an area of knowledge within organizational theory that studies models and theories about the way an organization learns and adapts.

In Organizational development (OD), learning is a characteristic of an adaptive organization, i.e., an organization that is able to sense changes in signals from its environment (both internal and external) and adapt accordingly. OD specialists endeavor to assist their clients to learn from experience and incorporate the learning as feedback into the planning process.

Several models have been proposed that facilitate understanding of organizational learning:

- Argyris and Schon (1978) distinguish between single-loop and double-loop learning, related to Gregory Bateson's concepts of first and second order learning. In single-loop learning, individuals, groups or organizations modify their actions according to the difference between expected and obtained outcomes. In double-loop learning, the entities (individuals, groups or organization) question the values, assumptions and policies that led to the actions in the first place; if they are able to view and modify those, then second-order or double-loop learning has taken place. Double loop learning is the learning about single-loop learning.

- March and Olson attempt to link up individual and organizational learning. In their model, individual beliefs lead to individual action, which in turn may lead to an organizational action and a response from the environment which may induce improved individual beliefs and the cycle then repeats over and over. Learning occurs as better beliefs produce better actions.
- Kim, as well, in an article titled "The link between individual and organizational learning", integrates Argyris, March and Olson and another model by Kofman into a single comprehensive model; further, he analyzes all the possible breakdowns in the information flows in the model, leading to failures in organizational learning; for instance, what happens if an individual action is rejected by the organization for political or other reasons and therefore no organizational action takes place?
- Nonaka and Takeuchi developed a four stage spiral model of organizational learning. They started by differentiating Polanyi's concept of "tacit knowledge" from "explicit knowledge" and describe a process of alternating between the two. Tacit knowledge is personal, context specific, subjective knowledge, whereas explicit knowledge is codified, systematic, formal, and easy to communicate. The tacit knowledge of key personnel within the organization can be made explicit, codified in manuals, and incorporated into new products and processes. This process they called "externalization". The reverse process (from explicit to implicit) they call "internalization" because it involves employees internalizing an organization's formal rules, procedures, and other forms of explicit knowledge. They also use the term "socialization" to denote the sharing of tacit knowledge, and the term "combination" to denote the dissemination of codified knowledge. According to this model, knowledge creation and organizational learning take a path of

socialization, externalization, combination, internalization, socialization, externalization, combination... etc. in an infinite spiral.

- Nick Bontis empirically tested a model of organizational learning that encompassed both stocks and flows of knowledge across three levels of analysis: individual, team and organization. Results showed a negative and statistically significant relationship between the misalignment of stocks and flows and organizational performance.
- Flood discusses the concept of organizational learning with Peter Senge and the origins of the theory from Argyris and Schon. The author aims to "re-think" Senge's The Fifth Discipline through systems theory. Where Senge's work has been critiqued as a sort of an organizational guru's self-help book, the author illustrates how advanced the concepts are by integrating them with key theorists such as Bertalanffy. Conceptualizing organizational learning in terms of structure, process, meaning, ideology and knowledge, theory development with the philosophy of science would further the discussion of how the theorists have been influenced by twentieth-century advances from the classical assumptions of science.

The work in Organizational Learning can be distinguished from the work on a related concept, the learning organization. This later body of work, in general, uses the theoretical findings of organizational learning (and other research in organizational development, system theory, and cognitive science) in order to prescribe specific recommendations about how to create organizations that continuously and effectively learn. This practical approach was championed by Peter Senge in his book The Fifth Discipline.

Diffusion of innovations theory explores how and why people adopt new ideas, practices and products. It may be seen as a subset of the anthropological concept of diffusion and can help to explain how ideas are spread by individuals, social networks and organizations.

The world seems to be changing faster and faster—from the technologies available to us, to the increasingly global scope of our interactions. Moreover, the problems facing us as a global community seem to be growing ever more complex and serious. How do we navigate such change and address these problems—not only in our work lives but also in our families, communities, and schools?

We believe that organizations—groups of people who come together to accomplish a purpose—hold an important key to these questions. The field of organizational learning explores ways to design organizations so that they fulfill their function effectively, encourage people to reach their full potential, and, at the same time, help the world to be a better place.

This field is rooted in a set of powerful principles, values, and disciplines. As Peter Senge wrote in his seminal book The Fifth Discipline: The Art & Practice of the Learning Organization, an organization is learning when it can bring about the future it most desires. In the business community, learning is much more than just a way to create the future you want; in today's fast-paced, highly competitive work world, it may actually give your organization the edge it needs to survive—and thereby keep fulfilling its purpose.

Organizational learning focused originally on the practice of five core disciplines, or capacities, of which systems thinking forms the cornerstone:

- Systems thinking
- Team learning
- Shared vision
- Mental models
- Personal mastery

Let's take a closer look at these disciplines:

Systems thinking is the art of seeing the world in terms of wholes, and the practice of focusing on the relationships among the parts of a system. By looking at reality through a systems thinking "lens," you can work with a system—rather than against it—to create enduring solutions to stubborn problems in every arena of your life. Practicing this discipline involves learning to recognize "signature" systemic behaviours all around you, and familiarizing yourself with some special terminology and some powerful tools unique to this field.

Team learning is what happens when a group of people working on something together experiences that rare feeling of synergy and productiveness that happens when you're "in the groove." When a team is truly learning, the group as a whole becomes much more than just the sum of its parts. Practicing this discipline involves startlingly different kinds of conversations and a remarkable degree of honesty and mutual respect—all of which you can learn to do through familiarizing yourself with specific tools from this field.

Shared vision emerges when everyone in an organization understands what the organization is trying to do, is genuinely committed to achieving that vision, and clearly grasps how his or her role in the organization can contribute to making the vision real. Practicing this discipline involves knowing how all the parts of the organization work together and being clear about how your own personal goals align with those of your organization.

Mental models are the deep beliefs and assumptions we hold about how the world works. These models shape the decisions we make in life, the actions we take in response to events, and the ways in which we interpret others' behaviour. Practicing this discipline involves surfacing and testing your deepest assumptions and beliefs, and helping others do the same. Again, there are specific tools available from this field that can help you with this practice.

Personal mastery is the art of identifying what mark you want to leave on the world during your lifetime. That is, what's your unique purpose in life, and how do you want to go about fulfilling that purpose? Practicing this discipline involves some honest exploration of your own life experiences and desires and a willingness to take some risks.

These five disciplines were originally outlined in 1990 in The Fifth Discipline and are core to many organizational learning efforts. We also believe there are many other disciplines that support and expand on the above five, including:

Corporate culture is that intangible "something" that influences the environments in which we work every day. Technically, culture is an anthropological concept. But in the field of organizational learning, it refers to the policies, beliefs, activities, and rituals that determine an organization's "personality." A company's culture can support or hinder learning, encourage or stifle creativity, and so on. Fortunately, we can shape our organizations' culture through careful attention to how we do things and treat one another in the workplace.

Corporate social responsibility addresses the question of how the business community fits into the larger social picture. Specifically, what responsibility do organizations have beyond just their own industries and arenas of competition? How do the actions of a particular organization or industry affect neighbourhoods, the public sector, educational institutions, and families? It's tempting to compartmentalize these dimensions of human life, but of course they all influence each other. The discipline of corporate social responsibility focuses specifically on these interconnections and ways in which businesses can make the larger social world a better place for everyone.

Dialogue focuses on new communication forms that strengthen a group's collective intelligence. This discipline offers several intriguing tools and techniques that may seem strange to you at first but that, with practice, will transform the way you talk with others, stimulating questions and insights that we often miss through traditional forms of conversation.

Leadership in the field of organizational learning takes on a particular focus. Specifically, the discipline of leadership explores how managers—and leaders at every level in an organization—can unleash the full potential of each and every employee in the organization. Often this involves moving away from more traditional command-and-control management structures and toward more fluid, self-organizing leadership. This discipline is truly redefining the role of management for businesspeople everywhere.

Sustainability, as a discipline, entails being thoughtful stewards of the natural resources on which our organizations depend. After all, if we use those resources without regard to their limits, we may deplete them permanently—and our organizations can't survive that. Sustainable management practices help us design organizations that respect and balance human needs with the natural cycles and limitations of our planet.

Work/life balance is another area receiving increasing attention in the organizational learning field. More and more, people are seeking to design their work so that they have room for the other important dimensions of their lives—family, community, self-development, and so on. At the same time, the boundaries between work and home life have blurred in recent decades. The discipline of work/life balance seeks to explore the ramifications of these changes and address the question of how to set priorities and find meaning in both our work and non-work lives.

Because everything really is structurally connected (systems thinking again!), an organization committed to true learning practices all of the above disciplines in some form, rather than tackling them in isolation. After all, they each reinforce one another, and when they come into alignment, the organization truly soars! And as we move into the 21st century, we'll no doubt see new disciplines emerge in this dynamic field.

## CHANGE MANAGEMENT

Change management can take many forms and include many change environments. The most common usage to the term refers to organizational change management.

Organizational change management is the process of developing a planned approach to change in an organization. Typically the objective is to maximize the collective benefits for all people involved in the change and minimize the risk of failure of implementing the change. The discipline of change management deals primarily with the human aspect of change, and is therefore related to pure and industrial psychology.

Many technical disciplines (for example Information technology) have developed similar approaches to formally control the process of making changes to environments.

Change management can be either 'reactive', in which case management is responding to changes in the macroenvironment (that is, the source of the change is external), or proactive, in which case management is initiating the change in order to achieve a desired goal (that is, the source of the change is internal). Change management can be conducted on a continuous basis, on a regular schedule (such as an annual review), or when deemed necessary on a programme-by-programme basis.

Change management can be approached from a number of angles and applied to numerous organizational processes. Its most common uses are in information technology management, strategic management, and process management. To be effective, change management should be multi-disciplinary, touching all aspects of the organization. However, at its core, implementing new procedures, technologies, and overcoming resistance to change are fundamentally human resource management issues.

Attitudes towards change result from a complex interplay of emotions and [cognitive] processes. Because of this complexity everyone reacts to change differently. On the positive side, change is seen as akin to opportunity, rejuvenation, progress, innovation, and growth. But just as legitimately, change can also be seen as akin to instability, upheaval, unpredictability, threat, and disorientation. Whether employees perceive change with fear, anxiety and demoralization, or with excitement and confidence, or somewhere in between, depends partially on the individual's psychological makeup, partially on management's actions, and partially on the specific nature of the change.

An early model of change developed by Kurt Lewin (1951) described change as a three-stage process. The first stage he called "unfreezing". It involved overcoming inertia and dismantling the existing "mind set". Defense mechanisms have to be bypassed. In the second stage the change occurs. This is typically a period of confusion. We are aware that the old ways are being challenged but we do not have a clear picture to replace them with yet. The third and final stage he called "refreezing". The new mind set is crystallizing and one's comfort level is returning to previous levels.

An individual's attitude toward a change tends to evolve as they become more familiar with it. The stages a person goes through can consist of: apprehension, denial, anger, resentment, depression, cognitive dissonance, compliance, acceptance, and internalization. This emotional framework is a derivative of work by Elizabeth Kubler-Ross in her book "On Death and Dying" which dealt with the phases people experience when faced with the loss of family member or friend. Many employees, however, may not experience these phases, as their attitude toward change is heavily dependent on their view of the current state. When employees have a negative view of the current state they may anticipate and embrace change early in the process.

The ADKAR model developed by Jeff Hiatt (1998, 2006] for individual change management presents five building blocks that an individual must obtain to realize change successfully. These include awareness, desire, knowledge, ability and reinforcement. It is management's job to create an environment in which people can go through these stages as quickly as possible, including:

- Building awareness of why the change is needed
- Creating desire to support and participate in the change

- Developing knowledge of how to change
- Fostering ability to implement new skills and behaviours
- Providing reinforcements to sustain the change

Organizations are ruled by laws of complexity (The systemic/complexity principle) Emerging evidence from systems thinking and complexity science indicates that large systems show a different behaviour from their single parts. System theory talks about organizations as "non-trivial machines" (like the human body, etc.), whose behaviour cannot be predicted or calculated by a computer. These new sciences are applied to organizational development and change, for example in Appreciative Inquiry, Open Space Technology, Systemic Constellations, etc.

We are living in a field which is a whole (The quantum principle) Most of our day-to-day assumptions are still based on classical Newtonian mechanics, which usually are applied to working with organizations. For example, most people would assume that if A is true, B is false. There is a growing number of thinkers who relate change in organizations to Quantum Mechanics, which teaches us that if A is true, B is equally true - just another side of the coin -, and that A could not exist without B. Observers (or consultants, or leaders) are always part of a field, which they influence but by which they are influenced themselves instantly. Some examples for the application of Quantum Mechanics to Change Management: - Process Oriented Psychology by Arnold Mindell, talks about the field in which each human relationship exists. Its application field, Worldwork, intends to transform systems by shifting roles that people unconsciously hold in a system. - Dialogue (by David Bohm) is a new form of communication in large groups which is based on the suspension of assumptions, thus letting the common knowledge of 'container' emerge. - Appreciative Inquiry, one of the most frequently applied approaches to organizational change, is partly based on the assumption that change in a system is instantanously.

Below are several well known concepts in which the Change Management practice is rooted. There is some overlapping in these concepts and its practice, the tools derived from these ideas are often used interchangeably.

- Process Oriented Psychology
- Theme Centred Interaction
- Transactional Analysis
- Systems Thinking / Family Therapy
- Neurolinguistic Programming
- Communication Theory
- Whole Systems Change
- Total Quality Management
- ADKAR (a model used in Change management that connects organizational change management to individual change management).
- Change Management Excellence: Putting NLP to Work

The Formula for Change was developed by Richard Beckhard and David Gleicher and is sometimes referred to as Gleicher's Formula. The Formula illustrates that the combination of organisational dissatisfaction, vision for the future and the possibility of immediate, tactical action must be stronger than the resistance within the organisation in order for meaningful change to occur.

Management's first responsibility is to detect trends in the macroenvironment so as to be able to identify changes and initiate programmes. It is also important to estimate what impact a change will likely have on employee behaviour patterns, work processes, technological requirements, and motivation. Management must assess what employee reactions will be and craft a change programme that will provide support as workers go through the process of accepting change. The programme must then be implemented, disseminated throughout the organization, monitored for effectiveness, and adjusted where necessary.

Proper management of change to industrial facilities and processes is recognized as critical to safety, since complex processes can be very sensitive to even small changes. In the US, OSHA has regulations that govern how changes are to be made and documented. The main requirement is that a thorough review of a proposed change be performed by a multi-disciplinary team to ensure that as many possible viewpoints are used as possible to minimize the chances of missing a hazard. Change management in this context is referred to as Management of Change. Management of change is just one component of Process Safety Management. There were several large industrial accidents in the 60s and 70s that could be seen as the impetus for this regulation. As other examples, poor change management most likely played a part in the plane crash that killed John Denver, and was questioned in modifications to the fishing vessel in the book The Perfect Storm that may have made the ship less stable.

## Chapter 8

# Administration in Hotel Management

### PERSONAL DEVELOPMENT

People are not born understanding their society's morals. Instead, these understandings develop and mature over time. Psychologist Lawrence Kolhberg's famous work has provided us with a developmental mapping of how moral understanding tends to progress through childhood and early adulthood.

- According to Kohlberg, infants have little or no moral sense, because they are not born with an understanding of the nature of human relationships. As children reach elementary school age, they enter into the first major stage of moral understanding, known as the "pre-conventional" stage. Pre-conventional children are essentially selfish in orientation. They do not think about what behaviours will serve the greater good, but rather think in terms of what will most benefit themselves. They respond primarily to power, and think of morality as a matter of following rules so as to avoid punishment.
- As children grow into adulthood, they typically enter into the stage of "conventional" moral understanding. Some children will be developmentally delayed in this regard and become adults who have the moral understanding of children; we call them sociopaths,

narcissists, and anti-social personalities. The majority of people that do make it to the conventional moral understanding start thinking in terms of duty; a duty to do what is necessary to promote the greater good. They orient towards behaviours that are most likely to gain other people's respect and admiration. Part of conventional morality is the duty to behave lawfully. Some people take this duty further and understand it as a duty to conform to what other influential people around them want.

- Most adults never actually achieve the final stage of morality, known as post-conventional morality, mostly because in order to get there, people have to throw off their sense of duty to what others around them want, and reinvest their moral sense in higher principles, such as (but not limited to) "honesty", "reciprocity", and "social welfare". Such people become willing to take unpopular stances and make unpopular decisions simply because those decisions represent the right thing to do. For example, a post-conventional CEO might decide to offer full medical coverage for all employees because it is the right thing to do (to use the company to raise up all participants), even though to do so would anger shareholders who might see this as a drain on profits. It is very difficult to achieve a post-conventional morality in what is largely a conventional world. The CEO in our example would probably not last long, unfortunately.

People are not born understanding their society's morals. Instead, these understandings develop and mature over time. Psychologist Lawrence Kolhberg's famous work has provided us with a developmental mapping of how moral understanding tends to progress through childhood and early adulthood.

- According to Kohlberg, infants have little or no moral sense, because they are not born with an understanding of the nature of human relationships. As children reach elementary school age, they enter into the first major stage of moral understanding, known as the "pre-conventional" stage. Pre-conventional children are essentially selfish in orientation. They do not think about what behaviours will serve the greater good, but rather think in terms of what will most benefit themselves. They respond primarily to power, and think of morality as a matter of following rules so as to avoid punishment.

- As children grow into adulthood, they typically enter into the stage of "conventional" moral understanding. Some children will be developmentally delayed in this regard and become adults who have the moral understanding of children; we call them sociopaths, narcissists, and anti-social personalities. The majority of people that do make it to the conventional moral understanding start thinking in terms of duty; a duty to do what is necessary to promote the greater good. They orient towards behaviours that are most likely to gain other people's respect and admiration. Part of conventional morality is the duty to behave lawfully. Some people take this duty further and understand it as a duty to conform to what other influential people around them want.
- Most adults never actually achieve the final stage of morality, known as post-conventional morality, mostly because in order to get there, people have to throw off their sense of duty to what others around them want, and reinvest their moral sense in higher principles, such as (but not limited to) "honesty", "reciprocity", and "social welfare". Such people become willing to take unpopular stances and make unpopular decisions simply because those decisions represent the right thing to do. For example, a post-conventional CEO might decide to offer full medical coverage for all employees because it is the right thing to do (to use the company to raise up all participants), even though to do so would anger shareholders who might see this as a drain on profits. It is very difficult

to achieve a post-conventional morality in what is largely a conventional world. The CEO in our example would probably not last long, unfortunately.

## SELF DEVELOPMENT TIPS

As long as you are still alive, you are capable of changing and growing. You can do anything you want to do, be anything you want to be. Listen to some positive thoughts on how to continue your self development and then apply them in your own life.

- Accept personal responsibility for your own growth; no one can do it for you. What you do today will determine your readiness for tomorrow.
- Take time every day to do something for yourself.
- Take classes to stay current in your field of expertise. The world is changing rapidly and you must learn to manage change to avoid obsolescence. The way Will Rogers put this was that "Even if you are on the right track, if you just sit there you will get run over."
- Listen to cassette tapes on personal and professional growth topics.
- Never look back to the past-you only can control your actions in this instant, so what should you be doing right now?
- Learn from "other people's experience" rather then having to try everything for yourself. It shortens the time needed to learn.
- Dealing with a problem helps you learn patience and strengthens your management skills; it is good mental exercise.
- Analyze, in a non-judgmental way, mistakes in which you were involved. It will help you to prevent these in the future.
- Reward yourself when you catch yourself working on the most important priorities.
- Never say something can't or won't be done. Keep looking for ways to do it.

- After attending a seminar, report to your boss or other people in your organization, what the most important things are that you learned from the programme.
- For all learning experiences, whether it is reading, seeing, thinking or attending, apply the R squared, A squared formula: Recognize, Relate, Assimilate, and Apply. These actions will help you grow in the direction of your goals.
- Eliminate one time waster a week from your life.
- Read a minimum of one chapter of a book a day.
- Read a minimum of one book a month.
- Be hungry for what life has to offer and go for it.
- Decide what you really desire to do-then do it.
- When you have the option of reading a book or listening to the cassette tape version of the programme, listen to the tape. It will be more to the point and can be done while you are driving, jogging/walking, or getting other routine things done.
- Develop a "master mind" group of four or five people with whom you can openly discuss ideas in a nonjudgmental way.
- Develop yourself as a resource for others by networking. Find out who does what, when, and for whom. You may find excellent contacts for your future needs and for the needs of others you meet.
- Work for balance in your life goals: family, financial, professional, social, spiritual, recreational.
- Always keep your goals in mind as you start a new activity.
- If you do a lot of work with the calculator, run the machine with the hand you don't use for writing.
- Do not be afraid of failing at something. You can learn and change as a result of it.
- The most difficult projects are opportunities for your biggest successes just as the most difficult people could become your strongest allies.

- Put up pictures of your dreams and goals where you will see them frequently. They will remind you and aid you in focusing and visualizing your goal.
- We all have the same 24 hours in a day. Learn from those people who get more done than you do. Perhaps you can find a way to improve what you are doing.
- Find a nonjudgmental mentor who will help you by providing feedback, suggestions, challenges and support.
- Identify some "models" and observe their style and actions. Do not copy them but learn from their experiences.
- Learn from the errors you see others make as well as from their successes.
- Fill your mind with positive ideas, thoughts and inspirations and you will have no room left for the negative.
- Trade jobs with someone so you gain additional experience.
- Ask for and accept lateral moves in the organization so you learn more about the entire operation.
- Do more than your "self doubts" say you can.
- Have confidence that you can get through and learn from anything and everything you experience.
- Reward yourself with a treat when you have completed a learning objective.
- Keep a daily journal, recording your thoughts, ideas, feelings and personal growth progress.
- Ask questions, listen, then ask more questions. You will learn as well as help others learn.
- Ask yourself, "How can I manipulate my fate?"
- Do things with someone you respect. They will be supportive of you and you will learn from interacting with them.
- Seek new information on projects for which you have responsibility. Look for new "ah ha" ideas all the time.

- Challenge yourself to learn something new every day.
- Remain flexible and constantly adaptable.
- Be open to others and sincerely interested in them. You can learn from everyone you meet.
- Mentally rehearse a new skill. Your subconscious does not know the difference between actual practice and mental rehearsal.
- Keep a record of what you accomplished the previous day(s)/week. If you did not accomplish as much as you wanted, it gives you extra incentive to do better in the next time period.
- Make notes of the questions you want answered. Then as the answers come to you, jot them down next to the question.
- Work on overcoming personal, nonproductive habits; for example: overeating, smoking, gossip.
- Keep an "Idea File" ring binder or notebook in which you record all new ideas. At least once a week in a standing appointment with yourself, review your ideas.

## KNOWING YOURSELF

Not everyone is cut out to be an entrepreneur. It takes a special talent.

Some owners of small businesses have it and some don't. Before you invest time, energy, money and a piece of your heart, it's important to do some serious self-analysis. To answer such questions as: Am I prepared to work hard and make sacrifices? Am I self-disciplined? Do I have management ability? Am I experienced enough in this field? What do I want out of life? Are my goals realistic and attainable?

Studies have shown that entrepreneurs are persevering and not easily defeated. They thrive in a challenging environment and have a tremendous need to be in control. They turn diversity into opportunity. They are risk takers. They welcome responsibility, and they are willing and able to make decisions.

Moreover, successful entrepreneurs are patient and able to wait out the sometimes slow beginnings of a business. They also are able to learn from their mistakes, trust their own judgment and have an optimistic outlook.

Take a good look. Do those traits describe you? "Know yourself and be willing to work 60 hours a week. Starting a business is one of life's biggest commitments," advises Roy Nordman, director of Emerging Business Services Practice for the San Francisco office of Coopers & Lybrand.

Small business owner Nancy Wansick, of Wansick Graphics, echoes those sentiments: "My business has become my whole life. Day becomes night and work has become play."

It's obvious: you have to love you work. And if you choose a business that meshes with your personality (the answers to the above questions should tell you about your personality), those extra hours spent won't be as difficult. The key is to identify what you enjoy doing the most and then find a business opportunity that makes use of your skills and interests.

## METHODS FOR CHANGING BEHAVIOUR AND THOUGHTS

It may help to start this section on methods you can use to change behaviours by offering a definition of behaviour. A behaviour is something that you do; some action that you take. Conventionally, a behaviour is something that you act out physically, such as taking a walk, or smoking a cigarette, or rolling your eyes when your spouse is complaining. However, behaviours can be subtle, non-physical things too. Thinking can be considered a behaviour, for instance.

A very few behaviours are directly instinctual and designed into the human condition. A infant's rooting reflex (how it knows to orient its mouth to the breast) is one, and human being's preparedness as infants to learn languages when exposed to them is another. Most other behaviours are learned. Non-instinctual behaviours become established according to the regular principles described in learning theory, that most scientific of all psychological theories.

The principles of learning theory apply equally well to both human beings and animals, because all animals (human beings included) share a common basic design. All animals, from the highest and most complex to the lowest and simplest, have basic needs they need to meet and are designed in such a way so that they know how to meet them. All animals get "hungry" in some fashion and search for food, and all animals know to avoid extremes of temperature, predators or other environmental threats to their continuing existence Another way of saying this is that all animals have in common that their behaviour is motivated. Any animal that can be motivated, can be manipulated according to the principles of learning theory, so as to shape the animal's behaviour.

There are two types of animal motivation: the motivation to approach something, and the motivation to avoid something. These two opposed orientations are caused by ancient brain systems that most all animals share in common. In learning theory, approach motivations are described as "rewarding", and avoidance motivations are described as "punishing". Something that an animal desires to approach can be considered to be a reward for that animal, while something the animal desires to avoid can be considered a punishment.

Things don't innately have rewarding or punishing properties; rather these properties are things that animals assign to things, each according to its own needs. What is rewarding to one animal, then, may not be rewarding to the next. Similarly, what punishes one animal, may not punish another. Animals are born with different temperaments (genetically determined basic personalities and dispositions), and each individual animals temperament helps determine what they will respond to.

To make things more complicated, there are two kinds of rewards, and two kinds of punishments Positive reward and positive punishment occurs when an animal is confronted with something they either desire, or wish to avoid, respectively. Negative reward and negative punishment occurs when an animal was confronted with something they desired, or wished to avoid, and then that thing is taken away. A negative punishment is not punishing! A negative reward is not rewarding! Instead, negative punishments are actually rewarding, and negative punishments are actually rewarding. This is is a complicated idea, so an example will help comprehension.

## BUILDING TRUST

Mutual trust is a shared belief that you can depend on each other to achieve a common purpose.

More comprehensively trust defined as "the willingness of a party (trustor) to be vulnerable to the actions of another party (trustee) based on the expectation that the trustee will perform an action important to the trustor, regardless of the trustor's ability to monitor or control the trustee."

"People sense how you feel about them. If you want to change their attitudes toward you, change the negative attitudes you have toward them." Building relationships requires the building of trust. Trust is the expectancy of people that they can rely on your word. It is built through integrity and consistency in relationships.

If you listen well people will trust you. "You cannot establish trust if you cannot listen. A conversation is a relationship. Both speaker and listener play a part, each influencing the other. Instead of being a passive recipient, the listener has as much to do in shaping the conversation as the speaker"

One of the golden rules of the therapy profession is that everyone needs at least one person with whom they can openly and unashamedly discuss every little detail – happenings, desires, fears – of their life, whether it is from the past, present, or future. There are other psychological needs – to be accepted unconditionally, appreciated, recognized, respected, desired, valued, approved of, or complimented – that affect the way we communicate with each other. Listen carefully, ask questions to show that you are genuinely interested and you'll be amazed at the spin-offs from becoming a good question asker and a good listener. People appreciate, respect and value others who are great listeners.

Most people simply listen to the words that are being said to them, but words contain only 10% of the message. The remaining 90% is hidden in the body language and the tone of voice. Understanding body language can help you look beyond what people say to what they really mean.

To remember better what's being communicated to you, try to engage all your senses whilst listening as human brain stores pictures, feelings, smells and tastes more effectively than words. Understand you preferred mode of thinking, your mental map: whether you are a visual ('see' the world), auditory ('hear' the world), or a kinesthetic ('feel' the world). If you are a visual, when you're listening to someone, first of all make what they're are telling you into a movie. As brains remember better things that are out of the ordinary, you can try distorting pictures or making them funny. To enhance the effect, add sounds, link feelings to your movies, put the taste and smells in. And exaggerate everything.

Often we have too much difficulty listening to other people because:

- We "know" what we are going to hear;
- We are seeking confirmation, not information;
- What's being said is getting in the way of what needs be said.

Active listening involves playing back your own interpretation of what has been said in acknowledgement - 'As I see it, what you mean is...'

Socrates used this technique more than 2300 years ago. He pretended ignorance in order to encourage others to express their views fully.

Today, many world's smartest and fastest businesspeople have perfected this art – consciously or unconsciously – of paying dumb. "People who try to impress by pretending to be smart generally aren't. Truly smart people know that by playing dumb and asking the other party to repeat or explain things several times, asking lots of questions, they'll be better prepared to respond and then make a fast decision."

Successful people have the ability to develop relationships that last. Building relationship requires the building of trust.

Your relationship with yourself is your closest and most important relationship. What kind of relationship with yourself have you chosen – a judging, a coaching, a fearful, or a loving one? "Ask yourself in meditation what kind of friendship you want to nurture with your own self – do you want an inner friend who constantly judges you and denies you love, or do you want an inner friend who accepts you just as you are?" advises John Selby.

Your life can only be in balance when giving and receiving are in balance. Every interpersonal relationship is built on this fact of life. He who always gives acts against this principle just as much as he who only takes. This basic truth is valid without exception everywhere where people deal with people.

"You can make more friends in two months by becoming interested in other people than you can in two years by trying to get other people interested in you," advised Dale Carnegie.

Resolve to focus your energy on helping others feel valued and appreciated. Show your appreciation with a thank-you, or a smile. Call up someone you haven't spoken to in a while, just to catch up on how they are. If you have children, give one child at a time your full attention for an afternoon. Write a note of appreciation to someone who is important to you.

Think of the way you'd like to be remembered by those around you, and give of yourself accordingly throughout the year. Practice a random act of kindness every day. These little moments, over time, have a huge impact. The added benefit for you is that you'll be in a more positive frame of mind overall.

A relationship is two people eliciting responses from each other. If you want a change in response, then you must change your own actions.

As a business professional, you should ask yourself: "What business am I in?". The answer is quite simple: if your business has anything to do with people - and all businesses do - you are in the business of building relationships. "Some people think that if they sell things, they are in the business of selling. They aren't. They are in the business of building relationships – because that's how you sell things. Those in management are also in the business of building relationships, because that's how you get things done."

Managing collaboratively means managing not people but relationships. Good managers listen more than they talk and ask questions more than give orders. They also distribute management functions so that responsibility goes to whoever shows initiative.

Emotional intelligence (EQ) is a key to effective leadership. It refers to your capacity to recognize your own feelings and those of others, for motivating yourself, and for managing emotions well in yourself and in your relationships. Emotionally intelligent leaders are more likely to achieve results and are effective in dealing with the complexity involved in leading change and organizational transformation.

Negotiation is the game of life and business, the lifeblood of relationships, and a positive way of structuring the communication process. Whenever you attempt to reconcile differences, resolve disputes, manage conflict, influence others, establish or improve relationships you are negotiating.

To communicate effectively, don't try to say all you know – say only what your audience needs to know. Sort out relevant data from a huge amount of available input and convey only what helps your audience take productive action. Turn data into information that has clear meaning and relevance to your audience.

When asked what they consider the single most important factor for business success, many business leaders come up with listening. Your cannot establish trust and build relationships if you cannot listen. "In selling, there is probably no grater asset", says Mark McCormack, the author of What They Don't Teach You at Harvard Business School.

## DECISIONS MAKING

In his classic work, "Think & Grow Rich", Napoleon Hill stated that 98% of people are in the jobs they have through indecision, i.e. because they never made the decision about what they wanted to do in their lives in the first place. Indecision explains why many people feel that they have a life purpose, but have no idea what it is.

Decision is the key to transformation. It is one of the key character traits distinguishing high performers from the vast ranks of the mediocre. Decision is, by definition, behind every truly great achievement anyone ever makes. Interestingly, the most successful people make decisions quickly and change them slowly. They persist with the decisions they have made. However, failures are very slow to make any decision at all (most never make any), and they change the ones they have made very rapidly indeed. Which description applies to you?

Decision making is a process of first diverging to explore the possibilities and then converging on a solution(s).

The Latin root of the word decision means "to cut off from all alternatives". This is what you should do when you decide.

The Six Thinking Hats proposal analysis tool invented by Edward de Bono is particularly useful for evaluating innovative and provocative ideas. While most of our thinking is adversarial, the six thinking hats technique overcomes these difficulties by forcing everyone to think in parallel. As participants wear each hat – white, red, yellow, black, green, or blue – they all must think a certain way at the same time.

### Determination and Positive Attitude

Decide, and then act as if you could not fail. Interestingly, this attitude of mind attracts to you forces from the universe that are fully capable of supporting you and bringing your decision into manifestation. If you ask a lot from life, you will receive a lot. If you ask a little, that is what you will get.

Interestingly, the universe has no favorites and does not care either way how much or how little you ask for. As and you shall receive, is the way it was once expressed.

## Recognize Impact of Your Beliefs and Values

Beliefs are the assumptions we make about ourselves, about others in the world and about how we expect things to be. "These assumptions determine the way we behave and shape our decision-making process. They are often based on emotions rather than facts. We tend to notice 'facts' that reinforce our beliefs."

The 80/20 Principle tells you that you should choose an option that produces 80% of outputs from 20% of inputs, and gather 80% of the data and perform 80% of the relevant analyses in the first 20% of time available.

There are many models for understanding and characterizing the styles of interaction different people prefer to employ. According to the widely used Myers-Briggs Type Indicator (MBTI), people are divided into thinkers and feelers:

- A Thinker tends to use reason and logic
- A Feeler tends to use values and subjective judgment.

While the situations that fuzzy logic addresses are ambiguous, fuzzy logic itself is a very defined methodology. New business leaders use the managerial equivalent of fuzzy logic to address the ambiguity of the fuzzy front end.

Technology leaders have an analogous form of logic that they use to address the ambiguity of the fuzzy from end.

This technique is called the "master method" of decision making. Ask yourself "What can go wrong in this situation? What is the worst possible outcome?" and decide whether or not you can live with those consequences.

Fast companies that have demonstrated the ability to sustain surge and velocity all have established sets of guiding principles to help them make quick decisions. Abandoning theoretical and politically correct 'values' and bureaucratic procedures in favor of a practical, down-to-earth list of guiding principles will help your company make the decision-making process much faster. Only one question will need to be asked of any proposed course of action: Does it fit our guiding principles?

### Judge the Probabilities

Probabilities are basic to the art of decision making and arbitrage. The principle of arbitrage is to estimate the probable result if a given event occurs.

Warren Buffett, the world's most successful investor, is a master of judging the probabilities. He says, "Take the probability of loss times the amount of possible loss from the probability of gain times the amount of possible gain. That it what we're trying

"In leadership, it's important to be intuitive, but not at the expense of facts," writes Michael Dell, Founder of the Dell Computer Corporation. "Without the right data to back it up, emotion-based decision making during difficult times will inevitably lead a company into a greater danger. There is a very easy way to test whether you're making decisions based on emotions. When you come across data that are strikingly different from what you previously thought, how long does it take for you to shift your thinking? Do you deny the data and say, "Well, I don't believe this?"

## ORGANIZATIONAL COMMUNICATIONS

By internal communications, we mean the steps groups take to keep their members, donors, and supporters informed about their work. Internal communications tools include newsletters, web sites, mailings, magazines and other publications, and hotlines. By external communications, we mean the publicity relations activities groups rely upon to deliver their message to their target audiences (which may include members and supporters, but also include key decision-makers, other organizations and individuals, and the media). External communications tools include news releases, media events, speaking engagements, advertising campaigns, public service announcement campaigns, brochures, fact sheets and reports. There is frequent overlap between internal and external communications, but it helps to think of them separately when developing a communications strategy or determining how to improve an organization's overall communications capacity.

Most experts on organizations, management and leadership, assert that effective communications is the foundation for effectiveness in any type of organization. They assert there can't be too much communication. Some leaders misinterpret communications to be the same as paperwork or bureaucracy and so they're averse to a high degree of communications. As leaders and managers mature, they realize the need to effective convey and receive information, and efforts at communications (internal and external) increase substantially.

Herbert Simon introduced the concept of bounded rationality which challenged assumptions about the perfect rationality of communication participants. He maintained that people making decisions in organizations seldom had complete information, and that even if more information was available, they tended to pick the first acceptable option, rather than exploring further to pick the optimal solution.

Through the 1960s, 1970s and 1980s the field expanded greatly in parallel with several other academic disciplines, looking at communication as more than an intentional act designed to transfer an idea. Research expanded beyond the issue of "how to make people understand what I am saying" to tackle questions such as "how does the act of communicating change, or even define, who I am?", "why do organizations that seem to be saying similar things achieve very different results?" and "to what extent are my relationships with others affected by our various organizational contexts?"

# Index


### A

Accountancy 170, 171

Accounting 06, 170, 171, 191

Advertising agencies 144, 152

Alliances 54, 128

Alternatives 26, 29, 30, 71, 81, 85, 240, 241, 244, 252, 253, 255, 286

Attitudes 32, 102, 125, 282

### B

Benchmarking 87, 116

Brochures 121, 124, 289

Bureaucracy 53, 289

Business analysis 11

### C

Channels 39, 110, 111, 128, 145, 151, 202, 203, 204, 205, 206, 207

Collaboration 106, 176, 213, 231, 233

Comment cards 122

Communication 46, 60, 72, 75, 89, 91, 95, 110, 114, 118, 143, 151, 154, 155, 157, 176, 182, 237, 252, 266, 270, 285, 289

Community 16, 50, 66, 67, 69, 94, 101, 102, 112, 153, 212, 213, 214, 215, 216, 217, 231, 236, 260, 264, 266, 267

Complaints 90, 94, 108, 111

Concierge 90

Conscious 59, 70, 233

Conservation 36, 146

Consumer analysis 155

Contract 80, 92, 93, 96, 97, 104, 227

Control 71, 79, 87, 116, 172, 193

Customer 107, 108, 110, 111, 125, 126, 127, 138, 181, 195

### D

Daily operations 88

Data collection 110, 135

Delegation 73, 74, 76, 77, 79, 84, 115

Demographics 100, 108
Dependent 29, 148, 199, 269
Descriptive 68, 196, 200
Discrimination 100, 129
Dissolve 225
Distribution 125, 126, 128, 202, 203, 204, 208
Distribution channels 128, 203, 204

E

Economic environment 178
Employee training 108
Environmental scanning 155, 161
Examining 226, 232, 235

F

Fact sheets 289
Feedback 75, 105, 110, 121, 238, 261, 278
Financial risk 20
Franchising 204

G

Generic 185
Goals 24, 26, 38, 56, 60, 61, 70, 73, 74, 77, 86, 115, 116, 120, 155, 163, 164, 165, 179, 181, 183, 259, 265, 277, 278, 279
Graphical editors 187
Graphical metaphors 188

H

Human resources 97, 99, 101

I

Impacts 139
Income statement 86, 115
Indirect channels 203
Integration 106, 160, 163, 166, 192, 193, 204, 207, 208, 218
Intermediaries 203, 204, 205
Intermediary 204
Interpretation 99, 283

J

Judgement 28, 29, 106, 189, 241

K

Krypton 88

L

Liabilities 117
Litigation 87, 116

M

Macroenvironment 155, 268, 271
Mailing lists 260
Market demand 55
Market segmentation 131
Marketing environment 29
Marketing management 133
Marketing mix 33, 134, 135, 136, 202

Marketing planning process 25, 31, 34, 35
Marketing research 33, 133, 138, 166
Merchandising 32
Motivation 55, 76, 176, 179, 205, 206, 271, 281

## N

Negotiation 84, 106, 285
New products 17, 39, 139, 262
Newsletters 121, 214, 288

## O

Obesity 152
Objections 240, 252, 253
Organisation 19, 29, 30, 37, 52, 64, 92, 96, 100, 101, 124, 150, 189, 213, 271

## P

Perceptions 32, 46, 104, 214, 227, 228, 233, 240
Performance 24, 28, 40, 59, 64, 74, 85, 104, 115, 161
Personal selling 135, 143
Personnel 84, 92, 97, 122, 127, 162, 206, 209, 210, 250, 262
Politics 49, 52, 244
Pollution 7
Population 22, 157, 220, 255
Positioning 34, 120, 129, 140
Principal 68, 93, 96
Process 18, 23, 25, 29, 31, 33, 34, 35, 39, 40, 43, 46, 47, 51, 55, 60, 61, 62, 64, 79, 103, 106, 110, 113, 125, 131, 132, 133, 135, 136, 138, 143, 154, 160, 186, 187, 188, 189, 190, 191, 192, 193, 194, 195, 196, 197, 198, 199, 200, 203, 208 236, 239, 240, 241, 243, 244, 246, 248, 249, 250, 252, 253, 255, 256, 257, 258, 259, 261, 262, 263, 268, 269, 271, 285, 286, 287, 288
Profit 20, 21, 23, 24, 26, 35, 63, 86, 90, 94, 107, 112, 117, 130, 133, 164, 165, 172, 183

## Q

Qualitative 29, 236
Quality 14, 87, 105, 116, 128, 158, 175, 185, 271

## R

Reference groups 231, 236
Regulation 71, 144, 152, 272
Requirements 32, 50, 58, 92, 96, 106, 111, 131, 147, 158, 167, 169, 173, 187, 197, 201, 208, 209, 210, 211, 213, 271
Research studies 22
Reservation systems 203
Retailing 135

## S

Sears 144
Seasonality 28
Strategic business units 165
Strategic planning 123, 162, 163, 164
Suppliers 27, 36, 90, 93, 96, 124, 126, 142, 158, 188, 205, 207, 209, 210

## T

Target market 133
Travel agent 5
Trout 131, 134

## U

Up-selling 109

## V

Validity 18, 33
Value proposition 142

## W

Wages 21

## Y

Yvonna Lincoln 239

## Z

Zero-based 243
Zero-level 204